A dysfunctional Hampstead childhood 1886–1911

The memoir of Phyllis Allen Floud, née Ford

*To Martin & Lisa
with love from
Cynthia   Sept 2018*

© Cynthia Floud, 2018

ISBN 978 0904491 97 5

Printed and bound in Great Britain
by Marston Book Services Ltd, Oxfordshire

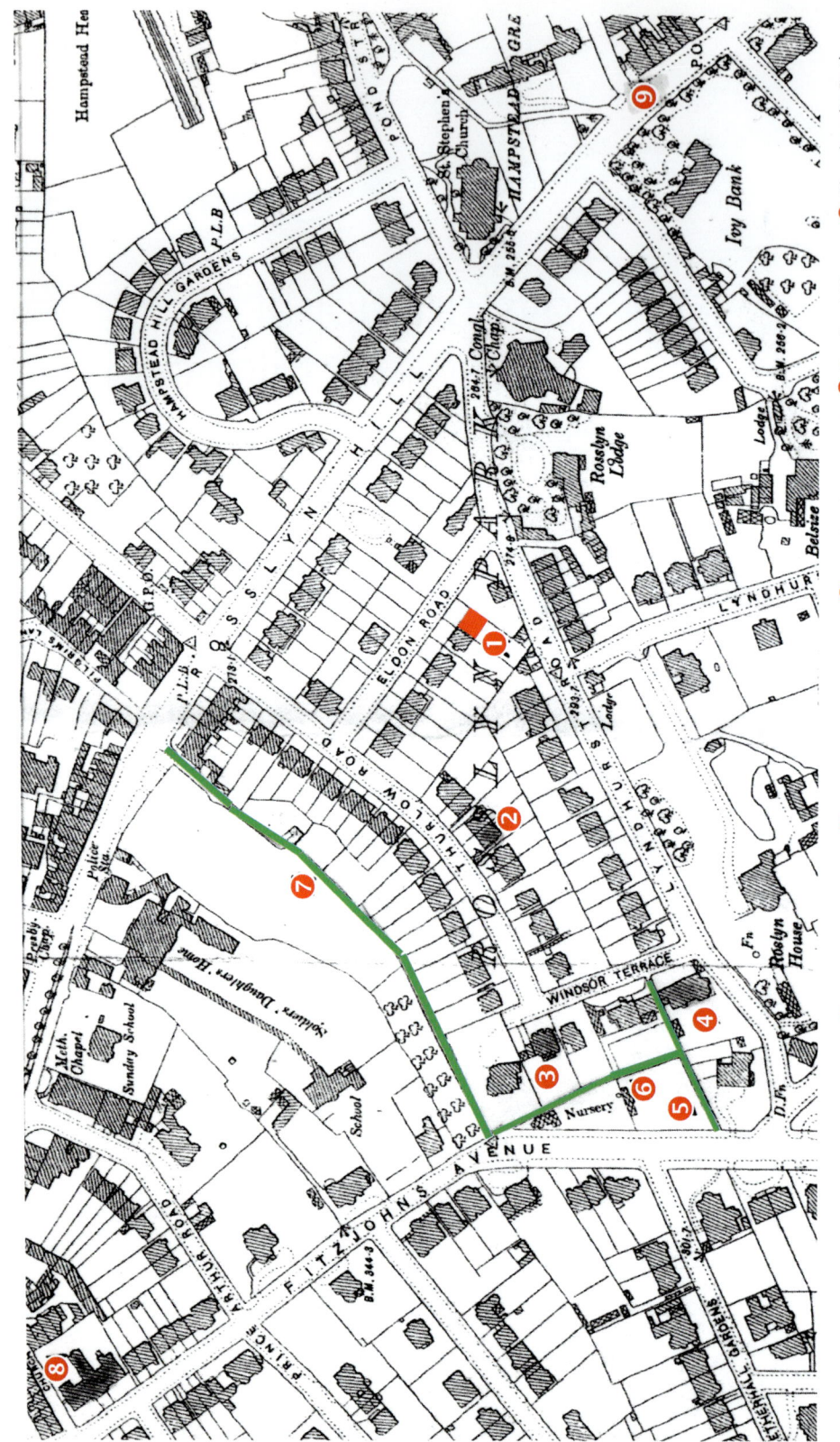

'Rosslyn Park', Ordnance Survey, 1896 ❶ the Fords' home ❷ Miss Pollock's school ❸ Ashbridge House ❹ Bayford House ❺ Shepherd's Path ❻ Spring Path ❼ Shepherd's Walk ❽ Sailors' Orphan Girls Home ❾ The George

A dysfunctional Hampstead childhood 1886–1911

The memoir of
Phyllis Allen Floud, née Ford

edited by Cynthia Floud

Designed by Ivor Kamlish
Published by Camden History Society
Editor of Publications, David A Hayes

Introduction

Phyllis Allen Ford was born at 2 Eldon Road, Hampstead on 10 February 1886, to Everard Allen Ford and Rachel (née Hammick). She spent her entire childhood there. In 1908 she married Francis Lewis Castle Floud, a civil servant, and they lived at Rosemount, 75 Flask Walk, where she gave birth to twins, Mollie and Peter in 1911. This account of her childhood, adolescence and early married life in Hampstead was written in the 1940s.

Phyllis recalls in lively detail the daily life of a middle-class family for whom the importance of social class was expressed in small differences of choice in the churches patronised, the hats worn, where wedding clothes or party dresses were made, the closeness, or otherwise, of chaperones, schools attended, the types of entertainment offered and indeed in every aspect of their lives. She records their attempts to cope with the new challenges afforded by the advent in Hampstead of cycling for women and the Suffragettes, while yet living in a world where Mother still made decisions on whom they could "know" and on whom she could "call".

Her mismatched parents and their extended families are the subject of her often withering criticism, but she is by no means complacent about herself, her intellect and her attempts at social success. She considers that everything is constrained by the family's conviction that they do not have enough money to maintain their rightful position in society. Her woefully inadequate education in Hampstead's private schools, which is the direct result of her mother's having had a governess, the sex pests in Hampstead's streets and the excitement of travelling in a horse bus down through the 'slums' of Camden Town are all vividly recounted. We also learn about bonfire night in Belsize Park, tennis parties in large gardens near the West Heath and the etiquette at the many dances which Phyllis enjoyed in her search for a suitable husband. She can laugh at herself when talking about her good works in Lisson Grove with poor children. Although not from an intellectual family, she met many of Hampstead's interesting and artistic inhabitants and pronounces her verdict on their housekeeping standards and styles of dress.

Her handwritten script was typed at Essex University, where Professor Leonora Davidoff hoped to use it in her work but died before she could do so. It was then scanned and became somewhat muddled. I have set it in order and then edited it with the considerable help of David Hayes. We have inserted explanations of people and places in italics within the text. The square brackets are Phyllis' own. I have omitted the sections on Phyllis' later life in Epsom and Canada, as they digress from her main story of life in middle-class Hampstead 1886-1911.

I would like to thank Hannah Westall, archivist of Girton College, and Jackie Sullivan, archivist of Roedean School, for the information they supplied; and to thank Sophie Pelham for designing the family tree.

We have inserted photographs and other pictures. The early family photographs were hard to trace: David Feeney, the]current resident of the Vicarage in Milton Abbot kindly showed me the alterations made to the house to fit in all the extra bedrooms for the Hammick sons and daughters, and provided the photo of the Vicar and his family outside the Vicarage. From within the family I would like to thank Phyllis' granddaughter, Esther Bagenal, and great-grandson, Marcus du Sautoy, for their help in transporting and opening boxes and albums to unearth the relevant photographs; and my husband, Roderick Floud, for his encouragement and his historical perspective.

Cynthia Floud,
Haddenham 2018

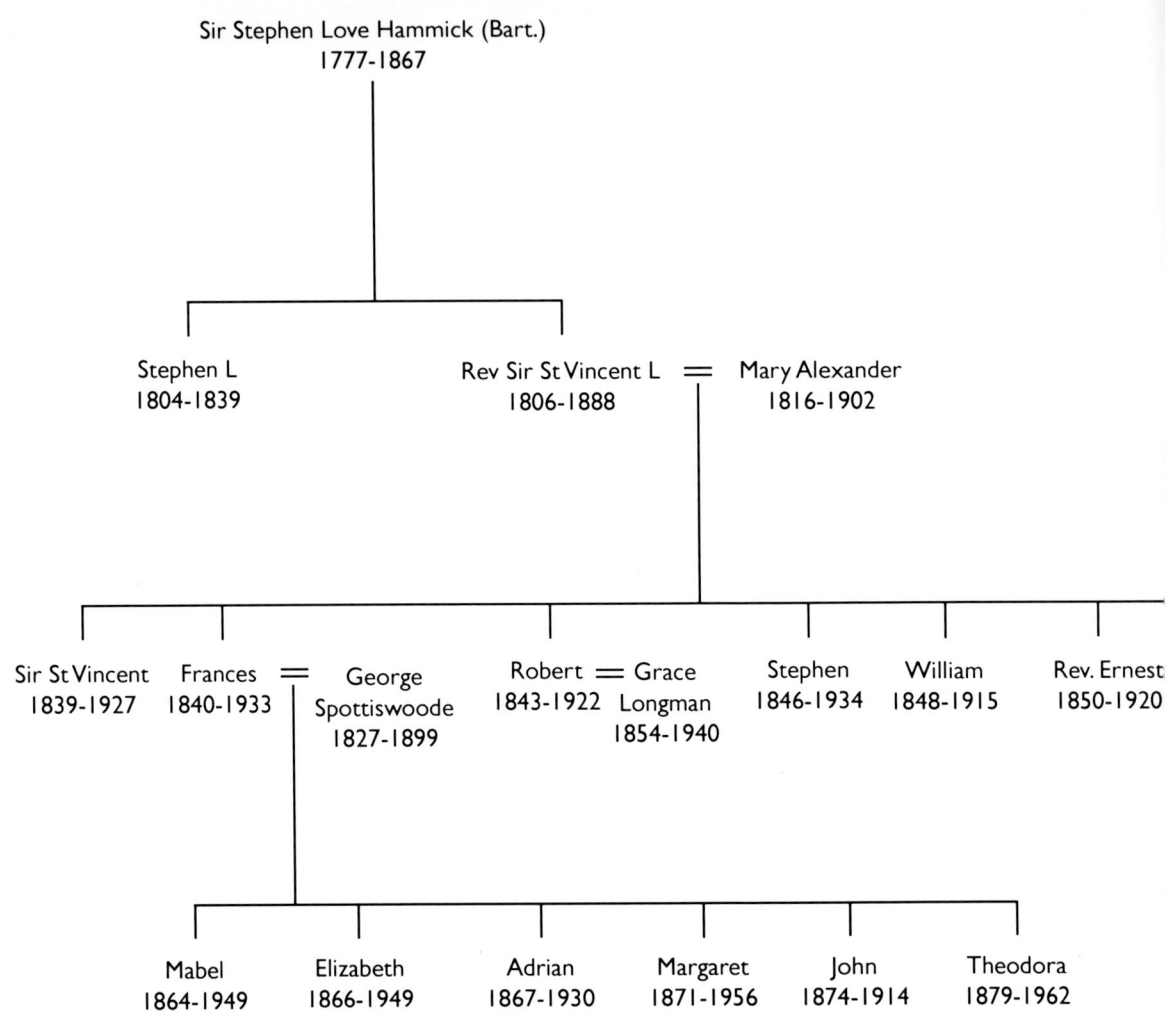

(Contains only those mentioned in the text)

Family tree

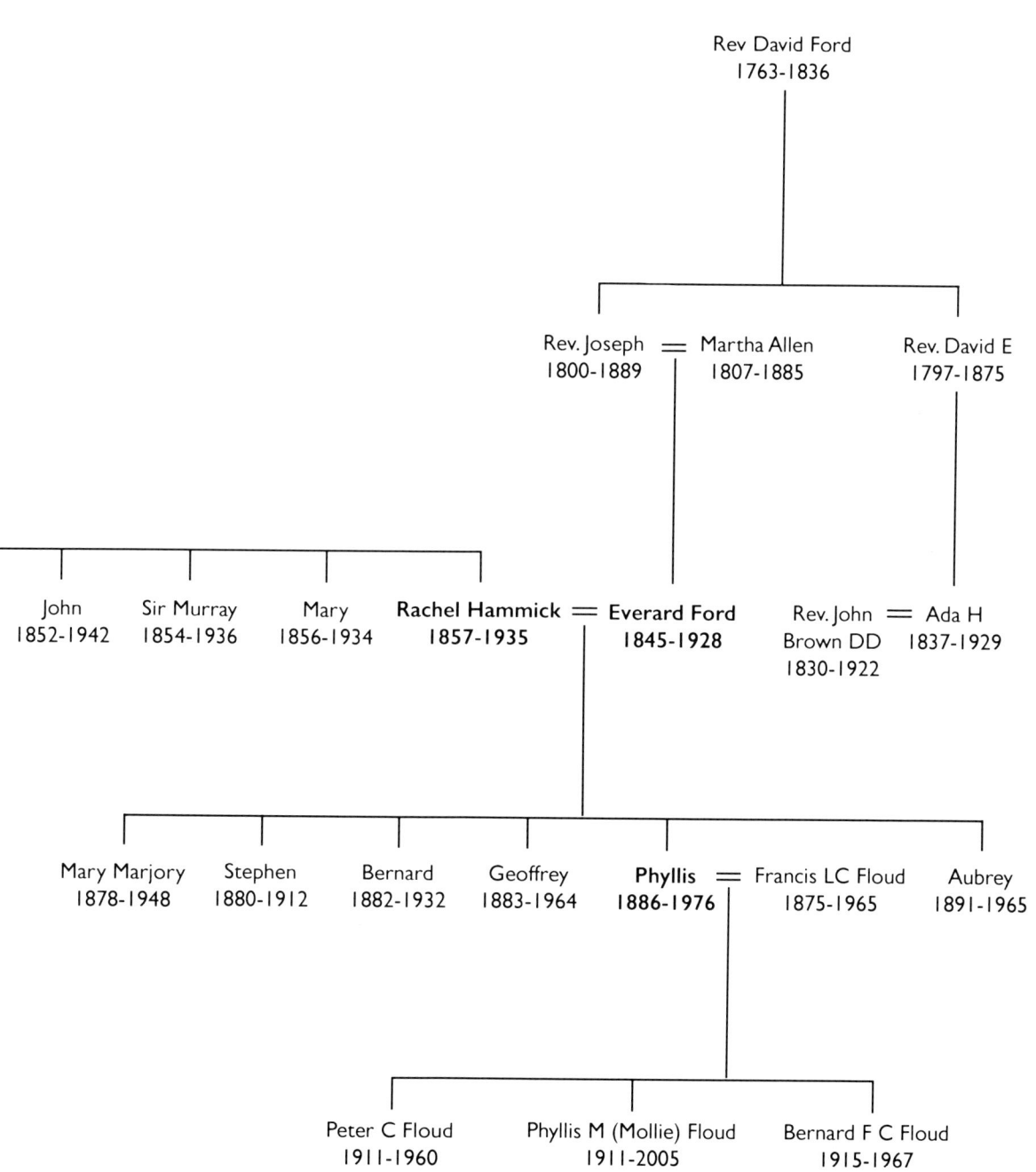

The memoir

Beginning

So many books have been written by people who were born with silver spoons in their mouths. They make me full of envy. "Envy, hatred and malice and all uncharitableness" – that is me, though perhaps I might leave out hatred, that is too strong. The wonderful descriptions of large, gracious, well appointed houses. Loving mothers, aloof but dignified, and kindly fathers, adoring retainers. Beautiful gardens, ponies to ride, orchards full of fruit. How enviable. Then at the other extreme are the people who managed to climb from the gutter. The little boys sold papers and ended by owning half the newspapers in England. Their lives in the gutters were hard, no doubt, but exciting and varied.

The rich or the poor; surely, I used to feel, the lives of those were better than Middle Class respectability. We came in between."Why didn't you send me to a Council School? If I had started at the very bottom I might have climbed to the top." I never envied the poor. It was the rich and the self-contained. The ones who always behaved as they should. Most children long to be of a pattern – to be like the rest – to be conventional and un-peculiar.

Never would I go back to my childhood if I could. Certainly never below the age of 16 or 17. I don't really ever like thinking about it. I avoid it. (No, we were not cruelly treated; we weren't starved.) To all intents and purposes I suppose we appeared a happy family, but we weren't. There was a rotten core to our home life and yet even that seems an overstatement. I think perhaps the state of our family life was more negative than that. It was just that there was little or no love in our home. And that again is an overstatement because my father worshipped my mother in a strict Victorian sense. They were an ill-assorted pair, again an overstatement.

The Hammick family

My mother *(**Rachel Hammick**, 1857-1935)* certainly looked down on my father. That was gently obvious to me even as a child. My mother's father *(**Rev. Sir St Vincent Love Hammick MA**, 1806-1888)* was a Baronet, and her mother *(**Mary Alexander**, 1816-1902, daughter of Robert Alexander of the Indian Army)* a Northern Ireland heiress. *(The Alexander family came from Londonderry originally but Mary's grandfather, William Alexander (1725-74), married in England and moved to England before he had completed his family. Robert, Mary's father (1771-1861), was born in Acton, Middlesex. The family were well-off, but as one of three siblings it is unlikely that Mary was an 'heiress', more that she received a large marriage settlement.)* The Baronet had a most distinguished face, in fact both he and his wife were a distinguished looking pair. He was a country parson and was rector in the same village *(Milton Abbot, Devon)* for 52 years and both he and his wife were adored.

St Constantine Church, Milton Abbot, Devon

My grandmother was, from what I have heard, the perfect clergyman's wife. Both of them visited continually. The people of the parish came to them for comfort and advice and, if there was an accident, my grandmother was called out at once to do first aid. She was very young when she married *(aged 20)* and had never had any training but she faced anything. My mother told us of some of the gruesome wounds she had to tend. Fingers caught in saws and once a man's eye hanging out by a thread. Whether that is possible or not I don't know, but it was mother's story. But then mother had some wonderful stories. At one time the whole village was swept by small pox and my mother said there was not an unmarked villager in the place.

I used to picture my grandparents turning out of their home on a stormy night and making their way across the fields to some lonely cottage. My grandmother must nearly always have been pregnant, as she had 13 children. My mother was the 13th. My grandmother was the perfect vicar's wife (activities were all for the parish) but my mother scarcely knew her. She always talked about her with a sort of detached air and with no affection. My mother and the sister next to her *(**Mary Caroline Hammick**, 1856-1934)* were practically handed over to a German governess. She saw very little of her mother. In the evenings the family collected in the drawing room and grandmother read aloud to them. She had devised a way of making rugs. A piece of string was fastened across the room. Old woollen garments were unravelled and washed and the wool cut into short equal lengths. While they were being read to, the children knotted these pieces on to the string. When enough had been done the string would be sewn in parallel lines on to a piece of canvas or sacking.

There was plenty of money but they lived very plainly with no luxuries. The vicarage was a large stone building. *(Newly built in 1837 when the Hammicks moved in as newlyweds, its design was overseen personally by the 6th Duke of Bedford, who granted the living to Rev. Hammick.)* Apart from the heated sitting rooms, the house was icy cold. My mother used to describe to me the misery of going to bed in the winter. Leaving the fairly warm room downstairs and mounting up, a candlestick in hand to the freezing summit. No cardigans to be slipped on in those days. Bare arms with little puffed sleeves.

My grandfather would read to himself every evening and, reading a review of 'Alice in Wonderland' *(published 1865)*, he ordered it. Every evening he set himself down to read a chapter and every evening he would put the book on one side with a sigh, saying to his wife, "I cannot think, my dear, why this book is supposed to be amusing".

The Vicarage, Milton Abbot

Rev. Sir St Vincent L Hammick and his wife in the 1880s, with probably at least two of their grandchildren

The rug-making and the reading make a pleasant picture of a happy home. But my mother said she saw very little of her parents and told me she really didn't know her mother at all. That is not surprising. This was the family: 10 sons and 3 daughters *(ten sons were born but two died in infancy.)* The first son *(St Vincent Alexander, born & died in 1838)* died as a baby and the second *(St Vincent Alexander, b.1840)* died at about the age of 14. *(He did not: this story is a mystery; he became a Colonel in the army, dying in 1927.)* He was at school at Marlborough. He went there and back by coach, staying on the way with friends of his parents. He started home from school for the Christmas holidays arriving at the house of the friends. He felt ill and his hostess, to her horror, saw that he was covered with a rash. She wasn't going to risk keeping him with scarlet fever in her house with her family, and next morning she bundled him into the coach. He died soon after getting to his home in Devonshire. My grandmother never forgave her.

The eldest daughter of the family (**Frances Grace**, *1840-1933)* was a woman of very forcible character. There were 8 sons who survived, followed by 2 more daughters. They were a remarkably fine lot. All lived to a good old age. The only delicate one of the family being Mary, the sister next to my mother. She developed what was called hip disease and had to wear a high boot. She was the only one of the family who did not marry. Oh yes, Uncle Jack too (***John Eustace Hammick***, *Lloyd's underwriter)*.

The sons, all except one, were 6ft tall, and the two daughters up to 5ft 8ins, a considerable height in those days. They married and all had children. Their sons were practically all of them swept away in the first war. They were my first cousins. I had 30 of them, 15 of each sex *(evidence for only 20)* and, when I was adolescent, we had some superb combined holidays with them. My mother's village *(Milton Abbot, Devon, population in 1851 1,202)* was 5 or 7 miles from the nearest country town *(Tavistock)*, yet she was never taken there until she was 12 years old. She and her delicate sister *(Mary)* were left to a German governess to bring up. My grandmother was a very busy woman and saw very little of her young daughter. I suppose the Governess had to teach every subject. Anyway my mother spoke German fluently, of course, French not so well. She painted in hard dry water colour and played the piano very modestly well. She learnt nothing of cooking or gardening or natural history or domestic work. Money was plentiful and labour cheap. When many years later I spoke of vaccination in a slighting way, objecting to having my babies done, my mother said, "You wouldn't have talked like that if you had lived in our village. When I was a child there was scarcely a person there who was not cruelly scarred with small pox."

My grandmother seems to have had an unusual outlook on life at that date. The children were not made to do fancy work. They learnt to sew, to darn, etc. [My mother (Rachel) was a beautiful darner and taught me. My husband's trousers are generally a beautiful exhibition piece of darning.] On one occasion a visitor came to call on my grandmother. She asked a lot of questions about the daughters and what and how they were learning. When she had gone, grandmother thought it all over.

Obviously the girls were not learning dressmaking. They must begin. She bought two lengths of good material, handed it over to the governess and said, "See that the girls make a Sunday dress each for themselves."

The girls were about 14 years old. The governess knew little more than they did about making dresses. She had no pattern and the result was too terrible. My mother never forgot those dresses, and, having made them, they had to wear them every Sunday to church. No, mother never learnt to be a dressmaker. That is, she never was able to teach herself dressmaking, though her sewing was fine and beautiful. I suffered terribly from the dresses she made me. In those days with good material, dresses were an investment and were expected to last for years and they did. Mother and Aunt Mary felt themselves a veritable spectacle and I suppose they were, in dresses with hems up on one side and down on the other, gaps between the buttons and buttonholes.

A niece of mother's was very strong minded. Her mother was my mother's eldest sister (*Frances Grace Spottiswoode, née Hammick, who lived to be nearly 93*), and a formidable woman. It was she who, when I went to visit her one day, aged 93 – sitting up in bed asked, "And how is your dear mother?" "Fairly well thank you Aunty", I replied, "But then she is getting on". "Getting on, getting on," said my Aunt, "Your mother is a mere child." My mother was 20 years younger than she, which bears out the truth of the statement that old age is 14 years older than you are yourself. To return to the cousin and her abhorred dress. She wore it and then decided she would no more. She poured ink down it. No good, they turned it. Desperate, she pushed it down the lavatory. The drains got choked but she had won the battle. She wasn't made to wear it again.

I never heard of any other instructors but the German governess. My mother used to tell with amusement of a visit to the village of a German band. Great excitement. They came up the drive and sat and played and the two girls were enthralled. They had never seen or heard stringed instruments played, except by one man in the village. But my mother disgraced herself. Thrilled at being able to show off her German, she waited till the end of a piece and then went up to them to engage them in conversation, and in her ignorance, she addressed them *(familiarly)* as "du". Horror on the part of the governess, my mother was ignominiously sent indoors.

My mother's hair was never washed. No woman's was, or so I gathered. It was brushed. Brushed and brushed. Everyone had time in those days. Grandmother did not allow them to use Macassar oil on their heads, but occasionally one of the servants would give them a little of theirs to add a shine
to their already shining tresses. Long straight brown hair. They could sit on it – that was the workhouse description given in those days of a good head of hair. "She could sit on it." The fashion for continual washing of the hair is evidently quite a modern theory. My mother, as I say, was not allowed to have her hair washed. It was not done. I, as a girl, had mine washed about twice a year until I took the matter into my own hands.

I don't think I remember anything else that mother told me about her childhood. I only once went to my grandparents' village. I recognised the old Rectory from photographs. I was nosing around, when a villager came up to me and enquired if I was looking for the grave site of the murder. I couldn't make much out of his account of it but it was a recent event, long after my grandfather reigned there. When I could get the old chap to listen, I asked if he could remember my grandfather, "Oh aye," he said, "Those were good days. He were a gentleman, not like the Rectors they have now."

My grandfather had had a number of servants. *(In 1861, when only Mary and Rachel were at home, there were seven live-in servants: the German tutor, Swiss lady's maid, cook, parlourmaid, housemaid, child's maid and kitchenmaid.)* "He 'kept house'. He was a fine gentleman". I thought of the poor Rectors trying to live on their stipend in that great house. It was different for my grandfather. He had money and plenty of it. Five sons at the University. I asked the old chap if he knew my mother. Oh yes, he knew Miss Rachel. I said, "I am her daughter, I think I am rather like her". "Oh, no", he said with vigour, "Miss Rachel was a fine upstanding young lady, she was." I went into the old church and there was a memorial to all my cousins who were killed in the first war. Nearly all my 15 boy cousins had gone.

What else do I know of my mother's childhood? Very little. My sister *(Marjory Ford)*, 8 years older than I and the eldest of the family, must have known much more than I ever did. She went with my mother to stay in the old Rectory, and mother must have talked about her life there, I imagine. I wonder. One thing I heard about their life there many, many years later. It was not until after I was married that I heard of my grandfather's great fear. He was terrified of dogs. This was a great disadvantage to a country parson and it was a misery to himself. I never knew about this, nor did I know that my mother felt the same. One day she said, "I've always been so careful not to let any of you know. My dear father was terrified of dogs and I am too." So there was never a dog kept at the old rectory

The Hammick brothers and sisters

nor did we ever have a dog in my parents' home.

My mother's father was a Baronet. *(He was the second baronet. His father, Sir Stephen Love Hammick, 1777-1867, who was awarded the baronetcy, was Surgeon General to George IV and William IV and a member of the first Senate of the University of London.)* My Grandmother was fond of singing and so was my mother. She used to sing to us nursery rhymes and songs she had learnt from her mother. She would put the baby on her toe and dance him up and down while she sang. We had our regular favourites as children. "There was an old man who lived in a wood as you may plainly see. They said he could do more work in a day than his wife could do in three." That had the verse about his being kicked by the cow, and the blood ran down his clothes. *(Actual chorus: "But Tiny hitched and Tiny twitched, and Tiny cocked her nose. And Tiny gave the old man such a kick that the blood ran down to his toes.")* We loved that. One of mother's songs was about the Jenny Wren and it began "Let's go to the woods says Billy to Robin, Let's go to the woods says Jack o Malone". *(The wren boys tradition still lives in certain parts of Ireland. Boys would go out on Christmas Day and kill a wren, and on the next day, St Stephen's Day, they would go from house to house, singing this song and asking for money "to bury the wren".)*

Rachel's marriage, January 1877

My mother must have been very attractive. Her eldest sister *(Frances)*, 20 years older than herself, had much more regular features. My mother and aunt Mary had slightly crooked faces. Large dark hazel eyes and run away chins. That does not sound attractive but she must have been. Good colouring, bright cheeks, which persisted until she was

The young Rachel and Everard

elderly, full lips and a tall upright figure. Five feet eight inches; that was tall for a woman in those days; she must have looked fine on her horse. She rode a great deal and hunted. She married at 19. It came about in this way, as far as I could make out, her marriage I mean.

Frances, the eldest sister, had married 20 years earlier, a pillar of the church *(George Andrew Spottiswoode)*. That is how I always heard him alluded to. He ended by being buried in St. Paul's or somewhere like that. They lived in a big way. A large house in Cadogan Square and a country house in *(Axminster)* Devonshire. He mulcted my parents of half their inheritance. He also lost half of his own as well. *(He left £100,800 in 1899, so it is unlikely that he lost half his money.)* This pillar of the church was a big man with a beard. He was chairman of some church society called the Lay Helpers Association of the Diocese, I think, or some such. Mr. Spottiswoode wanted a secretary for this and secured the services of my father as a voluntary worker.

Everard Ford, 1845-1928

My father was 32 years old, unmarried and with a predilection for Church work. He had quite lately been converted and had joined the Church of England. His father was a Presbyterian minister, who had a living in Scotland. My father, an only child, was brought up there and went to the Edinburgh Academy *(an independent school, opened in 1824.)* There is a photograph of him, in the family album, standing dressed in a frock coat by a stile with a top hat and cane in his hand. A weak, good looking man. A tall slim figure and drooping moustache and less chin than is advisable. After turning over the pages full of pictures of my mother's brothers, it is a shock to come on the one of my father. He looks small fry, not out of the top classes, as my mother so often said of people, though I never heard her use *(the expression)* about her husband. About his parents and his relations she certainly did, if not out loud, in her mind.

I know little about my father's early years. All I know is from a chance remark I made. I said I did so like a velvet smoking jacket; why didn't my father wear one in the evening? My father put on an air of sanctity and said "I cannot even bear to think of velvet smoking jackets. They bring to my mind my unregenerate days – days that I wish to forget, the days before I was converted." That is all I have to go on and I used to think about it a lot.

Everard Ford in Church Lads' Brigade uniform
Church Lads' Brigade. Photo: CLCGB Historical Group

The Ford Family

My father's father *(Joseph Ford, 1801-89)* was a retired, I suppose Scottish, (Presbyterian) Minister *(born in Long Melford, Suffolk)*. My father was their only child. They must have had some money, because they lived in a large house in Belsize Park *(6 College Terrace, now Belsize Terrace)*. His relations were in cotton I think. I do not remember that lot of grandparents. All I remember was my parents going off to the funeral of the last surviving one *(Joseph, who died in 1889)* and our young skivvy telling me she was sure we ought to pull down the blinds in the house; I felt very important and we went round the house pulling curtains and drawing blinds and I felt really a person. I had been very disappointed when my mother had not even suggested that I should wear mourning. Mother was so irritating in those sort of ways, so unconventional and alas so, to me, painfully economical. I thought to have some new clothes would be wonderful and to have black ones would make me out as "somebody", a thing I always longed to be. I used to watch them come into church, a family lately bereaved, like a solemn row of black beetles; no one could avoid noticing them, no one could overlook them. Oh blessed state to be bereaved and wearing black! But it was not for me. Having drawn all the curtains, I began to be afraid we had done the wrong thing, so the skivvy and I went round drawing them all back.

I remember the paperweight on the table in the drawing room in the grandparents' house. I literally loved it. I would have done almost anything to possess it but I don't know where it went. I never saw it again after the grandparents died. But years later I collected paperweights myself. Their house was stuffed full of Victorian objects. My father's taste was very bad.

The Ford cousins

On occasions we saw his cousins. They were fat short women, north country and very second rate. My mother never disguised her aversion to them and I think she had some excuse. They were truly dreadful. One of them *(Ada Haydon Ford, 1837-1929, Everard's cousin)* must have had capacity. She founded the Ada Leigh homes in Paris. She also married a Bishop. *(In fact, she did neither: Phyllis has confused two Adas. The Ada Leigh homes, or hostels, were founded by Ada Leigh, later Lewis, 1840-1931, for English and American girls living in Paris without any family there. In 1873 she moved to France from Lancashire and set up a hostel for women in need. She married John Travers Lewis, Bishop of Ontario. Ada Haydon Ford's husband was John Brown DD, 1831-1922, a prominent theologian and Congregational Minister, and Pastor of Bunyan's Meeting, Bedford. They retired to 10 Upper Park Road, Belsize Park.)* When he died, she wrote to my father saying she proposed to put up a life-sized angel over his grave *(In January 1922 he was buried in Hampstead Cemetery, Fortune Green, but without the angel)*. How my parents laughed at breakfast when that letter came. I was rather shocked and pictured a huge angel brooding over the tomb. The joke, a life-sized angel, was lost on me until it was duly explained. I was slow witted then.

One of these fat aunts fancied herself at the piano. My mother went to call on her one day in London; the maid opened the drawing room door and announced her, but the aunt was too immersed in her piano playing to notice her, so there mother had to stand until

Rev. John Brown, DD

the lady would come to, affecting great surprise and expressing regret that she had not noticed mother, as she was so enrapt by her own piano playing. Mother told me that she knew all the time that the whole scene was a show off.

I ought to mention that the Bishop's widow was staying with us, and it was a Sunday. We sat in the drawing room and I was sent to the piano to pass the time. Presently Aunt Ada asked, "Did I not sing?" "Oh yes," said mother, "Of course I sang". I did. All our family did. Six of us. All lovely voices.

Every Sunday evening we sang hymns. My father sat at the grand piano in the drawing room and we all clustered round. My mother as well. Hymn after hymn. I loved that: almost the only bearable thing on a dreadful day. Also I found the singing in church did alleviate the dreariness. After the hymn singing, which went on a long time, we knew all the hymns by heart, we would sit down to be read to by my mother. As it was Sunday, she read a deadly book. Either deadly or gruesome. I didn't listen to the deadly one and the gruesome ones I couldn't help listening to, though they made me sick. Somebody's *(Fox's)* Book of Martyrs was a favourite and mother would read the parts about saints being heartily tortured and then turn to us and say, "Which of you would suffer like that for the sake of Christ?" and I thought not I, and neither would you. I think I felt always there were two mothers, one natural one and one who posed as being religious and wasn't a bit. Father, I think was. He was in fear of the judgement, but mother had too much sense of humour to take all that seriously.

When that aunt tired of my piano playing, she asked me to sing. My mother came over to the piano to play the accompaniment. I must have been 17 *(1903)* or more and emancipated, because my mother picked out some secular song for me to sing to the aunt. I hadn't any other sort. For years and years we were only allowed to play Sunday tunes on Sunday and read Sunday books, but by the time I was 17 things were changing. I was the only one left at home and the strings were slackening. My mother put a piece of music up on the piano. It had the sentimental name of "Love lies asleep in the Rose" *(see overleaf)*.". [I sang it at an evening party once and a young man came up to me afterwards and asked why was love lying asleep in the road like a tramp?] I was just going to begin when my aunt said, "There's nothing I like better than a nice piece of sacred music on a Sunday evening". Quickly mother searched the music stand and produced "Angels ever bright and fair" and one or two others in an album. Then we were stuck. The Indian Love Lyrics were the very latest and these I had learnt. Also, mother could get through the accompaniment without breaking down, a distinct advantage. As she put the book on the music stand, she whispered to me "mouth the words" and off we went quite successfully. The Aunt had no idea I was invoking Allah.

These aunts did not loom large, at least only at intervals. Their families hardly ever came to see us. My sister once went to stay with one of them in Bolton. She came home full of contempt. The second daughter had spent her days literally playing with a dog, sitting on a window seat looking on the road. She was about 21. The elder sister was the same age as my sister. Their surname was Butler.

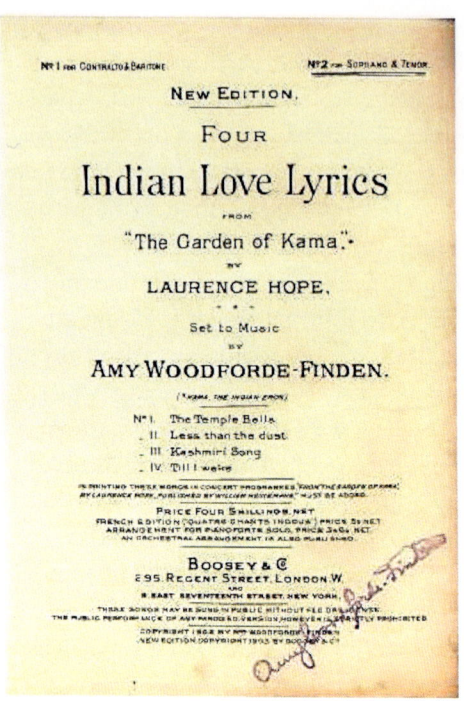

Lyrics: Kashmiri Song
Pale hands I loved beside the Shalimar,
Where are you now? Who lies beneath your spell?
Whom do you lead on Rapture's roadway, far,
Before you agonise them in farewell?
Pale hands I loved beside the Shalimar,
Where are you now? Where are you now?
Pale hands, pink tipped, like Lotus buds that float
On those cool waters where we used to dwell,
I would have rather felt you round my throat,
Crushing out life, than waving me farewell!
Pale hands I loved beside the Shalimar,
Where are you now? Where lies your spell?

(No Ford relative seems to have married anyone called Butler. Phyllis has most of her facts about the Ford aunts and cousins slightly wrong. One daughter of Ada Haydon Ford, Edith, married a rich cotton manufacturer from Manchester; but another, Florence Ada Brown, far more distinguished, went to Newnham College, was Mayor of Cambridge and was mother to John Maynard Keynes. It seems extraordinary that Phyllis did not know this, but she and her mother rated people by their social class and not their *education or intellect.)* The second girl, who was vast and who played with the dog, got engaged to be married oddly enough to a Butler, I mean a man called Butler. Mother and my sister were very sarcastic about it, the reason being that the Butlers' 2nd daughter was engaged before my sister, though I doubt if either of them realised this. Mother Butler said her daughter and the fiancé were no relation, but they had found some common ancestor in the past. My sister afterwards remarked that no doubt they were both descended from Pharaoh's cup bearer. The elder sister married an elderly widower some years later. "Nothing but a housekeeper," said my mother. My sister asked if they could lend her a copy of Ruskin, when she was staying with them. She herself admitted it was a snobbish thing to do. The Butler daughter answered "You'll find the poets in that book case".

There was another aunt, one of the sisters who visited my mother on rare occasions. I don't wonder they came so seldom. They must have realised surely as much as I, a schoolgirl, did that mother considered them impossibly common. They may have come from a sense of duty. The least noticeable of the aunts came with a paid companion one afternoon for tea. We were in the drawing room and, after tea, the aunt said to the companion, "fetch the little parcel please". She went into the hall and brought back a brown paper parcel about the size of an ordinary book. I was thrilled. I hoped it was for me. But it wasn't. "I have brought you one of my little art pieces," said she, handing the parcel with much solemnity to my mother. Mother looked as if she had been handed a stinking fish. She guessed what was in it; I was aghast at mother's ill manners. Why couldn't she smile and say, "Oh, thank you so much, how exciting, a present for me", like other mothers would have done? And then she opened it in a casual way as if no treasure was to be revealed. How I wish I had still that sacred gift. It would be unique nowadays, thank goodness. When mother got the paper off, she said nothing and the aunt, feeling the pressure of atmosphere, murmured, "Just one of my own little pieces, we have to use the hands God has given us". "Oh do let me see," and I took the object from mother's lap.

It was truly wonderful. A box had apparently been covered in purple velvet, the very blue purple. It was tightly stitched and smooth. It stood up and was framed. On one side was the picture. It was a conventional spray of flowers in white, so that the white spray on the purple velvet looked funereal. And the spray was made of fish bones! It was hard to believe at first glance, but looking into it one saw the ingenious device. Flat flower petals, leaves, everything. I had no idea one could get so many shapes of fish bones. And I wondered if she and her paid companion were doomed to eat fish twice daily, carefully sorting it on their plates with their forks (fish knives and forks were not used in those days, at least not in our house. Just a fork used in the right hand). Then what excitement when you got a bone in your mouth, licking it clean, and seeing whether you had got another stamen or a bud.

One thing more I remember about those sisters. The one *(Ada)* who *(proposed to)* put up a life-sized angel to her husband, lived in London *(10 Upper*

Park Road, Hampstead) when a widow. She gave a dinner party. It was a terrible affair. My parents went and there was quite a distinguished gathering. But my aunt seemed utterly lost and the hired butler she had got in was dreadfully drunk. At the meal food came in and out like in a pantomime meal. Some people were eating soup and others fish, at the same time. The butler came up to my father, knocked his arm with a dish of food and said, "Why don't you have some of this? It's very good". That was about all my father got to eat and my mother had practically nothing. People were almost fighting to get something. This aunt detached herself from this world and stared up to the heights in high-flown pious praises. The whole evening was a nightmare.

1897

Two of my mother's brothers were in the Indian Civil Service **(Stephen Hammick MA and Sir Murray Hammick** *KCSI, CIE).* They sent home silks and shawls and their wives seemed to us to live glamorous lives. I used to see them on the rare occasions when they came home on leave. They came and stayed with us and our servants were awful, our food solid and dull and our house icy cold. No-one seemed very happy. My mother used to dread these visits. On one of these occasions I was in the dining room with a most beautiful aunt. She was home from India. She was really beautiful, tall, yet frail-looking with perfect features, curly hair, little tight curls round her face. One of her daughters was just like her. From the drawing room, the whist room, came sounds of a child crying. "Who is that crying? Oh dear" said my aunt, evidently distressed, "What is that noise, who is that?" "That's only Aubrey doing his violin practice with mother", I answered. "But does he cry when he practices the violin?"she said with a voice of horror. "Oh generally," I said in a laconic fashion. This conversation imprinted itself on my mind. I felt that there was something wrong. I myself cried very often when I practiced the piano, that is, if mother was within hearing. I felt how deeply shocked my aunt was and I could feel her unspoken criticism of my mother. I must have been quite 11 years old by then and I felt how crude and rough we were.

At that age mother would reduce me to tears by violent argument, but Aubrey, who was younger (he would have been about 7 years old), would have got an irritated smack, as I had done – I still remember a cracking box on the ear I had from my mother. But her know-it-all arguments used to get me down. I loved to draw. In the nursery or in my bedroom I was always drawing. During those long eternally long church services, I was drawing in my mind all the time. I drew because I liked drawing better than anything and I didn't much mind what I drew - I copied pictures out of children's books and particularly sacred pictures of the Virgin and Child, but mother quite correctly said that was "poor stuff". She would give me a book to copy and she gave me one with pictures of old men lying on tombs, they were by Michael Angelo *(sic)*, but they didn't interest me and I wanted to be left to myself to draw and paint what I wanted. It was the same with the piano. "Don't mess about. If you aren't going to play properly shut the piano and go away." "Oh, your father has just come in, stop playing the piano". Or "What is that you are practicing?" "The dance of the Elves". "It sounds to me more like the dance of the Elephants". "Well, Miss Stuart told me to practice it like that, slowly and loudly, as my fingers run away when I try to do it fast." "Nonsense. I never heard anything so ridiculous". Argue, argue. I, nearly in tears of rage. When my lesson day came, mother straight at Miss Stuart. Miss Stuart very meek to her employer. "Yes, Mrs Ford, I did tell her to practice like that". Arguments from mother who eventually turned to me and said, "I evidently was mistaken about it". So it ended.

Whether or not my father had played the fool in his young days I don't know, but, if that was so, it is easier to understand why his two eldest sons turned out as they did. Why my father had been converted *(his father was a Presbyterian minister)*, I do not know, but to belong to the Church of England was infinitely better class than to be a Presbyterian, That may have been the reason; it may not, but at any rate it was detrimental in his meeting my mother. I think it very probable that the conversions may have been for snobbish reasons.

My father adulated the well-born. He easily mentioned his school days. He did tell us that, at the Edinburgh Academy to which he went, the game they played was marbles. My brothers were all at the best public schools in England where cricket and football were worshipped. So to hear my father say he played marbles was very embarrassing. Only "cads" would do such a thing. That awful word: how often it was used in those days. How it showed up the snobbish attitudes we were brought up in.

Father was mean. Mother found out later he never worked at Lloyds, but had a man to work for him; he promised Stephen a bicycle if he won scholarship to Winchester from the Dragon School – he did win the scholarship – father bought him an old bone shaker.

My father married my mother because he loved her. Admittedly when my mother married my father, he benefitted both socially and financially. My mother married my father for a complexity of reasons. She wished to get married. My father came from London. He was more interesting than the young men she met out hunting. The young man she was really getting very fond of had just gone to India for 3 years. She wasn't going to wait 3 years for anybody. Who knows when he came back, if he did, she might have changed. He might not want to marry her. It would be a risk. She was 19. High time she got married and got away from the Country Parsonage and the country life for which she had no liking.

My father, an impecunious but apparently virtuous young man, was invited by my aunt *(Frances Spottiswoode)* to go to *(Axminster)* Devonshire to stay there with them for a week. How my aunt ever came to do such a thing I cannot imagine. My mother and her cripple sister were the only ones left at home out of that large family. She must have taken my father there to stay in order that he should fall in love with my mother and yet, when he did, she "created", as they
say in this village. She created fit to bust. Which seems unreasonable, but then she was unreasonable. Her reason had been disturbed.

Because, when my first confinement was on, I asked my mother once, "Is there insanity in our family?" "No, no, my dear, whatever makes you ask such a question?" "I was thinking of the Spotts (*Spottiswoodes*)", I said. "They're all potty, at least nearly all of them". My mother got very red and hesitated and then said "Well there was a reason for that. Your aunt was very fond of going out and of entertaining. The house they had in Cadogan Square was large and very well appointed *(No.3 on the east side of the square)*. They kept carriages, butlers and footmen. Now your aunt thought it was most indelicate that, when she was going to have a baby, it should be noticeable. One couldn't go to parties if one showed. So she tight-laced, and she didn't show. But, my dear, I think it was very wrong of her. You see she had eight miscarriages and six children and you know what they are like". So my Aunt Frances was not always entirely balanced and her strange behaviour to my father may have been accounted for in that way.

She must have known him before she invited him and she must have realised that he was no doubt a worthy young man, but ineligible, and very different from the young men my mother was accustomed to meeting. But it was that very difference that made him attractive to my mother. Her friends lived on horseback and she did too. They hunted together. My father was a man from London. He was a man with ideals, with a devotion to duty and to service to his fellow men apparently. My mother told me he was on a plane above all the young men she

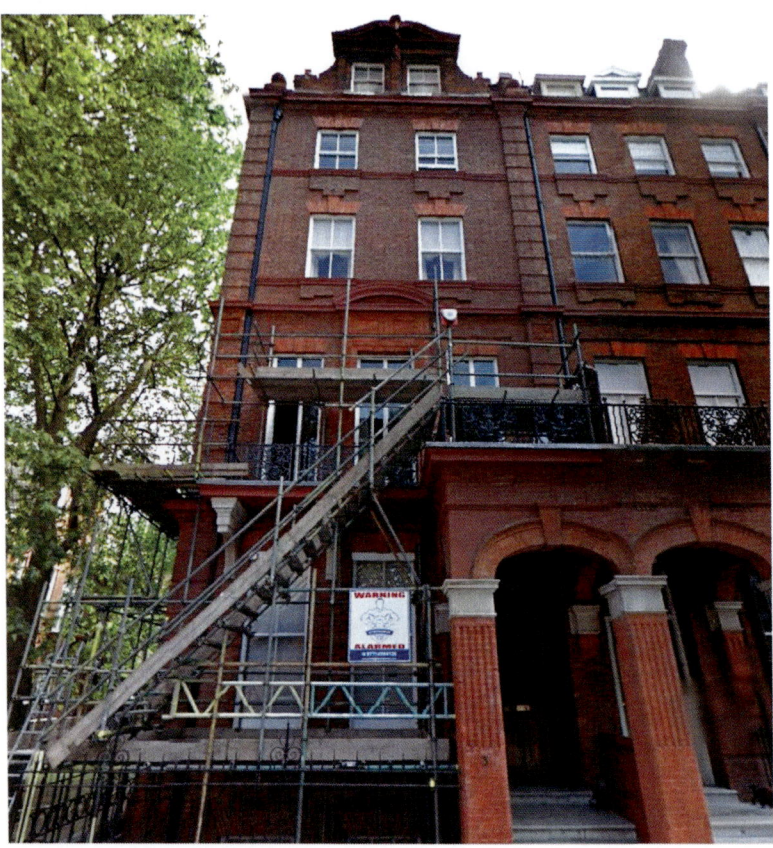

No.23 Cadogan Square today

met. So she thought then. But also the time was propitious. Her best young man, an army officer had just gone to India. Did he propose before he went? I think so. But I don't know. When she was arguing with me many years later that I should not get engaged to a young man, who was just going to India, the argument was one she must have used with herself. She told me once, "It's a mistake to get engaged to a man going abroad. How do you know he will want to marry you when he comes home? He won't have changed, but you will have. You will be five or 3 years older or whatever time it is and you will look it. Girls don't stay young forever you know. Then you may have grown apart; you will have different interests. It's a great risk."

"I could have got engaged to a young man going to India if I had liked." Her eyes lit up and her face looked sweet and gentle. "I could never understand, you know. Your brother *(Geoffrey Ford)* met him in India, of course years later, and he said he was known as being the ugliest man in the Army. I could never understand that because as a young man he was very, very good looking," and her eyes went into the distance and her voice trailed off. She pulled herself up and remembered what she was trying to convince me of. "It would have been a mistake to have got engaged to him. You understand don't you?" I felt I did."And then your father came along, so interested in world affairs and church affairs, I felt that was a new world opening up to me. He was so interesting and so different from the other men I knew. Well, I didn't marry the young man who went to India. I wasn't sure enough. I was very miserable for about 3 months. I had been brought up to think that India and the Civil Service were the highest one could attain to."

I know nothing about that week which father spent at mother's home. They became engaged and straight way Aunt Frances turned upon father and treated him like a pickpocket, which no doubt she thought he was. Their engagement was short: 6 months. Mother stayed for part of that time, at any rate, with her sister in Cadogan Square. *(Mid-Victorian etiquette held that brides-to-be could live with their future in-laws; cf. Lucy Morris, who ought to move to live with Frank Greystock's parents in Anthony Trollope's 'The Eustace Diamonds', 1871)*. One might imagine that there she and her fiancé might have grown to know one another a little. Their knowledge of one another was almost nil; not that that matters much, I think. But Aunt Frances, whether in conformity to the ruling fashion, or because she had a grudge against my father, or because she herself was unbalanced and peculiar, for what exact reason I don't know, ruled that the two young lovers should never be left alone in a room together. Perhaps she thought, as a young friend of mine did, that a kiss from a man could make a girl pregnant. Once, father and mother defeated the authorities and ran away together to Hyde Park to lose themselves in the great crowd at the Exhibition. *(This might have been for the unveiling in 1876 of the Albert Memorial, where Albert is shown holding a catalogue of the Great Exhibition of 1851.)* And after that they had to wait until their wedding day in order to have a word together alone. Mother was emphatic to me that a long engagement was a disaster, five months were quite long enough she used to say.

Aunt Frances' three elder daughters were the bridesmaids. The wedding was at Milton Abbot *(in early 1877)*. On the day before the event, all the bridesmaids came out in a rash. Aunt Frances said "Nonsense, of course it was nothing". So they all appeared in church and my mother spent her honeymoon having chicken pox. Where they went I do not know. Mother never mentioned such a thing. Father developed, or already had, a passion for foreign travel, but I don't know if they went abroad for their honeymoon. Marriage was an unavoidable state and a honeymoon was the unavoidable. Honeymoons were things that servants talked about; ladies did not mention them. Introduction to "it." Least said about all these unpleasantnesses the better. I still feel embarrassed over the subject, just as she was. I suppose chicken pox was finished with. What a thing to have on your honeymoon!

2 Eldon Road, Hampstead

The next thing I heard of was the entry into Hampstead. That is where they had decided to live. My father's parents lived there but that could not have been an inducement. They drive to their new house via St John's Wood to Swiss Cottage, where they wait for the turnpike gate man to open the gate, and then their horses, and the carriage lent by her sister, climb slowly up the hill along lanes through fields, no houses, just fields, my mother told me. No houses to be seen between Swiss Cottage and their house. *(Not quite lanes: Fitzjohn's Avenue was made in 1875 and ornamental trees planted. Applications to build 70 houses in Fitzjohn's Avenue were made between 1877 and 1879. Thus this 1877 drive occurred only just before the houses were built and when the trees were saplings.)* When I think of it I can hardly bear the vandalism. Those houses would have been ugly in a town, but they were put in fields, surrounded by fields. An oasis of ugliness. And there they still are.

Then they came to the house they had bought. That is to say, the house that mother's trustees *(the trustees of her marriage settlement, i.e. the money her father had settled on her at marriage)* had bought with her money. The trustees had been very careful. Nothing old and shabby, nothing too new and shoddy. Something solid and respectable, that was what was wanted. Some neighbourhoods and roads were definitely out of the running, not to be looked at or thought of. Two such were the Vale of Health and Downshire Hill, both of which were later to become the most fashionable and sought after properties in Hampstead. Whether they would have been good long term investments I do not know; the repairs and general upkeep must have been very heavy.

The house the trustees produced and which was approved by my parents was not at all like Downshire Hill or the Vale of Health. It was very solid, very ugly, very inconvenient and entirely respectable. *(2 Eldon Road, off Lyndhurst Road, Hampstead, now Eldon Grove.)* My parents lived there until my father died *(in 1928)* at the age of 82. The houses faced east and west.

They were semi-detached and each pair close together, so no house got the south sun. Our house had a great advantage over the others in that it was the last of the road and it had one whole side of it facing south. Not that it made much

No.2 Eldon Grove today, showing the front steps and where Phyllis climbed out of the staircase window

difference to the rooms, as none of them faced that way. Only the staircase, that interminable staircase, got the sun. I realised this one day as a child when I climbed out of a window on to the leads on the roof of the downstairs lavatory. Here was hot grilling sun, but I was quickly chased indoors and told not to be stupid. But, besides getting the sun, we had a garden beside us. I suppose on that side of us instead of another grey, dark grey stuccoed wall. In that garden stood a house by itself *(1 Eldon Road, on the site of modern Eldon Court)*. A great distinction. It was as ugly as ours and was built by the same people I suppose. That house was at the lower corner of the road *(the junction with Lyndhurst Road)* and is now occupied by Agnes Evans.

    The house that my parents lived in filled me with revulsion. I lived in it from the time I was born and I hated it. I hated its ugliness, its discomfort, its terrible weary staircases, its descent into the basement. Its unkempt barren garden. Its view of other ugly grey houses. There was nothing about it to commend it. But my parents were, I believe, inordinately proud of it. Certainly my father was. He kept it in good order. It had a certain number of rooms "done" while we were away on our wonderful summer holiday.

    One of my father's pastimes was to walk to new building estates or to go to look at properties for sale. Though I went on these expeditions with him and enjoyed them, bringing back the treasures in my pockets, bits of stone and granite which sparkled to make a rock garden in my own scrubby bit of garden, I never remember having any conversation with him. I was a great talker with my friends, but I have no recollection of ever talking to my father.

His comments about the new houses were always derogatory. Very likely they were justified. He would walk about them saying, "nothing but a rabbit hutch", etc. The houses were "shoddy, not room to swing a cat in the sitting rooms and the paint bad quality". I liked all the new ones immensely. Fresh red brick, tiled fireplaces, no basements, etc. Probably jerry-built and shoddy, but I didn't notice that. I don't know if mother genuinely liked her new home. You couldn't tell with mother. If the cook made a particularly revolting tea cake, and she made many such at one period, mother would urge people to eat large pieces, of this "delicious tea cake". Or whether she really thought them delicious I don't know. Heavy suet puddings she devoured literally with gusto. When she said her house faced just in the right way, she may have thought so, The Victorians didn't like sunshine, so I suppose east and west suited them. Terrible waste of sun I used to think.

She never complained about the back staircase, though every maid we ever had, and we had an endless succession, cursed that staircase up and down. It was appalling. Steep, dark and narrow with a twist near the bottom. Heavy silver trays etc. and every tray had to be carried up and down that for a family of 6 children and 2 parents.

Years and years later one of her grandchildren was staying in the house; luckily her beloved nanny was with her. Granny gave the child a dish and told her to carry it down those terrible stairs. The child was 2 years old and fell. When she cried, she was roundly abused for being a baby. Nanny soothed and protected her and found the child had put out the joint of one of her fingers in the fall.

That was typical. No word of criticism must be made of that terrible staircase. Stairs, stairs, steps. Unending they seemed to me as a child. How my legs ached. You started on them straight from the pavement. A wall with a balustrade rose up from the pavement. In the wall was a door or gate. You opened it and walked up one step. Then two or three paces forward on the level, then up three steps. Then four paces along on a slight slope of gravel, then the formidable erection cursed by cooks who had to kneel on them and whiten them in all weathers, except when there was a frost (that would have made them dangerous for the gentry): eleven, 12, 13, possibly 14 front door steps. Then the level of the porch, then one more up and you were inside the house. Indoors. If you wished to descend to the basement you had twelve steps down, the same anyway as the front door steps; round at the back and down three steps.

The house inside was as uneventful as it looked outside. The rooms were very large and very high, but the entrance hall was nothing, nor was the passage that went straight to the drawing room. The room facing the road and due east was the dining room. Early in the morning the sun slanted into it. There was a large picture, or I should say canvas, on the wall. The picture had long faded. Nothing was visible but in the centre a yellow green 'Madonna and Child' appeared in dark surroundings of nothing. The cook had orders every morning, when she drew back the heavy green serge curtains in the window, to leave one slightly forward, so that the slanting rays of the early sun should not touch the precious oil paint. Painted by some relation of my father. When it appeared that I might be going to paint, my father pointed at that picture proudly and said, "Well it's in the family, that was the work of my cousin". "I hope if you do paint, you'll do something better than that", said my mother with great scorn.

The room at the back of the house, the drawing room, overlooking the garden (so called), was very large and long. It had two pairs of french windows, opening on to a minute balcony about one foot wide with an iron balustrade along it. Follow this narrow balcony along and some steps led down to the garden. More steps, of course, narrow and everything black with soot. This large drawing room, about 24 feet by 16 feet, had a fireplace at one end of it. The drawing room 'drawing the curtain ritual' took place also in this room, but in the afternoon. The sun got round the house, all its goodness wasted on the wall and staircase, until it began to shed its rays into the drawing room. Prompt action must be taken. The maid must draw all the curtains in order to prevent the chair covers from fading.

The layout of the house followed the same pattern upstairs and downstairs. There were no surprises. The bedrooms on the first floor were two large and 2 small, up above that the same. There was no bath room. We were six children and two grown ups and 2 or 3 servants. In order, I think, possibly to avoid too much trouble, I don't know, a hip bath was put in mother's bedroom overnight and a flat bath in my father's dressing room. These were filled with cold water. In the morning the boys went to father's and we two girls went to mother's and there, like it or not, we had to have a bath in the same cold water. I have known days when there was ice upon it. I don't know what the grown ups did about hot baths, but, once a week, a young maid would toil up from the basement to the nursery at the top of the house carrying two cans of hot water. With luck it was fairly hot when we got into it, my youngest brother and I. We all shared the bath water, one after the other. When I was older, I had a cold bath put in my bedroom. I never got into it; I soaped my hands and made the water soapy and that was all I had of my cold bath.

The heating of the house was simple. There wasn't any. A small coal fire in the dining room and the same in the drawing room, and nursery. Chapped hands, chapped legs – just above my boots, round the top, my skin broken and bleeding, always chilblains in the winter on my feet. The grown ups endured it, taking such discomforts as a matter of course and we must too. Never any grumbling allowed. It was good for us. Perhaps it was, if we survived and we did. Discomfort didn't matter; it was morally virtuous. Comfort was of the devil. My husband years later summed up my mother by saying she had got to the pitch of thinking that anything disagreeable was morally good.

I never saw a fire in a bedroom until, years later, gas fires were put into a few rooms and a bedroom was turned into a bathroom and a geyser installed. I remember the great event of electricity being put in. Before that we had iridescent gas. When my father had electricity installed, it was not taken up to the top floor. We must all continue to be ill lit, as it must not be taken into the servants' bedrooms. They would leave it on all night. Probably an excuse on my father's part for economy.

The kitchen floor was a semi basement. It was far better than the London basements where light never entered. Every cook in turn complained of the oven. The sheet of iron on one side was worn so that I gathered that everything was burnt. But it was years before Father would buy a new stove. The kitchen at my parents' house was gloomy by day. At night it was horrible. Go down the backstairs, lighting yourself with a candle, and into the kitchen. Stop quickly on the threshold – not one step further – the floor is alive, the whole room is alive, with one struggling mass of black beetles. Our kitchen could have been a cheerful room, only just below the level of the garden. Of course, a thick mass of laurels had to be planted bang in front of the window, so as presumably to prevent the servants looking out or the visitors looking in. There was no view onto the road, as the wall rising up from the pavement obliterated that.

My parents always seemed to me extremely proud of their house. My father certainly was. He kept it in good repair. Every summer, when we all went away on that lovely six weeks holiday, some part of the house was done up. Coming home again, after six weeks in the country and near the sea, I sat in the train in a state of abject misery, fixing my mind as hard as I could on something, in order to prevent my breaking down and crying. One thing to think of was that some room had had new paper and paint. That would be exciting to look at when we got home. It was a poor compensation for losing the country and the sea, but it had to suffice. Whether my mother was also proud of the house, I don't know. She appeared to be, but then mother was like that about any of her possessions. My mother used to say the house faced exactly the right way. That it was such an advantage to have a semi-detached house, as that kept one side of the house warm. That we really couldn't hear our neighbours. We could hear not much and, as our next door people were very fine musicians, the man especially being a brilliant pianist, we didn't mind.

The house I have described sounds paltry and small. Semi-detached houses nowadays are very small, but ours was a large house. That is a substantial house. I hated it quite definitely. I knew it was ugly and uncomfortable. I longed for a red brick house. When *(in 1898)* I was about 12, Willett and others were building in red brick. My parents never knew how I hated that house. One never said what one felt in those days. *(William Willett, assisted by his son, was the principal builder in the area. His solidly built red-brick houses, with their steeply pitched roofs, tall chimneys, dormers and gables, and elaborate ornamentation, set a new standard for speculative house building.)*

The Ford children

There *(in Eldon Road)* 6 children were born and bred. A very healthy family. My parents were never ill, except when my father caught influenza during the first epidemic and was very ill. I remember no time when my mother was ill until she was middle aged. And my father only that once. Children were born at regular intervals one every two years. Birth control was something my mother only had heard of. When I was married she asked me if I knew anything about it and then in great embarrassment said she didn't want to know. I felt embarrassed too and didn't want to tell her. She told me she and my father were only "married" when another child was permissible.

The eldest child was a girl *(**Mary Marjory Ford**, 1878-1948)*, a beautiful girl with a sweet mild face and large blue eyes. So she looked in the photographs of her. Very sweet and mild. *(Marjory became a teacher after getting her London University degree at Royal Holloway College. Initially she taught locally and was living at home in 1901, but by 1911 she was a Senior Mistress at Roedean, teaching Maths.)* Instead of visiting the slums *(as Phyllis did, see p 137)*, my sister earned her living. Mother did her best to make it sound as if it was entirely for the good of mankind and father talked in a high falutin' way, as if she was doing it to pass the time until she was begged to accept some marvellous post as headmistress. She had got a scholarship to Holloway College – she was there 3 years. My mother and I were there for some Annual event. The grounds were full of young women in the ugliest hats ever designed - boaters. We three stood together. A young woman came up, touched my sister on the arm and said "Bad luck, Teddy, a 3rd", and ran off. I couldn't bear to look at Marjory's face. The term after that she went to teach at a girls' school at Watford.

At breakfast in the first week my parents were saying how odd it was they had not had a letter. I said, "I expect we shall hear on Monday. They are generally allowed to write on a Sunday." Oh dear, a ton descended on my head from my father. My sister could write when she liked (which was true); did I not realise that she had only gone to that school as a stepping stone to an eminent position as headmistress. I was duly reduced, but at the same time thought "my eye".

As Marjory got more independent, she and father were frequently coming up against one another. Differences of opinion often arose when Marjory was at home. It was a good thing that she was away teaching most of the time. One evening there was a dinner party. It was given for the new Vicar and his young bride. I was too young to be there, but next morning at breakfast a slight storm arose. Father: "I must say I was very

Mary Marjory Ford

disgusted to see that Mrs Bates drank wine at dinner last night." Marjory: "Why on earth shouldn't she if she wanted to?" Father: Because women should not drink alcohol. Men like to look up to women as something purer than themselves." Marjory: "That's got nothing to do with it. Why shouldn't women do as they like? Why should they have to conform to some absurd ideas invented by men? They should do as they liked and not bother about whether men were pleased or not." A storm ensued, of which I remember little except that father made several remarks about old spinsters. The joke of it was that I knew perfectly well what had irritated father so much. Before dinner parties he always put out what he considered to be exactly the right amount of wine. Mrs Bates had upset his calculations and there wasn't enough to go round. Marjory was never even given the chance to have any in her own home. The waitress, hired in for the occasion, knew she must not offer it to her.

At one small party at which I was present, father in a playful way offered a cigarette to the lady next to him, rather a distinguished person whom he was anxious to please. Dismay when she said "Thank you", took it and asked for a light. Mother was watching and whispered, "You take one too", knowing that I already smoked on the quiet. Next morning father told us how shocked he had been to see that Lady so and so smoked, but terribly distressed to see his own daughter doing the same. Poor father.

Soon after this, Marjory came home saying that she was going to take part in a suffragette procession. Mother was quite amused and interested but father was very upset. "Have you got a seat in the Albert Hall?" Mother asked. "Where will you be sitting?" I happened to know where her seat was, and promptly answered, "She's in the arena. Didn't you know, she is going to be thrown to the lions?" Mother burst out laughing, but Marjory almost cried and said we did nothing but make fun of her. "We mustn't let Marjory get the school mistressy manner." I was proud to feel Mother took me into her confidence. She was actually discussing Marjory with me as if I were grown up. We decided we must save her if possible, but, by the time she had really got it *(that manner)*, we didn't dare mention it, and alas it had come to stay. "I really am rather frightened of your sister", mother said to me.

Marjory was living in a school *(this must be after 1901)* not very far from home. So she came back every Wednesday to spend the day. Her day or half day off. On a certain Wednesday a clergyman who was a stranger to me came to lunch. I had seen him once before on the previous week; he had been having tea with mother. He was a tall good-looking man, except that he had a beard. He was immaculately dressed, very clean and spruce looking. His conversation at lunch surprised me. He told us at great length about his mission. He spent much time in going round to race courses preaching to the people lost in sin. I couldn't picture him doing it but I thought it must need a great deal of courage. On the next two Wednesdays he was with us again and then he faded out. A little while later, I said to Mother, "Where's that clergyman?" Mother looked very knowing and said archly (I think that is the word), "Didn't you guess?"

I wondered for a minute and then said, "Oh, he was in love with you?" He seemed to me just about the right age for mother. "What an idea! No, he wanted Marjory to marry him." Some years before, he had been to our house, a cousin of a friend of father's I think. Now he had come into a lot of money and was a rich man and he had also been given a very attractive country living. He brought with him large photographs of the beautiful vicarage and garden. He now wanted a wife and he remembered Marjory and thought her age would be suitable. I didn't think it sounded very romantic.

After two of her free Wednesdays being spoilt, as she considered, by his unwanted appearance, Marjory, who had no idea of what was in the air, apparently turned upon mother and requested that he should not be asked again. Then mother told her the object of these visits. Marjory was most distressed and wanted to know if she had encouraged her suitor. The thought of that worried her, but mother was quite able to reassure her on that point. Mother owned to me that she was disappointed that Marjory was completely firm that she would have none of it. So that was the end of that. I thought it was a pity too, when I thought of that nice house and garden. Two years later the Rev. suddenly turned up again, this time bringing large photographs of his nice looking wife and baby.

Marjory: "I never go out to a party without feeling I'm the most unattractive and worst dressed person in the world." How amazing, I, so good-looking, thought, and she is. I was in bed again. My pain *(either a migraine or her grumbling appendix, see p 168)*. Marjory was going to a dance given by the people opposite – new – very common. Stephen *(see below)* called the daughter Gertie. Marjory came to dress in our bedroom and I lay in bed watching. Marjory's dress was an old one to be revived with one of mother's exquisite pieces of old lace, this time a wedding veil much too long, and, of course, it must not be cut. Marjory stood there while mother walked round her (doing a sort of maypole dance, winding the veil round and round). Because of the value of the really lovely lace, no pins must be put in it. The effect was truly awful and at last, hoping to make mother desist, I said, "You look like a sawdust doll with a china neck". Mother and Marjory both collapsed on the bed with exhaustion and laughter. Oh! that terrible box of old lace. How we both suffered from it. It did not matter what the fashion was but our dresses, already all home made, were cut almost entirely as a back-ground for some piece of lace that mother wished us to wear.

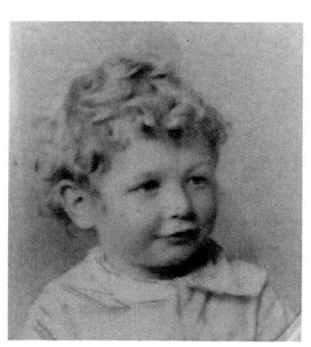

Stephen Everard Ford

Next a boy (***Stephen Everard Ford***, *1880-1912)*, but that was a different business, I believe. Mother was pregnant, the baby due in December. Father wished to go abroad, to Switzerland in the summer. He had a passion for travelling. He must go, he would go, and mother must come too. She didn't want to. They went. While there, mother had a threatened miscarriage. She was sent home and had to be on a sofa for the rest of the time, resulting in an enormously fat, heavy baby, a boy.

She had a difficult time one would have thought. But, when I was having my first child my mother was horrified. She said she never had suffered like that, nothing like it at all. She didn't know having a baby could be like that and she had had six.

The eldest son should have given great pride to his father, but somehow he didn't. Our father felt a grudge against him. Their precious holiday in Switzerland had been curtailed on his account. On his account his wife had had to be a semi invalid for 6 months. Then, when the child was eventually born, the mother was so overjoyed at it being a boy, so completely wrapped up in it that its father grew more and more jealous. I can only imagine all this. There was one thing at fault which only became apparent as the child grew up. His eyesight was bad. The oculists had said he had old age eyesight *(long-sightedness)*. When my mother was an old lady, she sometimes used the spectacles that that son had had when he was a boy. Very small lenses. He looked a jolly little fellow in photographs. Fat and jolly. He always stayed fat. His features were nondescript. Not like either parents that I could ever see. His bulk large and heavy and about 6 ft 2 in eventually. My mother loved him. My father not at all. None of his brothers or sisters liked him. I detested him. Never trust a boy who wears spectacles.

Bernard St Vincent Ford

Next came another boy **(*Bernard St Vincent Ford, 1882-1932*)**. Dark this one, dark brown *(hair)* and marmalade coloured eyes. Very like his brother in every way. The two elder ones had fair hair turning later to mousy brown – and both had blue eyes like their father. This new son was different: Mother's colouring, Mother's vivacity, Father's temper. He was a stormy mixture. Gay and generous. Never a penny in his pocket. So quick tempered he could be dangerous. He had more than his share of Irish in him. And if my mother had loved her first son, she adored her second. How the two would laugh together. He answering her back and she calling him a cheeky boy and laughing and laughing. He struck a chord in mother that none of the rest of us did. Father said he seemed always at loggerheads, but I adored him. He was very kind to me, generous with chocolates and presents, things I never had normally. He joined the Navy *(as a midshipman at the age of 15)* and had a freer life, except that he was always so hard up. I find it hard to believe, but he told me that when he went on his first cruise, father presented him with 2/6 *(two shillings and sixpence, or half a crown, worth £75 in today's values)* and that was the only tip he ever had from his paternal parent.

On one occasion, or possibly more often, Bernard during his leave went to stay in a country house with a ship mate, called Beckley. He wrote amusingly about the luxury of his surroundings. "I am lying in bed watching the valet go through my socks. He is trying to find a pair without holes." When he came home he told me about his visit; of how fed up he got sitting around all day talking rubbish with the girls, so he went off on his own, either walking or playing golf. Bernard's instincts were sound. He liked good books, and open air and walking and solitude. He had so much good in him, such humour, kindness and imagination. He ought never to have gone on the rocks. After this visit of his to the country house, my mother started the usual "we must return their hospitality". Bernard said nothing to me about it but we both knew it was quite out of the question. But mother persisted and she won to a certain extent. Mother arranged a bright and happy day for us all. The young man was staying in town. He must be invited to lunch and to play tennis in the afternoon. Bernard had to do it. He couldn't get out of it. Why did mother not see and understand? People who owned a country estate did not want to traipse out to a suburb, to a semi detached house, and play tennis on a sooty hired court between four walls. Perhaps I was a snob, but I felt strongly it was all wrong; but no arguments would have convinced mother. I don't think she had any idea that she was not a born hostess. Perhaps she was and it was just me that was all wrong. It was arranged that the naval friend should be asked to luncheon and that 4 of us should play tennis afterwards, but that's all there *(would be)* no drinks. We never had anything but wine and it would not have occurred to my parents to have wine for luncheon. Beer was unheard of – at least when I did hear my brothers mention it, I was horrified as no one but workmen drank beer, I thought. The day arrived, but the young man didn't, at least not at 1 o'clock when he was expected. We waited and waited and mother fumed because the lunch would be spoilt. At last about half an hour later, mother said he couldn't be coming and we had better eat. Bernard felt awkward. Lunch consisted of 4 cutlets, one each. By this time they were very dried up. We each had one and the fourth was sent downstairs again just in case the young man turned up, though Bernard had demanded that he should be allowed to eat it. I don't remember the pudding.

We had soon finished our festive meal and the front door bell went. Heavens above – the young man. He was pleasant and friendly and explained at length why he was late. His explanation boiled down to the fact that no cab would come out as far as our benighted neighbourhood and that he had had to take a bus and walk the rest. The cutlet was retrieved and offered to him and after that he changed – he had been carrying a suitcase, and we went up to the tennis court where we found poor Hetty *(Dalton, see below)* sitting waiting. No telephones in those days of course. I may not have mentioned the tennis court we hired by the hour. It was at the back of the little old public library. It was enclosed by a sooty wall. Very much enclosed, so much so that there was much too little run back. Owing to the blackness of everything the balls were soon as black as the few straggling trees. We played a little tennis and then were turned away by the next people who had hired the court so we trailed back to tea and the young man left as soon as he could. He and Bernard went in search of a cab and found one and we never heard from him again. Nor did Bernard receive any more invitations to stay in his country house.

(The father of "Hetty" – later described as Phyllis' "good friend" – will have been (Sir) Cornelius Neale Dalton, KCMG CB DCL, 1842-1920, who from 1897-1909 served as Comptroller General of Patents, Designs and Trademarks. He was also the author of biographies of Thomas Pitt (grandfather of William Pitt the Elder) and

of Captain Kydd. With his wife Margaret, née Gaskell, whom he married in 1873, Cornelius lived successively on Downshire Hill, at 11 Heath Rise, Willow Road (in the 1880s), and at Eskhaven (later numbered 8 East Heath Road) from 1899; then at 26 Belsize Lane (by 1911), and finally at 57 Belsize Avenue, where he died. The youngest of their four daughters, evidently nicknamed Hetty, was Catherine Esther Anne Dalton, born on 1 Feb 1886 and so exactly the same age as Phyllis.)

These sort-of entertainments in our own home froze me completely. After they were over I had to bear the criticisms of my mother, quite just ones. I had been uppish. But I never felt at my ease at home for one minute. I was just beginning to find that I could be a success when I went out, but at home no. Then my mother used to announce "I think we ought to ask so and so to the house". I prayed for deliverance but generally ineffectively.

Bernard after this told me of a strange visit he paid to another ship mate. This one lived in a very slummy part of London. Bernard wondered how people could breathe there."You could hardly see the sky," he said. I think he had been invited to lunch, but when he got there no meal appeared and there seemed to be no sign of food. The man's wife was a slummocky sort of creature. They sat in the parlour till the man asked Bernard to go outside with him. "I say old man", he said, when the door was shut, "Could you lend me 2/6?" "Of course", said Bernard and the man disappeared out of the front door. In a few minutes he was back and they were all sitting down to a festive meal consisting of a small tinned tongue. "Queer the way people lived", said B., "I couldn't live like that."

Geoffrey Noel Ford

Then another brother *(**Geoffrey Noel Ford**, 1883-1964)*. This one a seven months child; only 19 months after his brother. It was Xmas morning. My mother got onto a chair and started reaching down the presents which she had put on the top of a wardrobe. The baby started to come. The three children were whisked off to neighbours two doors away, there to spend their Xmas with two young women and their mother *(the Nevinsons)*. The new baby arrived very quickly and was born in a chamber pot. It was, compared with the others, delicate. A very pretty child with tight golden curls, marmalade eyes. By far the best looking of the family even from birth. He became a dazzlingly handsome man. But my mother had no use for him. Never, not even when he was a gentle little boy. My mother preferred guts and toughness. Geoffrey was admitted to be delicate. At the age of 5 he had an operation on his glands and so had to wear a sailor suit, as he could not wear an Eton collar. I only know of his miseries from what he himself has told me; he was sent to a convalescent home at Margate, a school for boys. It seems to have had one of those sadistic brutes as a headmaster. Geoffrey was only 5. The bullying from top to bottom of the school was brutal, and Geoff learnt every form of beastliness there was. Strange to say, Father went down to see him. Father never had visited one of his boys at school. He must have gone on this occasion, because mother was ill or something. Even he noticed Geoff's misery and he was brought home. When he arrived back, my mother found he was hardly able to walk. She had very carelessly sent in his clothes a pair of father's socks by mistake. The nurse doubled these over in his shoes and the poor child had to try and walk like that. I do not think my father removed him forthwith. They waited till the end of the term.

A somewhat similar thing happened to my brother in law. My husband's father *(Rev. Henry Castle Floud 1847-1937)* was a clergyman. When he married, the living he got *(Froyle, Hants., 1876-1897)* was worth £245 *(£117,000 today)* but, owing to tithe or glebe or something *(perhaps in 1894 when the Parish Council took over many functions from the Church)*, it was reduced. He and his wife were good managers, but they had a job to feed and clothe 4 children, and then came education. Frank *(Francis Lewis Castle Floud, Phyllis' future husband)* got a scholarship to Cranleigh. He had scarlet fever when he sat for the exam. There was no hope of a similar thing for Harold, who was charming to look at with large brown eyes, like a gazelle. Good at games but no use at work. A kind friend got him in to the Blue Coat School. It was then in London. *(Christ's Hospital was then in Newgate Street in the City of London. Harold was a pupil there at the age of 12 in the 1901 census.)* The public were allowed to come in and watch the children being fed. They were so badly fed that, when my father in law came to London to see his son, he was shocked to see his appearance. He looked, and was, starved. Mr Floud saw the headmaster and said he was taking his son away with him that day. The headmaster was furious and said he couldn't. The boy was not going away in the school clothes. All right. Mr F. went out and bought an outfit came back and retrieved the boy. *(£117,000 sounds like a good income to us, but the cost of a public school and university education for two boys was and is high. His parents offered to pay for Frank to follow his father to Wadham College, Oxford, provided he would agree to take Holy orders, as they could afford only one set of fees. Frank refused and went into the Civil Service straight from school. Harold agreed and went to Wadham.)*

Phyllis Allen Ford

Then came myself (**Phyllis Allen Ford**, *1886-1976)* and the less said of me the better. No looks at all. A strong likeness to my sister but my face irregular, whereas hers was regular. My eyes, unlike any of the others', bright green. My hair a chestnut brown and masses of it, bright cheeks. My father liked me well enough, far preferring me to my sister. My brothers, except the eldest one, were very fond of me. My mother had no use for me. The last brother and I seemed to have made some mistake in being born.

Five years then of peace and another boy came (**Aubrey Hammick Ford**, *1891-1965*). He grew into a good looking edition of the eldest brother; heavy in build, but a pleasant face and a very pleasant nature. The kindest person on earth. He and I spent much of our time together, quarrelling incessantly, but I loved him.

My brothers

I had 4 brothers but I had never seen them undressed, until one day, when mother was out, they captured me and gave me a demonstration of the male frame. Also satisfying themselves as to the female body. My eldest

Aubrey Hammick Ford

brother, whom we all hated and who frightened us, was the ringleader over that and similar episodes. I would never had dared utter to mother and I had no one else - the sailor's orphans *(servants, see p 65)* weren't much good. My brother used to pay me afterwards on the few occasions that these things happened. He paid me 1 shilling *(5p, perhaps worth some £5 today)* and he had a nerve.

One day he handed it over to me in full view of everybody at breakfast. I nearly died. "What's that for?" asked mother. I went scarlet all over. "I said I'd give it to her", said Stephen casually. "You're far, far too generous, my dear boy", said my mother. Things got to such a pass that I demanded a key for my bedroom. At once mother jumped to the conclusion that I was up to no good and I was quickly told that it wasn't a nice habit to lock oneself into one's room. As I couldn't have a key, I used a hat pin. When I was sitting in my tin tub, having a tepid bath, the door opened and in he came. I jumped out, wrapped a towel round me, and I seized one of the enormous hat pins (hats were one foot *(30cm)* across) off the dressing table. My brother turned to go and I darted at him and gave him two digs in the back. He called me a devil and quickly left. But even over that he managed to put me in the wrong with mother. At lunch he said "I do think, mother, you ought to teach that sister of mine to keep her temper. Do you know she jabbed me in the back with a hat pin – drew blood too?" Mother was shocked and told me so and again I blushed to the skies and said nothing. I suppose I was too upset at the thought of mother's distress, if she really knew what her beloved son was like. Also I couldn't talk about those sort of things, I never could. I tried to acquire knowledge by other means, the Bible etc, but I never could talk about such things or listen.

Stephen

I used to envy the freedom of my brothers. Their frequent comings and goings. Mostly goings. Stephen had a friend whose parents lived somewhere near the *(Norfolk)* Broads in a very luxurious house surrounded by park land. Towny men were always welcomed at such houses and, whenever he could, he used to get on his bike and be off. He was foolish and used to boast of riding to Norwich *(110 miles)* without getting off his machine. In our drawing room were two large vases with flowers printed on them. They stood on the floor, one on either side of the chiffonier *(see p 109)*. In these vases were tall rushes and honesty, and those delightful little red Chinese lanterns called *(Physalis)* were in some. Occasionally, when no one was about, one could burst a lantern, but it was a pity as one found one had just spoilt it. The bullrushes became a form of entertainment when they got tired of standing there and decided to moult. Just a little help, when no-one was looking, and the brown velvet cushion would almost melt away in one's fingers. This didn't happen often; in fact very rarely. Those bullrushes must have stood there for years on end and must have been quite filthy. When they were disintegrating on one occasion, mother began to badger Stephen. I use the word because it describes the process. When mother wanted something however small, she was going to get it, and she would go on and on with such insistence until she did. She wanted new bullrushes and she found out that they grew in profusion on the estate of Stephen's friends, the Roppeys. "Couldn't Stephen bring some home?" No, he couldn't bicycle with them. "Couldn't he cut some when he was next there and post them?" No, he couldn't do that without asking Mrs Roppey and then she could have them sent. That would put mother under an obligation to Mrs R and be very awkward. Well, mother won, as she always did. The bullrushes arrived most beautifully packed and then another argument. Mother must write and thank Mrs R and enclose the postage. But here Stephen won and mother didn't press the point. Stephen said that Mrs R had merely said to her head gardener, send off some bullrushes to this address and that was that. What was very annoying for Stephen was that he knew that bull rushes were no longer "the thing". Most of us were not to realise that till about 5 years later. Bullrushes and aspidistras went out at the same time. Every Saturday mother intended to wash the aspidistras, but very often they were forgotten. How I hated the things. One of them stood on a table by the huge dining room window. It stood in a brass pot. Washing them consisted in wiping their grimy leaves with warm water and a soft rag. I also detested the dirty laurels and the dirty holly. There is something super sensitive about the ends of my fingers. There were many things I could not bear touching. Velvets and also baize, the tops of card tables, for instance. I would not stroke the top of a card table with the ends of my fingers. The thought of it gives me shudders down my spine. Blankets too. But I never met anyone else who felt the same as I do. Dust was particularly unpleasant, I found. But in those days I never dusted a room. A chamois leather above all upset me. The only form of house work we ever indulged in was, on occasions, to clean some of the ornate silver. The huge silver tray and the large spoons with a letter embossed on them. I could not bear that job because plate powder drying on the tips of one's fingers, plus the feel of a chammy leather, was almost unbearable. And still is, the only way to endure it is to wear cotton gloves.

When *(Stephen)* went abroad, mother kept his bedroom exactly as he left it, waiting for the day of his return, which never came. I slept in that room, as the space was needed, but mother emphasised that nothing must be moved. His books were kept in order and she talked as if he would one day come home in rapture crying, "Oh, my own beloved little bedroom, my own beloved home, how I have missed you. How many a time have I dreamed of you and of you, mother dear." I know one thing: if I was glad when I got away from home, he was gladder.

Bernard

I must have been about 12 years old *(in 1898 when Bernard joined the Navy)* when an atmosphere of fearful anxiety pervaded our household, and mother at a moment's notice started off for Naples. "Your brother is seriously ill of typhoid," my father said. Mother's favourite son at the point of death! No wonder she looked like that when she left us to go as fast as she could to see him, not knowing if he would live when she got to him. The telegram she had received left her little hope. She ate nothing on the way, she told me afterwards. But when at last she arrived and saw her precious son wasted away, thin as a skeleton, her presence had a wonderful effect on him and from that moment he started to recover.

When at last he was well enough to travel home (Mother had been with him all the time in the hospital), he was to me almost unrecognisable. He had had his head shaved and a downy growth of tiny dark curls covered it. That was what struck me most – that and how tall he had grown. He was 6 ft 3in. It was very good to have him safe home, but somehow I did not feel that my parents were happy about it. I sensed there was something wrong but had no idea what it could be. It must have been a long while before he was recovered enough to go back to his ship. He was in the Royal Navy. One evening he did not come home. I went to bed and imagined he was coming in later, but next morning he was not at breakfast and the concern of my parents was obvious. Sometime later in the day he turned up. When he found me alone, he said, "Do you know where I was last night? I spent the night in prison. It was only for being drunk and disorderly, stupid of me. I always make such a hell of a row. I only tell you this in case you might think something worse of me." I was horror stricken and said nothing. But what did he mean by saying he might have been doing something worse? What could be worse? That was the beginning for me of a menacing cloud, a cloud that grew and was never dispelled.

It was shortly after my marriage *(1909)* that the blow fell about my second brother. He had been dismissed from the Navy. He was out in Australia at the time. Ever since his severe illness in Naples (typhoid), there had been a sort of cloud over him. He was hardly mentioned. Mother was ready enough to talk about him, but not father. My mother had told me at that time when she brought him back from Naples, with no hair on his head, only a little fluff and looking like a skeleton, that he had come under the evil influence of a naval officer. This man, she said, made a business of ruining young officers. My brother had been taught to drink.

I hated to see the drunks rolling about the street, they disgusted and frightened me — I didn't see much of him. He was in awe of Frank *(Phyllis' husband)* and felt awkward with him. I heard rumours about him. He had almost been had up for creating a disturbance at a political meeting in the street. Some young men whom we knew, the Marshalls, were very kind and dragged him away and took him home with them. It was very good of them, as they were a family mother had never called on. They were a family of four sons. Poor Mrs. Marshall. She was so desperately disappointed when her 4th child was a boy that she kept him wearing skirts and long golden ringlets until he was about 7. Poor child.

My friend, Gladys Griffith, told me about Bernard. She would come to see me and talk about him, telling me what he was doing. She was, from then on, devoted to my mother, the fact being that she had fallen in love with Bernard. Like all unsatisfactory sons of those days he was sent to Canada. Gladys became more and more restless and miserable. She had no happiness in her home life. The plain one among five sisters. She had a little money and she more or less ran away from home to Canada. There she took a job as mother's help on a farm. Having been brought up to do absolutely nothing domestic, she cannot have been a very useful help. She stayed for about a month in each job and eventually got married to the son of an English clergyman out there. So she never saw Bernard again, though she continued to love his memory.

Bernard was safely in Canada for life, I suppose my parents thought. My mother must have always been thinking about him. She did so adore him. he was certainly not making his fortune out there in Canada, barely a living, judging from the occasional letters that came home. Just casual jobs, that was all, with bad intervals between. *(He described himself as a surveyor in 1914)*. Then came the war. We *(husband Frank and I)* had luckily already moved away from Hampstead *(to Epsom)*. My brother joined up with the Canadian forces *(enlisting on 23 September 1914)* and was back in England. My father ill-advisedly thought that now was an opportunity for Bernard to clear his name and start afresh; he moved heaven and earth to get him taken back into the Royal Navy and at last he was successful. I write without very definite knowledge, as I did not any longer live near my parents. I think Bernard was posted to a battleship, but then we heard he was in command of a mine sweeper *(he had the rank of Lt-Commander in September 1915)*. He had said that he was engaged to a girl in Canada, Scottish, I think. One night, he told me later, he had been out on the booze and he suddenly thought how nice it would be to have this girl with him. He sent a cable telling her to come over at once, giving my parents' address. He then departed on his mine sweeper, and not a word was heard of him or from him.

The young woman *(Elizabeth)* arrived. She was a nice person, big and strong and cheerful and would make an admirable wife for a man in the Colonies. She was a lady, but not the incapable sort that I was. She arrived at my parents *(in Hampstead)* and found there was no letter or message from Bernard and that no-one had heard from him for weeks. She was indignant. "Just *like* him," she said. She would have nothing more to do with him. I was shocked, but then I didn't realise what it would mean to marry an undependable man. I was thinking that a marriage to a decent girl would be the saving of him. Time went on. No news. One evening Frank came home from London. He took me in his arms and said , "I have bad news. Bernard has been court-martialled and dismissed from the Navy."

He mentioned some crime but it conveyed nothing to me. My legs had crumpled up beneath me and he had to hold me up. Bernard had to all intents and purposes disappeared out of our lives. I was greatly concerned about the girl. Her position seemed to me tragic. After some time Frank wrote to a cousin of his in the police, a high up. He soon was able to tell us that Bernard had enlisted under another name in the Guards. *(In 1917 he was a Lance-Corporal in the Coldstream Guards under his own name.)* My parents were furious at what they called Frank's interference. I bicycled over to their headquarters, which were not far from us, and stood at the gates hoping to see him come out one afternoon. He came and we went off to a canteen or restaurant together and almost enjoyed ourselves. He amused me as he was so pleased, when I called the waitress "Miss". He had been to some quite cheap tea room with my sister one day and she had called, "Waitress, waitress," and he felt very ashamed. It was too snooty, he said. I left him with the understanding that I would get Elizabeth to come and stay and that he should come over and meet her. We parted and he, so he told me later, went off and got completely sozzled. Nervous reaction, I suppose - he told me with tears in his eyes that he would say to himself, "Mother, mother," knowing he mustn't drink and with the words on his lips he would go on drinking. It certainly wasn't that he didn't try. I got Elizabeth down to stay. She would not commit herself. She was still furious with Bernard. She would see what she felt when she saw him. Bernard arrived over to lunch and the meal went off all right and then I said I was going to have a rest and I left them in our little drawing room. When I crept down some time later, there was complete silence but, as I stood at the door, I was taken aback at a strange sound, like very heavy breathing.

I crept outside and looked in at the window. Bernard was sunk deep down in an armchair, his head back, his mouth wide open. He was fast asleep. She was sitting reading on the sofa. It appeared that, as soon as I left them, Bernard had fallen asleep. She was just beginning to tell him what she thought of him and she found he wasn't listening at all. He had dropped off. I saw it was useless. I could do nothing. He had lost all interest in her and I don't think she felt she could forgive him. I could do no more. She was a nice girl. She went into the forces and I never saw her again. Bernard went to France with the Guards and came back with a wound in the right arm. I heard he was in hospital at Shoreham and I bicycled down to see him. Owing to bad nursing, his arm had been left tied up for weeks, his right hand was almost useless. His fingers all curled round as they had been round the splint. In spite of treatment they never recovered. I bicycled to Shoreham from Epsom, forty miles, and got there at 10 pm. I was very pleased with myself as I did the ride without getting off my machine. Very foolish.

After he was demobilised, *(Bernard)* lived at my parents. The basement room was given over to him. He worked in a chocolate factory, we saw him occasionally. He arrived one night at our little house at Epsom. Frank was out doing warden's work or something. Alice had gone to bed. *(Bernard)* arrived rolling drunk. I put him into F's dressing room on a camp bed, the only room I had. He was sick over everything. It was awful.

Another time when we had moved to a bigger house *(23 Alexandra Road, Epsom)*, he arrived one afternoon, his face streaming blood. We had a tennis party on in our garden. It must have been a Saturday afternoon. He came in looking terrible but fairly sober. He had lost his way and come through the "splash", a small stream running across the road, but quite obviously then had run into a wall with his face. I began to realise then that drink didn't just make you get drunk, it demoralised you. He had changed. He was no longer the quick amusing man, fond of exaggeration but always out to find the truth, quick-witted, affectionate and gay. He was becoming morose and demoralised. If he wanted money, he would have almost done anything to get it. He would ask me for money. If I gave it to him, as I generally did, he would later on rave at me. I must never, never, never give him money if he asked for it. He only drank it. He became shifty, irresolute and his face, the face so like his mother's, the big nose, the too small chin, the high cheek bones, his marmalade eyes – mother's were dark green – had become lined and drawn. His face – a haunted infinitely sad expression – was full of sorrow, almost agony.

One day I heard that he was going to Australia. I went to the station, though how I found out when or from where he was leaving, I do not know. My parents were abroad at the time, I think. But I found out and I was glad I did. He was sitting on a great big old trunk on the station all alone. He was touched and quite overcome when he saw me. We sat together and had little to say. He was emigrating. *(He left Southampton bound for Fremantle via the Cape in August 1924.)* We said goodbye and we never saw one another again. We wrote to one another occasionally. He was clearing land. His twisted hand must have been a drawback but I suppose he was glad to get the disability pension. After he had been gone about two years, my sister wrote to Frank asking him to lend or give money, £200 I think, to Bernard to help him improve his land, or his shack or something. Frank declined very wisely. At the time I was a little upset about it. My sister was upset about it and said bitterly that she would have to send the money herself. "Well let her' said Frank,"if she wants to. I haven't money to throw away. If I were giving it to anyone, I should give it to my sisters."

The wonderful improvements to Bernard's farm were never made, I believe, I know little – my mother received an ill-written letter from a neighbour of his. Bernard had been celebrating on his birthday. He was taken ill. The neighbour had had to get him to a hospital. "He was yelling in agony every time the cart jolted." And so on. He died in hospital of T.B. of the kidneys, I think. *(Bernard died in 1932 at the age of 50 in Northam, 60 miles north-east of Perth, Western Australia)*. What belongings he had went to my sister. I heard little about it all, partly because we had all got out of the way of talking of him and partly because my sisters and, I think my mother, resented the fact that F would not lend him money.

Now, I understand, it is possible to be cured. At one time, not long before he went to Australia, I made enquiries about the possibility of a cure. I was recommended to a doctor in Harley Street and wrote to him, I think he was a psychiatrist. He said he was ready to try to cure my brother if he, Bernard, was anxious to be cured. I broached the subject to him tentatively – "Give up drinking," said Bernard with great force. "Give up drinking? It's my only pleasure in life". He talked about this emphatically for ages, he was a great talker. I came to the conclusion that I could do nothing.

Garden at Eldon Road

The garden was a bone of contention between my parents. It was the usual strip at the back of the house, but in our case a wide strip. A stable, not belonging to us, with rooms above it, thrust its stucco side up above one wall at the side of the garden. It was a good wall, the stable wall that is, for beating a ball against. The garden had trees and a few laurels struggling to grow up the left side against the garden wall. They did not struggle very successfully as they faced due north. The bed against the wall at the end was equally unsuccessful, as it faced due east. The bed on the south side had a certain amount in it. At the top end on the south side were rhododendrons. I did not like their sooty leaves, but I loved the lilies of the valley which grew in a thick mass nearby. There were a few standard roses and, near the steps leading up to the drawing room was strong smelling privet, put there lest the neighbours should see over. The best thing of all out of a not very attractive lot was the wisteria. It was always a mystery as to how that grew wherein it did. It had its roots near the bottom of the steps, and a great thick trunk. From there it wandered up the wall dividing. It started up the house. What a brave tree to try to climb that house. But not only did it succeed but it also covered the house. It was wonderful. It was our show piece. I loved it. It came right up to the nursery window at the top. It climbed all over the iron bars outside the window and it flowered all over itself from top to bottom. The sweet smell and the beauty of it.

The front garden had a piece of grass and the inevitable shrubs. In the back garden was a swing up near the end. The whole area was unkempt and untidy. Father knew nothing about gardening, nor did mother, but the garden was her province. I think I remember a man coming in once a week for a few hours to mow the grass and tidy up. Otherwise the gardening was left to mother. She used to argue, and she may have been right, that you either have to have a nice garden for the grown ups or a nice playground for the children. It was our playground and we used it a lot. It was dangerously near the windows and there were consequently occasional disasters. The grass in the garden got churned up by our boots, the ground under the swing especially.

My mother never liked having tea out of doors, I am sure the servants couldn't have liked it either. Trays to be carried either up from the basement or down a very narrow staircase from the drawing room. But on occasions she had tea out there if relations had come to see her.

Which reminds me of something that makes me feel quite sick. I don't want to think about it or write of it. Have other people these horrible poignant memories, poignant is the word, because they stab at one, leaving one flinching? I have so many more memories of that sort than happy ones. Many, many more.

One afternoon the wife of a nephew of my mother's had come to tea. The nephew *(Capt. Adrian George Spottiswoode 1868-1930)* was one of the dotty family, one of the Spots and he was very odd. It was said that he got sunstroke when he was in the army and he was consequently invalided out. He was a huge man with a round moon face, large vacant blue eyes and a moony manner. When he was about 50 *(actually 32 in 1900)*, he married a widow *(Jane Atwood née Wilson – Trissie – b.1864 in Manchester of Scottish parents)*. She was very badly off and, as she had a son *(Leslie Atwood b.1895)*, by her first husband, it was a relief to her to marry into a good family and to a man who had solid money behind him. She was a harmless, amiable, silly little thing with red fizzy hair and a very vivacious manner. Mother rather liked her and all her new relations accepted her kindly. With her to tea came her son *(this cannot be Leslie because of his age)*. He was a boy of about 12. I was about 10. We sat in the garden. I had a cat. I didn't really like cats but this one had been given to me and there it was. The boy, Tony I think he was called, stretched out his hand, caught the cat, lifted it onto his knee and gently stroked it. Talk went on, tea was finished and mother and "Trissie" went on chattering. Trissie with a very strong Scottish accent. I have always intensely acute eyesight. I miss nothing. My husband says I see through brick walls and often see things that aren't there. My children say it is like living with a detective in the house. I am putting off the horror but I must now come to it.

I glanced at my cat, which Tony was fondling, and was appalled by a strange look in its eyes. A look of terror and agony. Without appearing to look, I looked; I myself was sweating with fear. The cat's eyes started to protrude, literally they were popping out of its head, then I saw with one hand he was stroking it and, with the other placed under it, he was pressing with his fingers on its wind pipe. I was now in agony. I was sitting quite close and I stretched out my arms to the animal saying, "Pussy, pussy," calling it. Tony had to release it. He let it go. It was off his knee in

Phyllis and Mrs Nevinson *(see p 59)* at the base of the iron staircase to the Eldon Road garden, 1890

a wink, uttering a long, ghastly cry; it disappeared down the garden. I sat petrified with horror. I couldn't sleep. Three days later my mother was reading a letter. "Oh dear, oh dear", she said, "how distressing. Listen to this. Poor Trissie, you know she was here a few days ago. Poor poor Trissie. She had a cat, a great big marmalade Persian that she was devoted to, and what do you think? It crawled into her house shockingly mangled; oh terrible, its eyes hanging out on threads, most dreadful. She had had to have it destroyed. She is sure it must have been done by two boys she saw passing her house carrying tennis rackets. Oh dear, how very dreadful." I didn't say anything. Odd, I never told anyone, not my best friend, but I couldn't go to sleep that night nor for many nights to come. I knew who had done it.

Tears

One of the minor banes of my life was and is my proneness to tears. They flowed unwelcome on so many occasions, when they were not required. It didn't matter that I wept like a waterfall when I was sitting in an armchair reading a book at home, it didn't really matter if I wept at funerals, but at weddings it was embarrassing to myself and my mother. After my first wedding I was on the look out. I had firmly to think of anything and everything rather than the matter in hand. The first time that I disgraced myself was at Hetty's second sister's wedding. *(Mary Elizabeth Neale Dalton, b.1877 on Downshire Hil and known as 'Ellie', was the Daltons' second daughter. On 10 Dec 1901 – when Phyllis was 15 – Ellie was married at St John-at-Hampstead to Arthur George Cross of Holly Mount. Both bride and groom were registered as 'architects'.)* Asked by my mother for an explanation of my peculiar behaviour in the hall, when the bride was going away, I said I was so sorry for her mother – I was very sentimental and pictured the broken-hearted mother losing her cherished daughter. (I tried to pretend that my own mother would feel like that about me.) My mother said she had never heard such nonsense, that Ellie's mother was only too thankful to get her daughter married off. Which was quite true, as there were four daughters and no sons. The real truth was I felt deeply moved because of the solemnity of the occasion. The irretrievable "I will" was terrible, but I couldn't explain that, so I said I was very sorry for the bride's mother, which was partly true and easier to explain.

 I cried on many quite unpredictable occasions but, worse than that, I was frequently sick. Here there and everywhere. As the Americans so vividly express it, I threw up, and, just as my tears couldn't be regulated, nor could this other.
I was certainly no respecter of places. There were no cars in those days, but railway carriages nearly always did for me. They smelt so. It was, I think, quite natural that Chopin's Funeral March played on the organ in church should set me off, the bereaved family all standing enveloped in black; that was reasonable, but to burst into tears at fire engines! I really wonder mother didn't beat me. She must have wanted to. We had an invitation, she and I, to go to a County Council Fire Display in Battersea Park with the two very nice old sisters of a Councillor. We had very good places in a stand and the day was pleasantly hot. Towards the end of the

rather lengthy display, a dummy house was set on fire and dummy figures were rescued. That was very exciting and it was closely followed by a 'march past' of fire engines. The noise was terrific as they went roaring and clanging by – all their bells ringing. Hundreds of them tearing by in a flash. The thrilling excitement of it! I suppose that was what did me down. I knew nothing but the noise and clamour until silence came at last and one Miss M. said "Aren't you well, dear?" Said the other, "I don't think she can be well". Mrs. F.: "Do you think she would like an ice?" What was happening? What was the matter? Why were they looking at me so oddly? I apparently was not only crying but I was sobbing. The dear Miss Ms, they must have thought I was mad. They never mentioned it again afterwards. Nor did my mother, except to say when I was going to a play where there was a rescue from a fire, "Take plenty of hankies, you know what fire engines do to you, " and we both laughed. After that experience in Battersea Park, I was able, when on rare occasions a fire engine went tearing down the street, to hold tight on to myself and prevent the tears from flowing but it needed some doing.

My own Confirmation opened the flood gates. How thankful I was that I was being "done" in a strange church, in *(Christ Church)* Albany Street, NW1, where I knew nobody. Only my mother was present and she must have been fairly accustomed to my behaviour. This time the trouble was I had left my hanky in my coat and given it to mother, so I was saturated and couldn't do anything about it. How I longed to be quite ordinary and to behave quite easily without having to try so hard.

Parents and children

As far as I know, only one of my friends was fond of her parents and she, I think, had a most selfish mother. I asked one of my friends how her mother occupied herself. "She spends her time," she said, "running up and down stairs all day, calling people." As that was her main occupation, what a good thing that she lived in a four-storied mansion with 72 stairs in it. But how completely different the relationship of parents and children is now to what it was in my young days. Everybody and every generation can probably say the same. Yet, I wonder, perhaps things have not changed. Listening to a play on the wireless the other day, I was to hear a boy's point of view about boarding schools. This boy was devoted to his mother and his home. He, therefore, greatly resents being sent to a boarding school, just as our own children did. The boy says most of the other boys don't mind much being boarders because being at home is worse. So many of them are glad to get away from their parents. I persuaded two of my children separately to accept invitations to stay away with school friends. Both of them were miserable and they both had much the same story to tell. The parents of their friends bickered without a break and the children were expected to amuse themselves all day, without seeing their parents except at meals. Bernard *(Bernard Francis Castle Floud, 1915-67)*, aged about 10, wrote me a letter asking me to send a wire to him to return home at once – which I did.

Daily life in Eldon Road

Family prayers took place daily in the dining room. Father rang the bell. It was a large brass clanging bell which stood in the hall on the floor at the bottom of the stairs. We called it the hall but really it was a rather wide passage leading from the front door to the drawing room. The dining room was on the right and the staircase on the left. By the time the bell rang the whole family had had its cold baths. All the boys and father in one and the girls and mother in the other. Father, having finished his dressing, descended to the dining room. The cook who did the dining room had to quit and father engaged in prayer on his own, I believe. The round table was laid. A large cottage loaf, butter and marmalade to be eaten separately by the children. Porridge dishes for the varying sorts of mixture that was produced by the ever changing cooks. One egg cup for father, who had a boiled egg every day of his life. We had them on Sunday. I say he had them every day but occasionally he struck. When the eggs were so high that even he noticed them, the two rashers of bacon came up instead and I minded that because they smelt so good. The eggs varied as much as the porridge.
My mother, who was a country woman, never ate one.

They *(the children)* were also supposed to have washed their teeth. Mother said that if we washed our teeth every day we should get one penny at the end of the week. At one time she put a paper on the wall of her bedroom and we were supposed to sign it daily. I know I scarcely ever washed my teeth. I disliked doing it very much and still do. I didn't cheat, I don't think. Seven days' teeth washing and only one penny hardly seemed worth the trouble. How amazing that I have all my teeth now, except for one wisdom removed. Our weekly allowance was all paid, if I remember rightly, in that sort of way. Rewards for virtue. The result being that I never got any. I don't remember at the moment what horrible toils we had to perform in order to receive our pittance. Oh yes.

Nail biting

The blight of my young life was my habit of biting my nails. For years my allowance on Saturday of 3d *(threepence, £1.30 in today's money)* was not forthcoming, because it was only too obvious that I had been biting my nails.
I hated and loathed doing it and yet I did it. I would kneel beside my bed imploring God to keep me to stop it and find that, as I so knelt, I was gnawing at my fingers. To people who have not been addicts they cannot realise what a miserable curse it is. I hate now even talking about it. It makes my inside squirm to think of it. But I don't think most grown ups understand the problem. The thing is that once one has started to bite one's nails there is no stopping because there is always another little rough bit or loose piece to be removed. The wisest way of helping the child is to do what a friend of mine did. Take the child to a nice young manicurist who will trim off those loose jagged pieces and make the best of what is there, and encourage the child to take a pride in its hands. But the chief thing is to have the nails smoothed.

It is no enjoyment to bite one's nails. It is hell – one is so ashamed. Imagine at a party finding oneself compelled to play Up Jenkins. *(Up Jenkins is a party game in which players conceal a small coin (or in some variations a ring) in their palm as they slap it on a table with their bare hands. The goal of the game is for the players on the team without the coin to correctly identify which hand the coin is under).* Here you have to sit amongst a dozen of your contemporaries spreading your hands out on the table in full view of them all and keeping them there for most of the game. I loved Up Jenkins but how I dreaded playing it when my fingers were at their worst. Finding that I bit my nails while I said my prayers, I put on gloves for that occasion. The shame of it was so awful. I remember some lady, I don't know who, probably an aunt, asking me to put my finger on the string when she was tying a knot. Horrors. Another misery was to be told to untie a knot in string. Or more difficult still in one's boot lace. Almost impossible. My mother's methods were as usual drastic, but useless and I think cruel. A shout, a slap on the hand which made me jump out of my skin, because I didn't indulge unless I was thinking or reading. And then that awful letter I had to write. 'Dear Lady Dalton, I am very sorry I cannot come to tea with Hetty on Saturday as I have been biting my nails.' Lady D. *(Dalton)* didn't particularly like me, but I think she must have had a word with mother because that form of punishment was not inflicted again.

Daily life, continued...

We are now dressed, our teeth washed, or not, and the next proceeding is that we all, including mother, kneel down and bury our noses in the bed clothes of the large double bed in mother's room. A good deal of elbow fighting goes on surreptitiously. I can't remember what prayers consisted of at all, except we ended up with the Lord's Prayer, and then the big bell downstairs clanged. Still nudging one another and giving surreptitious kicks, we then go down to a freezing dining room. I must

The Ford children about 1903; (l to r) Geoffrey, Marjory, Phyllis, Aubrey, Bernard and Stephen

admit that I never noticed that it was cold when I was young, but it must have been. I did find it very cold when I had to practice the piano there before breakfast. But I don't remember feeling cold at breakfast. The fire no doubt by then gave out some heat. An old man with a beard looked down upon us from the corner above the wardrobe and I shut my eyes. A coffee pot hanging on a brass stand had a light put under it and it was intended that coffee would be ready by the time family prayers was over. It generally was. On a few occasions it behaved oddly, spattering and popping. This was highly entertaining as, when family prayers were on, no one felt it right to get up and deal with it. But such incidents were rare diversions. Family prayers followed the same pattern every day for years. Father in a large armchair on one side of the fire. Mother in another armchair facing him. They were upright sort of chairs, not for lounging in. I sat against the wall beside the fireplace on a small stool, until my young brother was old enough to come there. Then I was promoted to a chair. Next to my mother, the family in age dwindled down until it almost met the servants but not quite. When I turned round to kneel at my stool, my eyes were glued to the wallpaper. It was Morris' pomegranates. I knew every pip by heart, I could almost do it now. For 24 years that paper clothed the walls of the dining room. I was surprised one day when I saw a new piece of it. It bore only an outline resemblance to the sooty object I used to press my nose against daily.

(In 1881 Robert Edis published 'The Decoration and Furniture of Town Houses' and included a picture of his own drawing room with 'Pomegranates' wallpaper. The Fords were showing themselves persons of modern taste in having it. By the end of the 1890s Morris wallpapers were hung in the homes of the artistic middle class. According to the Daily Telegraph, 'university dons' were typical of Morris & Co.'s clientele, and 'when married tutors dawned upon the academic world, all their wives religiously clothed their walls in Norham Gardens and Bradmore Road, Oxford, with Morris designs of clustering pomegranates'.)

William Morris' Pomegranates

Robert Edis, *The Decoration and Furniture of Town Houses*

One morning stands out in my memory, when I was 5 and 2 months *(in April 1891)*. My mother wasn't there. Quite unprecedented. My mother was never ill, never even unwell. But my father beckoned my sister into mother's arm chair. All very odd and we began prayers with the usual bible reading, followed by the usual prayers, everyone suddenly getting up, turning round and flopping down on their knees, their behinds sticking out, their elbows on the chairs, their faces in their hands. The usual prayers were said and then I heard something new. The usual prayers conveyed nothing to me. They were just the familiar sounds. But here was something else and I distinctly heard my father read, "We thank thee, oh Lord, for this gift of a son" *(Aubrey Hammick Ford)*. I was thrilled. I could scarcely bear to go on kneeling.

As soon as it was over I jumped up. I approached my sister. "Have we really got a baby brother?" I asked. "Yes, of course shut up you silly little idiot, shut up". Thus I learnt that we were now six of us. Years and years later I told my sister of this incident, which she had of course forgotten. She excused herself on the grounds that she had known about mother's pregnancy and had greatly resented it. She thought there were plenty of children already. Her annoyance was heightened by the fact that, although she was 13 years old, she was ignored and no one seemed to think that she was old enough to know that babies did not come out of gooseberry bushes.

Servants

There were usually 3 of them, dressed in print with white aprons and white caps. But ours weren't dapper, like other peoples. I suppose the wages father gave did not encourage the better sort. Nor did mother's inefficient housekeeping encourage the neat and orderly sort. They generally looked a scruffy trio, always changing. I don't remember liking any of them.

The only one I loved was my nanny, Harriet, and, after she left *(in 1891)* no one. I was five and a half. I was in our nursery at the top of the house. Harriet was bathing my baby brother in a tub put on a stool. I watched. I was standing facing her. She was probably quite young *(Harriet G Bowyer, born in Highgate, was 17 in 1891)*. To me she was ageless. She was very prim looking, very neat. She had a tiny mouth like a little button. Her hair was no colour in particular, parted in the middle and taken very smoothly back into a bun. The bun consisted of long plaits wound round. This bun had a lot of hair pins poked into it. It wasn't a very large bun, I mean it was fairly flat and didn't stick out a long way. Harriet had a way of putting her hand up and with the palm pressing it any pins that were poking out. I thought this was a very grown up and attractive habit so I did it too, frequently, though my hair hung down my back and I had no bun and no pins to press in. It gave me a pleasant feeling and no one noticed it.

I only remember one incident. On this morning, when I stood watching, she lifted the beautiful fat boy out of the bath onto her knee, wrapping him up in a towel. She began to rub him gently and, stopping a minute, she looked steadily across the bath tub at me and said, "I'm going to leave, you know". I only remember the pain.

It was an unbearable agonising pain as if a dagger had been thrust into my heart. I don't think I said anything. I was too distraught to speak. This must not, could not be. To be left alone, utterly alone. She must have known. I knew she felt as I did. She wasn't callous. After that I remember nothing. I don't remember her leaving or anyone else coming. But to think of that incident still makes me wince. It wasn't an incident, it was a continuous situation of continual loneliness. Occasionally broken by the companionship of some scruffy orphan who was hired in to look after us. But the orphans and I only had one thing in common, a sort of unspoken war against my mother and sister. They were common little brats, poor things, and I learnt no good from them at all, but at least they were congenial companions. I preferred them to my critical and criticising mother and sister.

There was no tittle tattle in the family. I never heard much until I went to Canada *(1934)*. That was an eye opener. There was a certain amount of gossip. I find it hard to define. Mother was very downright and critical. She would say that Mrs Tattum, a very pretty neighbour, also very silly, who sang like a nightingale, would not admit that anyone could sing unless they had learnt with her own "special, wonderful" singing master. *(Mrs Florence Tatham, at 16 Lyndhurst Road, was a solicitor's wife.)* But such remarks were not encouraged by the children. Mother would say someone looked a perfect fright, but there it ended. There was no "And I said to her, and she said to me". That was reserved for 'below stairs'. I found it very intriguing if I heard the servants at it. It seemed dramatic and fruity, whereas mother's condemnatory remarks closed the door.

A friend of mine, one of a family of 6 girls and 2 sons, for instance, told me once how refreshing it was to come to our house, where we didn't spent our time picking people to pieces. She said, in their house, they talked of nothing but the stupidities of their neighbours. I recognised that the reason was that we were ladies and they were not. "Not quite," but rich enough to be acknowledged.

Breakfast

Our breakfast came after family prayers. While I was small, the cook came to prayers but, when I was about 16, the new cook struck. She said she couldn't get the breakfast up if she had to come. A great argument ensued between father and mother. He felt his authority was being undermined. This was the thin end of the wedge. The importance of prayers was being made light of; on the other hand, he did not like leathery toast. So the cook won. He did not say on that occasion, "I will be master in my own house." He only said or shouted that, if he was really het up. It amused me, because he and mother and I and all of us knew quite well that he was not master, that that was mother's role, and also that it was not his house, it was hers.

Our breakfast consisted of just porridge. It varied with the cook. I wonder why we changed cook and our other maids so often. A constant stream. We were never without, but we were always in the midst of them either coming or going. The porridge was made of the coarsest oatmeal and should have been cooked for hours. I scarcely ever went into the kitchen so I don't know if it was. Some cooks produced a thin slop; others a solid congealed mass. Occasionally we got someone who cooked it properly. It was a trial to me. When solid, I was unable to digest it and, as I grew older, I found it was one of the foods I should not eat. What to my mind made it so unpalatable was that we were not allowed sugar with it. Father had been brought up in Scotland and he knew. I don't think the question was ever discussed. People who ate sugar with porridge were very second rate. If some unwary visitor asked for sugar, we all eyed him and felt that the devil had suddenly got down to have breakfast with us. There was to me a constant irritation over the eating of porridge. My mother had her own peculiar method which disgusted me. Why couldn't she do things like other people? Why must she always be different? Why should she make herself conspicuous? I would have loved to have had a soft, dimpled mother, pink and white, agreeing with everything everyone said. Neatly, prettily dressed. Mother was so downright, so positive, so drastic.

[A generation later there was my daughter *(Mollie)* thinking just the same about me and, because she was a later generation, she not only thought it but said it. She pointed out that the mother of one of her young men had all the qualities in which I was lacking and that she went for beauty treatment to Elizabeth Arden, or somebody. I looked at the said young lady and wondered. I thought that she certainly had not spent half her days out on tennis courts in all weather, nor had she faced the biting wind on golf courses. Pleasures that I wouldn't have missed for the world. I also thought that if by some miracle they made my face smooth and pink, I could never behave according. It couldn't be done. I did sympathise with her.]

Every day I had to endure my mother eating her porridge as no one else did. I was sure of that; no one else in the world ate their porridge like that. Such a fuss. Cold milk in a large breakfast cup held in the left hand. A large spoon, a tablespoon in the right hand, dug out a piece of porridge; the spoon was then pushed into the breakfast cup – some milk was picked up by the spoon and then the whole thing went into my mother's mouth. The spoon was too large anyway. But mother took the most enormous mouthfuls of any food she was eating. She literally wolfed her food. She no doubt agreed with the lady in Punch: a mother is giving lunch to her daughter in a restaurant. The girl has just come from her boarding school. The mother says, "Don't eat so carefully, the best people just shovel it down."

After my mother's bicycle accident, this porridge eating became more painful to me – because her wrist had been so badly set that she couldn't get her hand round to the cup of milk, and the bone, which was all wrong, stuck out most unpleasantly. But she never took to eating porridge normally.

[The day after our wedding my new husband and I sat down to breakfast and we had porridge and, while my inside froze with horror, he went through all the same antics as my mother. He always had, he said. He liked the milk cold!]

As I have said, no one in our house ate sugar with porridge. I hated porridge, but I had to eat it or have nothing and when I was young I was always hungry, or at any rate had an appetite. When I was 15, I went away to stay with friends and had sugar with my porridge, as they all did. I liked the thin, sweet food and made up my mind. My first morning at home I got up from the breakfast table and went to the sideboard and took out of the cupboard the sugar pot. Returning to the table, I sprinkled it lavishly on my porridge and waited for the storm to break. My father looked across at my mother indignantly. My mother looked back with a reassuring, soothing smile and the matter dropped for ever.

Our breakfast started with porridge and went on to hunks of bread and butter. A cottage loaf was on the table and was cut up into great wedges. Then a boiled egg was brought up for father. On Sunday we all had a boiled egg except mother. She had given up eggs soon after marriage. The town eggs did not please her. In those days they were frequently bad. That was a tragedy, if on a Sunday your boiled egg of the week was bad. It happened sometimes. We ate masses of thick bread, never very new, and butter both at breakfast and for tea. The egg business was always a nuisance. No one's eggs were reliable. Mother was delighted by a scheme whereby we received eggs all the years round from a farm in the country. She was to pay 1d for each egg all the year round. But, when the season came when hens were off laying, no eggs arrived. Mother complained, because she was paying the exorbitant sum of 1d an egg when eggs were plentiful. Then they were liable also to be broken in the post. So I never had a really fresh egg as a child.

After breakfast, father sat at his desk writing and doing accounts until 11 o'clock. During that time he would call across to mother, who sometimes sat at her desk in the further corner of the room away from the light. Just as well perhaps, considering how untidy that corner of the room was. Mother's desk was absolute chaos inside. A sort of wicker table with two trays to it between her desk and the wall. These trays piled up with newspapers and rubbish – socks which needed darning and all sorts of rubbish. On one occasion when a dinner party was going to take place, my father, as usual, was going round trying to tidy up and, when he came to mother's corner, he playfully told her to clear up her dung heap. Fury and indignation. Father's sense of humour was not very subtle.

I've diverted again. Father would call across the room to mother, "I lent you a stamp yesterday. Will you please pay me back?" Mother: "I told you I hadn't 1d change last night. How can I have got change now when I didn't have it last night?" Father: "Well, please pay me as soon as you get 1d. It puts my accounts out". This doesn't sound true, but it was.

Money

I've never known much about what money we lived on. But this is the story as I pieced it together. My grandmother *(Mary Alexander 1816-1902)*, the Irish one, was an heiress. She brought a fortune into the family. There must have been plenty of money around, as they sent their 8 sons to public schools and the university or gave them equivalent educations. When my mother married, she was given a good marriage portion. My father *(Everard Allen Ford)* did well for himself. He married above himself, the daughter of a baronet, and she had money. I gather that when my parents married they were well off, no, comfortably off. Father's parents bought a business for him. An East Indian merchant he was, I believe. I do not know what he had been doing before that. He married at the age of 30. But he surely must have had a job before that? He did hint to me once that he had led a dissolute life before he was converted to the Church of England. The strange thing about father's business was that he never seemed to be there. He did not leave the house till 11 am and he was back again by 5 or 5.30pm. This was not only in his later years; it was, I believe, his regular routine. In other words, he went to the City, lunched at his Club, the Junior Carlton, and perhaps worked till tea. I don't know. I do know that our times of playing the piano and practising were severely restricted by the presence or absence of my father in the house. I don't know how much they had to live on, but certainly we did not live by the sweat of father's brow. Frank says £1,000 a year (£370,000 p.a. at 2017 values). All went well for a bit. My sister and my eldest brother had riding lessons. That alone shows that there was money about. Then came a crash and this is what I think happened.

My Aunt Frances, the eldest sister in mother's family, had married *(George Spottiswoode)*, "a pillar of the Church",

Everard Allen Ford

which perhaps was a useful thing to be in some directions, though it didn't help him to be a financier. But, because he lived in London and happened to be a man of the world with a very successful printing business of his own, the Hammick family entrusted all their money to dear Uncle George. Uncle George speculated in a publisher's firm and lost most of it. He lost his wife's money as well as my mother's. Father was quite naturally livid and threatened to expose his brother-in-law and bring him to justice. The family were horrified. I mean mother's family. No doubt, they said, this just showed that mother had married a cad; they had always thought so, but they had never before said so. Poor Rachel! I expect she was having a pretty rotten time over it all. Father, staring poverty in the face, wouldn't be daunted and threatened Uncle George. It was patched up somehow. All the family subscribed toward a sort of fund to pay back mother – really father, but nothing like the right amount of money could be raised this way and so father just had to go without. In order to placate him, Uncle George made him a member of Lloyds. And there was something about paying for Stephen to go to Winchester. At least, I think he said he would, but never did. Then he introduced father to some publishers and for some time we were flooded with children's books, published by Ward and Downey, of very poor quality *(see overleaf)*.

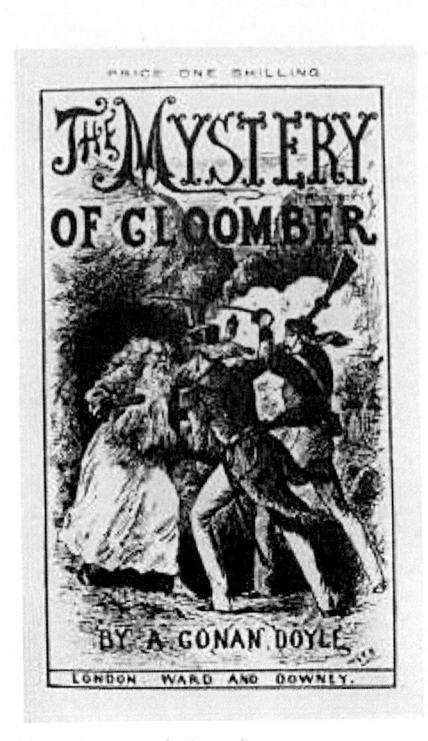

The Mystery of Cloomber,
published by Ward & Downey

One result of the whole caboodle was that mother's relations ceased to visit her for some years. Uncle George moved out of his mansion *(at 3 Cadogan Square)* into a small house of the same pattern in Egerton Gardens. *(This is incorrect: George died in Cadogan Square, and Frances moved to 38 Egerton Gardens and then to Onslow Gardens only after she was widowed.)* Uncle George then died *(1899)* and was buried in St Paul's Cathedral – or had a brass plate put up there. He also gave up his country house in *(Axminster)* Devonshire, the carriages were sold and the daughters went about in buses! After an interlude, Aunt Frances and mother started meeting again, and the daughters, but visits were always timed to avoid father.

I think I must have made a mistake about uncle George. The Spottiswoodes continued to live in style until after his death *(in 1899)* and then the bereft family found that they really were bereaved. Uncle George had left things in such a state that the whole family were heading for the workhouse, metaphorically. Like everything else they did, they went for their "poverty" head down. Attacking it with the greatest zest and I think they really enjoyed it. They brought economy to a fine art. I stayed with them at Charmouth after the crash. Their house at Axminster had been sold, and their carriage gone, and they had taken rooms above a confectioner's shop in the High Street. I don't think it could have been necessary to descend to rooms over a confectioner's in the High Street, but that's how they behaved. *(This was not their main house; presumably it was for holidays.)* I remember one meal we had there. We had had a first course, it was lunch, or as my Aunt would have said "luncheon". We all sat round the table and the second course was brought in. There were seven of us. It consisted of nine small, cold, jam tartlets. They were put in front of my aunt. Leonie quickly counted them and, in her shrill strident voice, she quipped, "Oh, she's sent in more than I ordered. I ordered 7 and she's sent in 9. Never mind we needn't eat them." So however hungry I was, I knew I mustn't have a second one and I was *very* hungry. Aunt Frances demurred. Of course we could eat them, if we wished. (There were only 2 extra anyway.) But Leonie was adamant. She was doing the housekeeping, etc. So we ate one each and no more.

If mother's brothers came along to see her it was always in the afternoon. I remember the carriage days of Aunt Frances. I would come into the drawing room for a few minutes and gladly escape. One day, when they were leaving, I joined the procession to see them off. Through the narrow hall and down the unending steps we slowly walk. As I stood on the top step I saw the magnificent equipage. It was a huge carriage which has somehow become distorted in my mind and when I try to see it now, I see a sort of Lord Mayor's coach. Well, certainly Aunt Frances didn't drive in a Lord Mayor's coach, but she did have a coachman and footman, both in livery, wearing top hats with cockades, for which Uncle George paid taxes. Also a coat of arms on the door – another tax.

On another occasion (I remember it because I put my foot in it as usual), we were slowly processing down the front steps. Aunt Frances talking in her high pitched London society accent, four daughters doing the same, and the fourth one *(Theodora, b.1879)* talking in a special way of her own, very loud, slow and insistent, because she was slightly mental, having been tight-laced before she was born. They were all years older than me. They were mother's nieces but, as Aunt Frances was 20 years older than my mother, her daughters were about the same age as mother, though they always called her Aunty Rachel. They were all devoted to mother, finding her a great relaxation after the conventionality of their own parents. As we walked down the steps that day, I saw no Lord Mayor's coach awaiting but I heard a shrill whistle. "What's that?" asked I, startled, "Who's that whistling?" Blank silence. I knew then that I had said the wrong thing. How was I to know that it was the footman, who had been left standing on the pavement outside the house, while the coachman kept the horses on the go up and down the road so that they would not get chilled? At the piercing whistle of the footman, they came clopping down the road, very magnificent, and I hid my confusion as best I could. "How very second rate of Phyllis not to know who was whistling," I heard them say in my idiotic, egotistic imagination. Not that they ever would say a thing like that. They were ladies, and I mean ladies.

I contrast that with the only time I had with them at Cadogan Square in the days of their affluence. I must have been about 8 or 9 and for some reason I went alone. I see the long tables polished and the silver and glass. Although it was only luncheon, it was very beautiful and impressive and the two liveried men, the butler and footman, waited at table. Had they powdered wigs or powdered hair? I can't quite remember but I think so. I was overcome with nervous agony as I sat there. The footman came to pour water into my tumbler. [I found the other day that a waitress at a restaurant where I was eating did not know what I meant when I asked for a tumbler. I suppose the word is old fashioned. It is an odd word anyway. I wonder what its derivation is.] *(Such glasses originally had a pointed or convex base and could not be set down without spilling.)*

I said to the footman, for no reason at all, "No thank you". He stood there; the water jug poised and waited. "You'd better have some water. You needn't drink it if you don't want", said my aunt. I knew that of course. At home one had to clear

Frances Spottiswoode, née Hammick

up one's plate to the last grain, but we did not have to drink down all the water in our glasses. But no. I had said no. I must therefore go on saying no and I did. The footman stood and waited and, in order to clinch matters, I spread my hand firmly over the glass and held it there. At that the beautiful creature walked away.
I couldn't look at anybody, I felt so awful, so stupid. I had made a fool of myself as normal. I knew that. I heard my aunt say in her high pitched society voice, "Oh isn't she a quaint little girl?" And I could have killed them all with pleasure.

After the great fall, when Uncle George had died I think, I said all the carriages etc were sold. My cousins were not the sort of people to cry over spilt milk. They had the same sort of guts as my mother who, instead of lamenting over some mishap, would enlarge on the enormous advantages it happened to have brought with it. Thus my cousins, all grown up, were suddenly freed from tyranny. The tyranny of having to behave as other young ladies in their class. No longer had they maids enough to dog the footsteps of them all. So they went out together, never alone. I think that would have been too risky.

Though the youngest one *(Theodora)* was slow witted, she did as a companion, and she and the one older *(Margaret Eleanor, known as May, b. 1872)* had the roaring excitement of boarding a bus, inside, of course, and driving up to see my mother. It was a new world to them. No longer did they have to accompany their mother on those terribly tedious afternoon calls. Nor did they have to wait until their mother decreed that it was time to go and see my mother, dear Rachel. On those occasions they would come en masse. Mother and 4 or 5 daughters; mother dominating all conversation, and the daughters sitting, not meekly but almost silently, because they couldn't get a word in. Now they were freed, liberated. No maid followed them along the streets and into the bus. They came on their own and when they wanted and, as they were very fond of my mother, and found her a great relief after the sticky atmosphere at home, they came quite often. Though they were nieces, they were not much younger than my mother though even the eldest one always dutifully called her "Aunt Rachel" They went inside the bus. No female went on top of a bus till years later.

Aunt Frances was a ruthless personality. Very handsome in a hard, well modelled way. Very ambitious I should imagine. She certainly was ambitious with her children. She nearly killed them because of it, driving them increasingly, no let up. The best masters and mistresses. They were all accomplished except the youngest. I mean the girls were. The boys weren't, but then there were only two of them *(Adrian George, 1868-1930, who at 33 in 1901 was already a 'retired printer'; and John, b. 1874, who died at Ypres in October 1914, an army Captain)*. Now I come to think of it, none of the girls painted as far as I know. That was odd in those days. All young ladies painted. They kept albums and decorated milk stools with cornflowers. Two of them concentrated on music.

The eldest one, 'Teeny' *(Mabel Spottiswoode, 1864-1945)* was learning singing with one of the most distinguished masters in London. She was the one with the shrill voice and the aggressive manner. She appeared to be biting everyone's head off. How well I can hear that insistent voice and how well I could imitate it, and I was allowed to, as 'Teeny' was the joke of all the aunts, uncles and cousins. She had hard flashing eyes, small, beady. Her faux pas were handed round the family. She was staying in Devonshire with her Aunt Mary, my mother's other sister. She was the one who was lame. They had several people to dinner that night. Dessert was on the table. Aunt Mary took an apple. "Fancy taking a nasty, stuffy apple, after all the dinner you've eaten", shrilled Teeny. As she let off in that way fairly frequently, it was not odd that no one was surprised that she seemed to be going to be a spinster, but, at the age of nearing 50, she became engaged to a little parson. *(She married Rev. Robert Stansfield Herries when she was 36 in 1900, the year after her father died)*. He looked as if his whole life was one big apology. At that time one was often characterising parsons and they were so like this little man. He seemed devoted to Teeny, and why not? She had all the characteristics that he lacked and, though the Spottiswoode daughters no longer were heiresses, owing to their father's mismanagement, they still each had a tidy sum. But what was so wonderful was that he passed muster. He came of a very distinguished family with a very distinguished name.

I went to the wedding. My cousin was approaching the age of 50 *(actually 36)*. Strange to say, she wore a white wedding dress. But she was so economical that she wouldn't tell the dressmaker she was getting married and that this was her wedding dress, so when it came it had on it a trimming of gold. No decent dressmaker would have done such a thing without asking her client, but this was a "little woman round the corner." Aunt Frances took mother on one side and explained it to her and they had a good laugh over dear Teeny's eccentricity.

The wedding service left out the bit about having babies. I can't remember a single thing about the rest of the performance. Towards the end of the wedding, just before the bride went away, I was standing in the packed dining room, and people were beginning to move towards the door to give the bride a send off. I stood alone and up came a very handsome middle-aged gentleman and spoke to me. He was dark and very good looking and quite obviously belonged to that world of society to which I did not belong. I was suburban and there was a marked difference that I always felt. It drew a line between me and the top notchers. I could pretend that I never was of them and it made me feel inferior (though I preferred my own freedom and thought and outlook). A freedom that I did not think they had. The middle-aged gentlemen. Yet I envied them.

Clothes

That wedding was a great occasion for me *(on 18 April 1900; Phyllis was 14)* as I had a dressmaker's dress for the first time. Up to then I had always worn my sister's old dresses, altered or not by mother, or occasionally a new dress made by mother. How I suffered from my clothes. Their looks and their feel, particularly their feel. I had and have a skin that is particularly sensitive to wool. I had a dark green blouse, for winter so it need never be washed. I hoped to get a mourning blouse when Uncle George died – no luck – my blouse was scratchy; I envied friends who had Viyella. Friends commented on the fact that my blouse was never washed. I brought it up with mother. She said, if I had had, say, a serge dress, it wouldn't be washed, so what was the difference? Elegant ladylike dressmaker – mother puts her foot in it by asking if the young woman with her is her daughter – her niece rather, she says, "The 'ook quite declines to go into the heye".

Any wool made me come out in a rash. No one took the slightest notice of this. I was dressed in wool from head to foot. Imagine, if you can, being in a state of intense irritation from head to foot daily. Now if I get the edge of a woollen dress touching my neck I am driven mad by it, but for years and years I had it all over me: Jaeger combies *(combinations were vest and pants combined)*. May Mr Jaeger be forgiven for the suffering he caused me. First, the combies. I found that, after they had been washed, they were more than unbearable, so, when I came to years of discretion and dressed in my own room, not in mother's, the clean ones went into the laundry basket every Monday and I continued to wear the dirty ones for weeks and weeks. I then had to put on a pair of warm home-made woollen stockings, but those were soon given up. It happened because mother had to go to Highgate.

I can't remember what for but she took me with her. We walked along the Spaniards Road and all along, as my legs got hotter and hotter, so the stockings tickled and scratched more and more and I would stop and rub them, and as I walked I would bang one leg against the other in the vain attempt to stop the itching. I was 6 years old. Mother complained and scolded, but I was beyond minding. At last she bribed and that did the trick. If I would walk along properly and not complain, I should have some sugar candy when I got home. It was a long time to wait and a long way to go and I didn't know what sugar candy was but I managed. Sweets were so rare for us that I would have sold my soul for them. I don't think I've ever seen sugar candy since. I think my mother must have had it sent to her from abroad. She scarcely ever bought sweets and this stuff was odd. It was like great lumps of crystal.

After that episode, the woollen stockings were removed and I wore cotton. I had terrible chilblains all the winter and, besides chilblains, I had a line or rawness just above my boot from chaps, and my stockings used sometimes to stick to the drops of blood on top of the combies. I wore another horror in the winter, even worse. A pair of navy serge knickers. I remember the feel of pulling them up over my stockings, and where the gap in the combies was I had rough serge against my flesh.

Mother was not interested in clothes. Her country vicarage had not taught her how to dress and the superimposing of Cadogan Square did not produce good results. I was looking at a photograph in the family album: an attractive picture of mother. She had on a large hat with an ostrich feather sweeping round it. The dress she said was cotton and had been made by a "little woman" she had discovered soon after she was married. On the cotton dress she fastened an old lace fichu, very lovely, given her by her own mother. Mother had been told by her sister Frances that the only place to buy hats was Sloane Street. So in Sloane Street she bought her hat. It was very expensive and looked it. Looking back at that photograph, mother laughed and said, "Such an unsuitable hat for a cotton dress." But the taste for expensive hats persisted, and I used at intervals to have one, which then I had to wear for several years.

The overwhelming policy in our house was economy. At first, perhaps when they were married, they enjoyed spending and the fearful close economy only came when Uncle George blew mother's money. It was certainly a well established rule by the time I came into the world. My husband says that, considering what my family had to live on, we could have been considered well off. But, though we were never hungry and we kept two or sometimes three servants, the general effect on us all was that the utmost economy was needed in order to make both ends meet and that we were badly off. The expression "can't afford" was used continually. My boots, I would have to wear them till the soles were right through because "I can't afford to have them mended just now". Other children had their dresses made by dressmakers. Mine were made by my mother, who had not improved greatly in the art. On one occasion I was found at a party with all the pins in the hem of my frock.

My cousin Teenie's wedding was a landmark, because I had my first dressmaker's dress. It was a green frieze, I think they called it *(frieze – French: fries – is a Middle English term for a coarse woollen, plain weave cloth with a nap on one side. The nap was raised by scrubbing it to raise curls of fibre, and was not shorn after being raised, leaving an uneven surface)*. I always longed for soft material but mother always got these scratchy things. But the dress was really so pretty I hardly minded the scratchy seams inside the sleeves and the scratchy bit at the base of the high collar. It was of a clear bright reseda green and exactly the colour of my eyes. It was trimmed, everything was trimmed in those days, with silver coloured silk braid and with a band of reseda velvet alongside it. I looked at myself in a long mirror. So elegant and chic. And the hat. The hat was a little darling. Green velvet perched on one side of my head, and curling round over one side 3 small white ostrich feathers, the relics of someone's presentation at court.

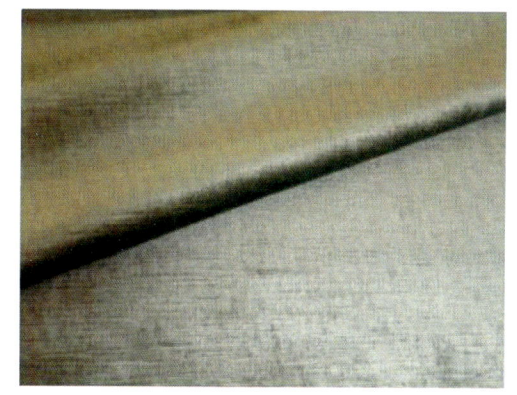

Reseda green velvet

The Misses Nevinson

(The Misses Nevinson, Mary and Elizabeth, were neighbours. They lived at 4 Eldon Road, next door but one, and were the sisters of Henry Woodd Nevinson, the journalist. In 1897 he became the Daily Chronicle's *correspondent in the Greco-Turkish War. He was known for his reporting on the Second Boer War, and slavery in Angola in 1904-05. In 1914 he co-founded the Friends' Ambulance Unit and later in World War I was a war correspondent, being wounded at Gallipoli. He became a socialist. His wife, Margaret Wynne née Jones, (11 January 1858–8 June 1932) was a British suffrage campaigner. She was one of the*

suffragettes who split from the Women's Social and Political Union (WSPU) in 1907 to form the Women's Freedom League (WFL). She wrote many articles for 'The Vote', the WFL journal, and also wrote many suffrage pamphlets including 'A History of the Suffrage Movement, 1908-1912, Ancient Suffragettes', and 'The Spoilt Child and the Law'. She taught at South Hampstead High School. Their children were Mary Philippa (1885-1950) and Christopher Richard Wynne (1889-1946), who was a British figure and landscape painter, etcher and lithographer and one of the most famous war artists of World War I. He studied at the Slade School of Art under Henry Tonks and alongside Stanley Spencer and Mark Gertler. At the outbreak of World War I, Nevinson joined the Friends' Ambulance Unit and was deeply disturbed by his work tending wounded French soldiers. Subsequently Nevinson volunteered for home service with the Royal Army Medical Corps. He used these experiences as the subject matter for a series of powerful paintings which used the machine aesthetic of Futurism and the influence of Cubism to great effect. His fellow artist Walter Sickert wrote at the time that Nevinson's painting 'La Mitrailleuse' "will probably remain the most authoritative and concentrated utterance on the war in the history of painting". In 1917, he was appointed an official war artist.)

C R W Nevinson in The Friends' Ambulance Unit

The Nevinson sisters' niece, Philippa, was 2 or 3 years older than I *(actually one year older)*, and her brother Richard, or Dicky as we called him, a year or so younger. He became the artist. These two children did not come to lessons. They appeared sometimes. Their mother looked like a dirty gipsy and the children also. My first introduction to Dicky was when he fell headlong out of the hammock. He was about 3 and still wore skirts, and, to my utter horror, he had nothing on underneath. They lived in squalor. Occasionally, through the years, I was forced to go to tea with Philippa. The Miss Nevinsons thought I was a nice child (I *was*, compared with her), and I was made to go that dreary walk to that filthy house beside the railway line. *(44 Savernake Road backed onto the Hampstead Junction Railway (p 87). Henry Woodd Nevinson had lived earlier at Scarr Cottage, 13 John Street (now Keats Grove), where 'Dicky' was born in 1889; the family subsequently moved to Savernake Road in 1896, and on to 4 Downside Crescent in 1901.)*

When I got to Savernake Road we did nothing. The afternoon was spent in Philippa's bedroom. It smelt. We stood and did nothing. I said little. She used a large variety of swear words. She also talked what I think was called smut. It made me feel very uncomfortable. I was not good, but mucky conversation made me feel rather sick. I heard enough of that at home from my brothers. We had nothing to do and I wonder now at her want of ingenuity. I was always busy doing something. All I know she did was to cut out some paper in patterns to go into a filthy candlestick. We stood in her bedroom and then we went down to tea. Her mother was out and the tea was non-existent. Those two children must have had a rotten time. Richard began painting when he was about 14 at school. She became a public singer for a bit. When she talked, she could be heard a mile away.

She married an architect *(Sydney B K Caulfield, in 1911)*. I met her in a tube lift at the beginning of the first war. She accosted me in her booming voice and in the same voice announced to me and the rest of the lift that she was having a baby: "Nothing else to do with the war on", that was why. That baby was born a complete helpless idiot. Later on she had a daughter. I saw Philippa near Selfridges one day, but dived to safety. She always made me feel uncomfortable.

[One day I was rung up by a person I know in a village about 3 miles from here *(Ickford, Oxon., see p 177)*. She told me on the telephone that she had been in despair about her large garden. Her own gardener had finished up. She had 3 acres of land. She had advertised in 'the Times' for a lady to come and live in her house and help with the garden. She said "I think you know the lady who has come. She says she is a friend of yours." When she told me it was Philippa Caulfield, who had been Nevinson, I had a contraction in my stomach. "I used to know her, but I haven't seen her for years and I really don't think there would be much point in my seeing her now, I never really was a friend of hers", I said. "That's what they all say", said the lady, "She seems to know someone in every village for miles round, and she talks of them as old friends and wants me to invite them here, but they none of them seem to want to come. It would be very kind of you if you would come. She seems rather an odd sort of person".

So I went, not at all wishing to. There she was, fatter and coarser, but much the same. We had nothing to talk about, except the war. Her son had died, I think, the idiot. Her daughter was on the stage, or going on. She was evidently very proud of her. Nancy. Then she began on her step-mother. When her mother died, her father married his secretary, or lifelong friend. It must have been a blessing to him at last, after that wife of his. Philippa bitterly resented this second marriage, and after a tirade about the second wife, she repeated over and over, "She's a virgin still", with much satisfaction. She looked at me sideways to see if I was shocked at her daring but I didn't respond. Last week at the theatre I saw her daughter on the stage. Large, fat, dark, coarse, but pleasant looking. Nancy.]

When bicycling came in, a school for learning the new art was started in the Hampstead Conservatoire *(64 Eton Avenue)*. *(From the mid-1890s onwards there was a rapid growth of so-called 'cycling schools'. An article published in 'Cycling' in 1896 described how 'it required the advent of the better classes into our ranks, especially the female portion thereof, to create the schools we have with us on all sides at the present time.')* Mostly ladies entertained an audience one day by trick riding. The performers were not at all glamorous. They were the local housewives – no, not housewives – the local ladies, among them Mrs Henry Nevinson. She was a clumsy looking, untidy

Mrs Henry Nevinson

woman, but she quite cleverly brought her bicycle to a standstill, balanced herself on it in that stationary position, and proceeded to bring out some knitting, which was in a bag hanging on the handle bars. Then wobbling slightly, she did a few stitches of knitting to the accompaniment of a violin, a cello and a drum. The drum rolled effectively during this performance. Mrs Nevinson must have been about 40 then. My mother, who had a caustic sense of humour, "very convenient for Mrs Nevinson when she gets into a traffic jam to be able to sit and do her knitting". Personally, having seen the inside of her house, which my mother had not, I felt fairly sure that she never knitted, or sewed, or did anything domestic at all.

Our Miss Nevinsons, Miss Mary and Miss Lizzie, were a family institution for us. It was to them that my sister and 2 brothers were packed off for the day when my third brother *(Geoffrey)* chose to arrive on Xmas Day. I think I mentioned that he was born in a chamber pot and he was a 7-months baby and delicate, but exquisitely pretty. The Miss Nevinsons had interesting treasures to show one and, above all, they kept pigeons so tame they sat on my finger, and that was unfortunate, as it then did its business down my frock; this was some special occasion and I had on my best frock. I didn't know what had happened, but the two ladies seemed fussed. And Mary, the elder of that family, scolded Miss Lizzie and said, "I told you not to give it to her, I knew what would happen". And I wondered what had happened and I wouldn't let my mind even wander to the possibility of that. One did not think of sad things. They happened, but one ignored them, at the age of 7. And Mary fetched a damp sponge and washed my frock and all was well. They were called by their Christian names by my mother and they were great friends. But my mother used to poke fun at them when they weren't there. Laughing at Miss Mary's fussiness and how if any subject cropped up that they didn't know about, they would run to their bookcases and look it up and read to you all about it. Quite true, that was just what they did.

Then Miss Lizzie's art came under mother's withering fire. I wonder why. Was my mother envious of that? Miss Lizzie's paintings were pleasant. Her copies were amazingly "like", I thought, but mother had no word of praise. She was like that over everything and everybody. She ran everything and everybody down, often with much wit. It is easier to be funny in that way, I know myself how easy it is. One can be very funny at other people's expense. But the thing is to keep the balance. Mother was intensely critical and nearly always adversely critical. My mother's tongue particularly ran away with her over music or art. These things she really couldn't pronounce on, having been brought up in a remote country vicarage with parents, who had no artistic talents, and taught by a governess, who made her pupils copy small watercolours out of a book. But mother had no misgivings about herself. Occasionally she would take me to an exhibition of pictures in London, not to the National Gallery or the Tate, but to some artist's show. She had probably heard of him. Round the gallery we went. "Look at those cows", said mother. She had a carrying voice. "Whoever would know they were cows?" Apparently *she* did. That sunset, oh, did you ever see such a sunset? It was as if we had gone to a fair and been asked to throw darts at all the pictures.

The worst occasion I had of going to a picture gallery with my mother was a visit to the Leicester Galleries to see the work of Richard Nevinson. *(The Leicester Galleries gave Nevinson a one-man show in October 1916. The show was a critical and popular success and the works displayed all sold. Sir Alfred Mond bought 'A Taube', which showed a child killed in Dunkirk by a bomb thrown from a type of German plane known as the Taube. Several famous writers and politicians visited the exhibition, it received extensive press coverage and Nevinson became something of a celebrity.)* As we walked in, I was suddenly thrilled. Here was painting such as had never been. The marching soldiers. Alive. I was exalted by it, but not so mother. She began at once. Henry Nevinson was standing about in the room and otherwise there was nobody there. I think it must have been at lunch time. Anyway, the place was empty, and mother began. I whispered, "Don't, Henry Nevinson is there, the artist's father". "I don't mind if he is. It's nonsense that people should think they can get away with this sort of thing – I'd be ashamed to draw so badly."

A Taube, C R W Nevinson (1916)

Returning to the Trenches, C R W Nevinson (1916)

Children's parties

It was a wonderful party. Opposite where Belsize Park Tube Station is now was a huge house and grounds. It belonged to a Mr Wood. *(Then soon to be demolished, Woodlands was home to Mr R B Woodd, a son of Basil Woodd, a wealthy wine merchant who had died in 1872, and whose benevolence and public-spiritedness had been inherited by his sons.)* [The Woodds] gave two large children's parties a year, though at that time the daughters were grown up, I think. The summer party was a hay party. All the fields were cut and we were supposed to make nests in the hay and bury one another in it. I never really liked that because the hay prickled so. Tea was a wonderful meal.

At one of these parties, a little girl like a charming doll – only more charming than a doll, she had golden red curly hair – came up to me and looked at me so intensely that I blushed. I thought something worse than usual must be the matter with me. She then put her hand in mine and thus we stood and watched. I had felt lonely. I was always lonely at parties like that. I felt too shy to contact others, just as I still do. If anyone else would make the advance I was only too happy to be friendly, but never could I start the ball rolling. This little girl made me intensely happy. She had chosen me and she chose to stick to me the whole afternoon sitting next to me at tea. I wanted to be liked or loved most desperately. This I know is quite a usual thing. But most of my friends were made on that basis. They liked me. That was enough. I would have done anything to be liked. Well, that little red headed girl made me happy but I never saw her again. Fortunately it was not until just before tea, when the fireworks were over that I had a setback. One of the Miss Woods *(sic)* was sitting on a sofa and I stood near her with the little girl. Miss Wood suddenly exclaimed, "Oh Phyllis, come here, do. Just look at your dress. All the pins are in the hem. How dangerous, dear, come here and let me take them out." She did and, as mother had forgotten to sew the hem, down it came and it wasn't cut at all even – in fact I looked like the typical beggar child. My little girl friend still stuck to me, so life was just bearable, but only just. I was indignant when I got home, but Mother just laughed and laughed. I said what would she do next? And I bitterly wondered. She seemed never to realise what one suffered and she also took a certain pride in being unusual. She was very anxious that we should all be original, with a touch of Bohemianism. But we weren't original, any of us. We weren't anything particular.

First school, servants and migraines (c.1891-92)

When I was at Miss Pollock's with the three boys, not my brothers, my father one morning asked me to tell him what lessons I had done the preceding day. It was hardly fair on Miss Pollock, as I was a scatterbrained creature and I gave a poor account of our lessons.

(Phyllis' teacher may have been Ella Violet Pollock, a solicitor's daughter brought up with at least 6 siblings, at 'Heathfield' off East Heath Road; Ella is recorded in the

1891 census as aged 31, unmarried, of no stated occupation, and living with her widowed mother and her two infant grandchildren, at 25 Thurlow Road.)

I was at Miss Pollock's class one morning a few weeks before Xmas. I was to have a great treat that day. Mrs. Cork – I can't remember her – had surprisingly offered to take me to London to see the shops. It was strange because there was little feeling of goodwill between ourselves and our ever-changing servants. We looked down on them and would have been definitely rude to them if we had dared. I was, in fact. One of my brothers, Bernard, I think, offered me 3d if I would say to a very florid, lusty housemaid we had, "you stink." I would have done anything for money in those days and so I did. Feeling rather sick, I said to her gently, having followed her about, "you stink!" She said, "That isn't a very nice thing for a young lady to say." I felt filled with remorse and self loathing. [A granddaughter of mine, aged 3, said to me "I don't like 'Obert; he called me a tinker". Robert was 4].

We never had the "loyal retainer" in our house. It was a floating set of young women. The youngest generally about 15. They generally came from the Sailor's Daughter's Orphanage. But they never stayed long. I suppose we didn't pay them well enough. *(The Sailors' Orphan Girls School and Home, at 116 Fitzjohn's Avenue from 1869, accommodated about 100 girls and trained them for domestic service. Situations were found for them when aged 16 (or sometimes earlier); outfits were provided and rewards given for keeping a situation. The girls continued to be supervised by the Home as long as they remained unmarried. The 1901 census lists three servants in the Ford household: parlourmaid Kate Bush (16), housemaid Minnie Hopkins (15) and Rose Grout (26), the cook.)*

On this one occasion a cook offered to take me to look at the shops. I quite realised that it was not done, that it was a thing my mother wouldn't do or take me to do, but I thought it would be wonderful, and my mother had given her permission. I went to my class as usual and went to have an early lunch. I came home sick from head to foot – overcome with a bilious nausea and a headache that no one could describe. I have had, since then, 1000 or more such headaches; they all follow the same pattern and each one was always the worst I had ever had, but I cannot describe them. But my face always gave me away – fixed in a grip of unbearable pain.

So I didn't go to London. The servants said it was because I had been sitting with my back to the fire at lessons. That was my first headache *(migraine)*, the beginning of a scourge that was to warp my young life. Any excitement or worry brought one on and I was knocked out for a day. By midnight I was demented, walking up and down the rooms, my head pressed back against the top of my spine, which brought some relief. Up and down, until I would suddenly start vomiting and then the pain was too acute to bear. After the sickness, it gradually subsided and slowly, slowly I would be able to sit – then propped up with pillows begin to doze off. Doctors knew nothing and still know very little. In time, when I was about 40, that is long after I was married, I began to cope with these *(attacks)* by taking drastic medicines and by then there were alleviating drugs. When I was a child, aspirin and such like things hadn't been invented *(aspirin was first manufactured in 1899)*. I, out of the 6 children, must inherit this affliction from my father. He suffered most of his life. I can see him now, that fixed, grey, far stare on his face. He would go to the mantelpiece, put his elbows on it and hold his head in his hands. Mine were much more frequent than my father's. He used to treat himself with Carter's Little Liver Pills. I have no doubt the best thing he could do. One day my mother was taking her eldest son *(Stephen)* out for the day. When they got into the train he said, "Those little round balls were nice". It transpired that he had swallowed half a bottle of Carter's before coming out.

Every now and then I was taken to a doctor. Mother had less idea of illness than anyone I have met. She just dosed us indiscriminately. From seven years old, my headaches and attacks of indigestion dominated my life. I do not mean that I was a poor feeble creature. I was intensely alive and active, but often smitten down. When I was up I was tremendously up and when I was down I was down. For some time, when I was about 8, mother dosed me with some stuff but, when at last she called in the doctor, he said, "Mrs Ford, this medicine is the worst thing you could be giving her". These interviews with doctors were agony to us all.
I had very little idea what the doctor was talking about. Bowels and flatulence meant little to me and mother never explained. It was all too indelicate. I know the doctor insisted on a visit to the lavatory before going to school, but I simply hadn't time, and I didn't know what I had to do there. I used to spend my day trying not to go, as I hadn't time. That was when I was at the big school.

Second school, 7-10 years (1893-96)

So next term I was sent to a big school. I was 7. It was a long walk *(Crossfield Road is a quarter of a mile from Eldon Road)*, at least I found it so. I had to come home for lunch and be back again at 2.30. In the morning I had a scramble to get there. Prayers were supposed to be at 8 o'clock, and, though father was a very punctual man, they varied in time a bit. Then at about 8.15, breakfast. I then had to get my things on, go round and call for a friend and get to school by 9. It was a rush and left no time for the lavatory. In those days clothes weren't so simple. The button vests we always wore were a misery. Buttons would fly off and, if two came off together, one simply couldn't go out in them. I had no one properly responsible for my clothes. I was as untidy as my mother. Every morning it was a rush round to collect my books and clothes. Gloves lost, scarves lost. The result on my health very bad – a constant state of trying to keep up. I couldn't remember that I ever walked to school with my sister, but I suppose I must have. I always went to a house round the corner and called for a certain K.Tatham, who was about 6 years older than I, and we walked together. We must have got on pretty good time because we never ran. *(Kathleen Tatham, of 16 Lyndhurst Road, was a daughter of the lady who sang like a nightingale, p 50.)*

My new school was a large building and the school was run in a High School way, but by two spinster ladies, Sarah and Rita Allen Olney. I rarely came across them. *(Rita Allen-Olney had been the first headmistress of the GPDST South Hampstead High School from its foundation in 1876 until 1886. Sarah had been the head of Blackheath High School from its establishment in 1880. The two sisters set up a school for general and higher education of girls in 1886 in St. John's Wood at The Elms, with some pupils from South Hampstead High. By 1889 they had moved to No 41 Belsize Park Gardens, and in 1891 they moved on to The Hall, a new house in Crossfield Road. They took boarding and day girls from the age of 6. Its buildings are still in use as The Hall School, a boys' preparatory school.)*

On the whole, take it all round, I enjoyed my time there. Though my sister was there, I never saw her and I think she and I can only have overlapped for a few terms. *(Marjory was 8 years older than Phyllis, so she would have been 15 when Phyllis arrived at the school. Marjory could have started at the school when it was on its earlier site.)*

The first class I went into was in the attic and there weren't a great many in it. It was taught by a Mrs Taylor. Short and fat with a booming voice. She always sang at school concerts and on one occasion was dressed as a daisy, a wonderful sight. She was a good tempered, vulgar young woman. I seem to have got on well at school. I never learnt anything consciously. I picked up things. I never sat down to a job and concentrated. I let things be and picked up what I could. But I was soon moved up into the next form. A large one, about 30 girls, sitting at desks, and a thin young woman, Miss Wicks, in charge. Here I pursued along the same policy quite unconsciously, and I got through all right without doing any work. Poetry I learnt so easily that I merely had to hear someone else say it and I could say it too. A good many of our lessons involved learning by heart the multiplication tables, the dates of the Kings of England and their wives. When we started off to learn them, their wives and their dates, we were told to buy charts with them on. Now, all the books we had to get for this school were to be bought at a shop on the other side of the Finchley Road, miles from my home. Mother wasn't going to walk down there to get them, so I either had to go without, or occasionally she would order them at a shop in the High Street. "Where is your chart?" I would be asked, and I would say I hadn't got one. A lecture on the subject. I was always getting into trouble in that way, and it caused me considerable misery. I learnt the dates by listening to the others. But the worst was when mother ordered a grammar book from the shop in the town, as we called it, and when it came it was a large expensive volume. I told her that I was sure it wasn't right and she said "nonsense". It was no good at all. We were told to do Exercise 6 for our prep and my Ex. 6 was quite different. I didn't like to say what was the matter and went on for a bit inventing excuses for not having done my work, until the burden of it all became too much, and one day my young brother found me bawling on my bed and told mother. Then my mistress, realising what was the matter, borrowed a copy from some girl and I was all right.

But on the whole I got on well there without consciously doing any work. I shone at drawing. I loved it. To me it was a joy, whatever we had to draw. At home I always was busy with a pencil or chalks. Always drawing. And at school I was the shining light of the class, just as I was at writing. My handwriting was always held up to the class as an example and I loved those absurd copy books, in which I wrote in enormous letters "Walls have ears", and I never knew what it meant. I don't remember disliking any lesson. Sewing I loved. We made a coarse apron, which went to some orphanage. The poor little girl beside me had a high voice and quite short hair which was then considered most odd. She was left handed. Every time the mistress came round the poor child was blown up, "Frances Matthew, put your needle in your right had at once". And as soon as the lady was gone, the needle went back into the left hand.

Classroom in The Hall, Crossfield Road, 1894 (English Heritage)

Most lessons were fun, and geography, science, botany were extra fun because I could always draw in those. We had also to write essays. It was called composition. We were set this subject: "What I would like to be". Which shows that this school was advanced, as it actually took it for granted that these young girls might one day "be" something instead of sitting at home doing nothing. I wrote, "I would like to be an artist. What could be nicer than to travel about the world painting pictures of what you see"? I still say amen to that. A rather highbrow pupil came up to me afterwards and said in an intense deep voice, "But do you think you will be good enough?" "Oh yes," I said with complete self assurance. That self assurance faded and died, leaving me so unsure that I thought I was no good at anything. I wonder why. Because it's true.

The lesson besides drawing that I also loved with my whole soul was physical exercise – only once a week, I think. We marched down to the large hall and there in lines we did exercises to the music of a piano. Then we ran and did mazies. *(A mazy run is a zigzag run with a ball.)* I loved it. The music, the rhythm, the feel of life in the finger tips. No jumping or stuff, then but it was wonderful.

And for about 2 years, I had painting lessons on a Saturday. Those were wonderful. Brushwork. I went to a private house in Keats Grove. There were 3 of us only and a wonderful teacher. I didn't like her, she dressed in willowy garments, rather William Morrisy, but she could teach. Then suddenly no more lessons. Economy as usual, I suppose. Dancing classes, which to me were even more entrancing than exercises. I went for one winter, or possibly two. And there I found that I was a born dancer, but then suddenly no more classes. And even for the dancing classes mother wouldn't buy me a pair of castanets. They cost something like 1/6 a pair. Mother said as usual, "Nonsense". You can flick your fingers. Hetty *(Dalton)*, my very good friend, was so kind she used to lend me one of her castanets, until the wrath of the mistress descended on her.

I omitted to say the drawing we did at that school was not progressive. We were handed out cards on which were printed complicated designs. Strawberries in a wreath shape, I loved doing the intricate pattern and getting it correct but most of the girls hated it. Then one day there was a great advance as we had a tea cup and saucer put in front of us. One for a large class. We were told to make a rough sketch in the corner of our drawing books. I, who had learnt about ellipses as well as perspective at my Saturday painting lessons, produced something that was highly commended.

I talk as if I had been a star turn at school. Far from it. I was a restless chattering child, very untidy and unpunctual and those things got me into constant trouble. I had no conceit in me. I thought always that I was a worm. I was plain awkward, too tall with very big feet. My hair, which later on was admired, didn't curl and so was no asset. It waved. The only conceit was one promulgated by my family. I believed I was socially superior to all my companions. Strange to say, my mistress at school emphasised that. "I didn't expect *you* to do such a thing," when I was seen by her to be making a face about something. The common class could make faces, but not me.

None of the girls were ever asked to my house or I to theirs. My mother did not know their parents, partly because we lived so far away. The girl I went to school with was the same; we were rather isolated. In the three years I was there I had better teaching than I ever had later on. My sister had left and gone to *(Royal)* Holloway College.

My mother had a set-to with the head mistresses of my school, which was rather a joke. Bicycling had come in and my sister *(Marjory)* had learnt to ride, so my mother sent her to school on her machine. An indignant letter came from the heads. Bicycling was an unladylike pursuit and would my mother refrain from allowing my sister to come to school on her bicycle, as it reflected unfavourably on the school. Mother had to acquiesce, but you can imagine her joy when the rumour went round, a few years later, and it was true, that the Misses Allen Olney had been seen taking cycling lessons in Regent's Park. Mother was not good at placating the authorities and it had its effect on us. A few incidents stand out about those three years; I learnt poetry with the greatest ease, no trouble at all, and I loved reciting it. I still remember some. Five years later I couldn't learn by heart if I was paid.

One stupid affair which upset me badly: my own fault, but a misunderstanding. I made up my mind one morning to reform. I could not chatter on, drop my book etc. and I would get through the day without getting an order or disorder mark, whatever it was called. All went well, until the last lesson, taken by Miss Wicks. At the end of the lesson she said, "Do pages 32, 33 and 34 for homework". I opened my side of the desk. We had some double desks and I shared with a girl called Elizabeth, who had eczema all over her hands. I looked inside. Balancing the lid on my head and searching for a pencil to make a note of the numbers of the pages, while doing so, I hummed gently 32, 33, thirty-four. A little song and, as I went on searching for my pencil, my song became louder without my noticing it myself. Suddenly I heard a voice, Miss Wicks', rap out, "Who is making that noise?" I stopped humming and waited. I wasn't interested and I wasn't involved. Someone had been making a noise but not me. Then the voice again.

"Who was making that noise? Own up at *once* whoever it was." Silence, and a horrible feeling crept over me. Had it been me? Oh, that was too much. I couldn't bear it. Hadn't I been so good all day? I had not got one bad, mark. Had it been me? "I shall keep the whole class in all tomorrow. You can now go home". Not daring to look at anyone, I got away from school as quickly as I could and walked home in misery. The misery increased. I had no one to tell, and the evening and night made it all worse. I had decided what I must do. I got to school and I noticed girls looking at me. Elizabeth, a very loyal child, though her eczema fingers always made me feel sick, whispered to me, "Some of the girls says you did it. You didn't, did you?" How kind of her, I thought and what a shock she will have. Miss Wicks came in. I walked up to the desk and said very quickly, "I made that noise yesterday". I couldn't explain that I didn't know I was doing it until it was too late to own up. Miss Wicks liked me. Again she expressed great astonishment. She would never have expected such a thing of me etc. etc., and the whole silly episode ended.

A new teacher was coming to that class and Miss Wicks was to go up to the Remove and teach there. It happened in the middle of term, I don't know why. The 3rd class was too full. Two girls would therefore go up to the Remove with Miss Wicks. Two girls whom she would choose. She chose me and Marion Layton, a very nice girl, very serious minded and a real student. My amazement and delight knew no bounds. I said nothing, but felt overwhelmed with delight that I should be one to be chosen. There was no sort of affection on my side for the mistress, nor on hers for me, I think. I was quick-witted and I suppose she liked it. Everyone liked Miss Wicks; the other girls were envious of me. I went home, not dragging my feet up those very hills this time, but walking on air. I told my mother and purred with pleasure inside.

I sat in a desk in the front row of Remove. I was years younger than the other girls. Marion Layton and I were the same age. During the day, in walked Miss Sarah Olney. I looked up as she came in and then went on with my writing. I was filled with joy at my promotion. The next morning my mother opened a letter at breakfast. It was from Miss Sarah Olney. She said that it was quite unsuitable that I should have been chosen to go into the Remove; that she noticed that, when she walked into the class room, I looked up. I had no mental ability. All of which was probably true. I would therefore go back to class 3. I broke down at breakfast and rushed to my room. My mother was sympathetic, but also furious, more furious with Miss Olney than sympathetic to me. I had a sodden face and she let me off school that morning but I had to go and face the music in the afternoon and, when asked by cheeky girls why I had come down in the world, I just said. "I'm sure I don't know". And why weren't you here this morning? "Because I had a headache."

My mother was raging against the school, because this incident was really a paying off of old scores by Miss Sarah. At the end of the previous term there had been a school concert given in the school hall. Each child was given one ticket to take home for a parent. I took mine home. Mother didn't want to go, so she asked the cook to go. This cook happened to be a neatly dressed, nice looking cook, but still she was the cook and no doubt looked it. We walked into the hall to take our seats, which were numbered. We sat down near the front. Miss Sarah observed us. She came up to us and I told us to get up and go with her and we were led by her to seats at the back and side. I understood nothing of what was going on. I wasn't worried at all. But next morning mother received a stinger from Miss Sarah, "Tickets weren't meant for people that sort", she said. My degradation from Remove to 3rd class was by way of retribution. I was taken away from the school a term later.

After that I had no education. That school had been tough and I found it very tiring, but the teaching was good. From the pupil's point of view it doesn't pay for the mother to be at loggerheads with the mistresses. What an obvious remark!

Indecent exposure

To get into that school one went down a steep set of stone steps from the pavement along a concrete path. A brick wall divided this path in half, so that, if one stood in the road and looked down, one would see the path to the side door, but not anyone standing behind this jutting out wall opposite the door. I suppose that wall had been put there so that people in the road could not get a clear view of the playground behind.

One day, afternoon I think, I came to school alone. I walked down the steps and behind the wall stood a man. He had his trousers undone and was "indecently exposing" himself. I learnt that expression from the police, when I was having a man up for so doing. Needless to say I did not know that expression then. I felt quite sick. As a family we were brought up to have no knowledge of the human body. It didn't exist. My mother was ultra proper. So on that day at school I rushed into the building, but said nothing, when I found a group of girls of my class discussing it in horror. "That nasty man" was repeated over and over, until Miss Wicks became interested and asked what it was all about. The upshot was that, for ever after as far as I know, a servant man had to walk up and down that piece of concrete path daily, morning and afternoon. Really I think the headmistress might have arrived at some more satisfactory arrangement. That nasty man was the first of a long series of similar encounters. I had and have the eyes of a lynx and can see an enormous distance. My husband says I can see through brick walls, and things that are not there. Quite untrue.

A sister-in-law of mine, who lived in Hampstead, has far more lurid stories than I could tell, but all of the same sort. Perhaps you will believe me when I say that any narrow lane was liable to be occupied by one of the exhibitionist creatures. They frequented the Heath in fairly large numbers. They hovered on the outskirts even of a group of us girls standing chatting in Belsize, at a corner on our way home from school. Twice while I was walking alone, once in Lyndhurst Gardens and once outside my own house, a man came up to me and poured filth into my ear. On one of these occasions, mother, myself and my young brother were walking home from church.

Mother with wonderful regularity took us to church on Sunday afternoons. She searched for an interesting service in vain, until she found Mr Newland Smith at St Mary's, Primrose Hill *(Rev. N Newland-Smith, curate)*. We loved his catechism class and wouldn't have missed it for anything. There I imbibed my first socialism. It was called Christian Socialism. It was a very weary walk home. Looking back, I can see there was not one beautiful thing to look at on that walk. Not one. Rows of hideous expensive houses. The only things were the lilac, may and laburnum that many people had put in their front garden.

We were not so advanced. We still had filthy laurels, but the more modern people, the ones in the red brick Willett houses, had lilac, may and laburnum. [After I was married, my husband suggested having lilac in our more or less country garden and I still feel that lilac, red may *(red hawthorn)* and laburnum are an abomination, as they remind me of those weary roads of my childhood.]

On our weary way home up Lyndhurst Gardens my brother and I, who had been quarrelling incessantly, got nearly to the pitch of open battle. My mother said she wouldn't stand it any more; would I please go on in front and leave them in peace? This I did and was glad to be away from them. I had not gone far, when a flashy looking young man came out of a side road and overtook me as I walked up the hill. He had just passed me when he turned took off his hat and asked the way to Rosslyn Hill. I told him and he walked beside me, to my annoyance. I realised at once that he was "common". The boys would have said a "cad". He talked quickly and described his coming up for the Guy Fawkes day celebrations; of how he had come up with his young lady and of how "they had gone to bed together afterwards, but not to sleep" – and at that something began to flutter in my inside – "but like your mother and father when they go to bed", the voice went on. I wanted to yell "Help". Quickly I turned and said, "I think I'll wait for my mother who is just behind". My word! That young man might have been shot from a gun. He vanished round the corner ahead in a second and no doubt ran for it when he got out of sight. I waited for mother as if nothing had happened. "My dear," said she, "Are you in the habit of talking and walking with strange men, whom you pick up?" She was evidently amused. "Well, he asked the way and then tacked himself on, but I didn't want to go on with him beside me, so I waited for you".

So ended that *(incident)*, but the one next to my house frightened me more, as it was nearly dark and suddenly a man come from nowhere saying horrible things that I half understood. I rushed indoors in a panic and told an orphan some of it. "Don't you tell me your evil", she said. And I didn't.

School clothes

I have no doubt that most children think that they are unsuitably dressed, but really we were. The boys had their suits made for them by a Mrs Hunwick, who lived in a slummy part of the parish. I say "the boys", but what really happened was the eldest one had a suit made for him and thereafter it was handed down till the fourth one got it. On one occasion, mother had a pair of knickers *(knee breeches)* for Aubrey and a coat and waistcoat of Geoffrey's suit. She sent him to school in those. The poor child was dragged on to the platform by the headmaster and the other boys (it was a large school) were made to laugh at him.

There never seemed to be any order at home and, though in books the wild Bohemian or Irish families seem to enjoy themselves, I think a well conducted household lends to the peace of everyone. One morning mother said my boots, evidently my only pair, had not come back from being soled. I must go to school in a discarded pair of my brother Bernard's. Now, boy's boots were considerably different from girl's boots. They were very heavy and clumsy. They were very short in the ankle. At the back was visible a black tag for pulling the boots on with, and the laces were wound round large hooks in the front. I felt to be made to go to school in those was the limit. I suppose I knew refusing was useless and so I put them on, protesting. They were so clumsy I could hardly walk in them and I shall always remember that day. I crept or rather stumbled along beside the walls.
I was wearing an old blue cotton frock of my sister's, unaltered. The dress being 8 years old was old-fashioned, and too large and too long. So I bent my knees as I walked and hoped that my dress hid the boots a little bit. Crossing the roads was the worst as I was right out in the open. I got to school late but was glad of that, as no one saw me come in. At playtime I shut myself in the lavatory. How could I run about the playground in those boots? When we came to dress to go home midday, I dawdled. I wasn't going out into the roads with those on among other children. So I again hid and eventually came out and started to put on my boots. Miss Wicks appeared. "What was I doing there?" I had no answer. She looked as if I had stayed behind in order to steal the coat racks. I crept out and crawled home and the uphill was hard going in those boots. When I got home, my mother said, "Your own boots have come back so you can wear them this afternoon". It seems so foolish and pitiful to have been so miserable but we were all brought up to admire uniformity.

Third school (1896-1902)

(The proprietors of Phyllis' unusual third school were Ellen Harriette Farnell and her younger sister Frances Elisa Dawson Ida Farnell, known as Ida. Their father, John Wilson Farnell (1817-74) was one of two sons of a landowning Leicestershire farmer, who had migrated to London and become drapers and silk mercers. John had then moved on to Wiltshire, where he married Harriette Pritchard, and traded in Salisbury, the birthplace of Ellen Farnell in 1854 and of three of her six siblings. These included Henry Dawson Farnell (1852-1923), who became a GP in Eastbourne and eventually a Fellow of the Royal College of Surgeons; and Richard Lewis Farnell (1856-1934), a classical scholar who was to serve as Rector (head) of Exeter College, Oxford and as Vice-Chancellor of the University in 1920-23.

The family subsequently moved back to the capital, at first to south London, where Ida was born in Clapham in 1859, and then by 1861 to Camden Town, living first at 3 Hamilton Street (now Greenland Road), and later at 89 Great (now Royal) College Street. No longer a draper, father John was now employed, "on a modest salary, as a brewery manager."

George Stanley Farnell was born in 1861 in Camden Town; he became a classical scholar at Wadham College, Oxford, and later a headmaster in Jersey, where he died in 1895 after falling off a cliff while out walking.

Ellen and Ida were brought up in Camden Town. Ellen was educated at a private girls' boarding school in Muswell Hill, before serving as a governess, at a country house at Royston, Herts., to the granddaughters of a peer, Lord Braybrooke.

Ida Farnell also worked as a governess, to a family in Hastings, before enrolling as an early student at Lady Margaret Hall, Oxford. There, in 1885, she gained first-class honours in French in the University's 'Examinations for Women' (this some 35 years before female Oxford students were first awarded degrees). Ida then sailed to America, where she taught French at a prestigious girls' school in Baltimore, before returning to England in 1891.

By that time her elder sister Ellen had opened her Hampstead school at 2 Thurlow Road, with six girl boarders listed in the 1891 census. By 1894 the school had moved 230 yards westward, to Ashbridge House in Windsor Terrace (renamed Lyndhurst Terrace in 1939), a larger, detached property today called Heath House and occupied by an independent language school. The Farnell sisters were both registered at Ashbridge House as eligible to vote in local elections, and were evidently the property's joint owners.

An advertisement in The Guardian (London) on 8 December 1897 read: "HAMPSTEAD. — HOME SCHOOL for GENTLEMEN'S DAUGHTERS, situated in the healthiest part of Hampstead, and conducted upon modern principles by two ladies (with high University honours). The intellectual advantages of London are used to the best effect. Highly qualified visiting teachers. Care of health. No over-pressure. Riding and tennis. – The Misses Farnell, Ashbridge House, Windsor-terrace, Hampstead, London").

My new school was unique. *(Run by)* two charming ladies and they were ladies of about 40, the nieces *(sisters)* of the Warden of Exeter and with a Doctor brother in Eastbourne, who decided to start out on their own and run a school. As one of their pupils, I have felt no sympathy with their project. About a year ago, I happened to meet a niece of theirs and she spoke of their bravery and initiative in striking out in a line of their own, *(at a time)* when doing anything of the sort was not done. There is that point of view, but there is also mine, that of the pupil. Looking back I can see, and I think I saw at the time, that it was a disaster for everyone concerned for a school to be started and run by people, however charming and cultivated, who were hopelessly incompetent, and that's what they were. We all of us realised that and we had no respect for them nor affection. A gentle antagonism was all we felt.

I started going there *(c.1896)*, when I was 10, I think. My mother happened to be away at the time and, at breakfast, before I started off to my new school, which was merely a five minute walk, I read her letter and I was moved to tears, though I don't see why. It said, "You are starting at a new school and you can now make a new start in life. I pray that God will help you to choose good friends and will direct you in your ways". Really, God didn't have much choice as, when I went there, the day pupils amounted to 4, or 5, or possibly less.

(In 1898 the school was again relocated, to Bayford House, at Nos. 1 & 3 Windsor (Lyndhurst) Terrace, on its southwest corner. Known since the interwar period as as Old Conduit House, the property is now listed Grade-II*. It was originally in 1864-65 built as two houses – Bayford House and Oswald House – with a connecting door between them, by and for John Burlison, chief assistant to the architect George Gilbert Scott; and his son-in-law, the stained-glass artist Alfred Bell. In 1870, Bell combined the two houses, and with Charles Buckeridge, another pupil of Gilbert Scott, produced the still surviving ornamented gothic interiors.)

The two ladies, Ida and Ellen Farnell, either rented

Entrance to Oswald House, later renamed as part of Bayford House; watercolour by Alfred Bell (Camden Local Studies & Archives Centre)

or bought (I don't know which – *actually, bought*) a most unusual house near Fitzjohn's Avenue. It was called Bayham Lodge *(sic)*, I don't know why. *(Bayford House was named after Alfred Bell's Hertfordshire birthplace.)* It had a large garden and open space round it. The house itself was built by an architect for himself. It was rather charming with little staircases and turrets and I felt it ought to have been occupied by the Lady of Shallot *(sic)* and not the pupils of St Trinian's.

It was charmingly decorated inside. Only one room looked like a school room with desks. The two ladies had good taste, but they were 'scatty'. The establishment, I think, started as a finishing school. It was intended for the daughters of rich foreigners. And they came. *(One boarder in 1891 was from Ontario and another, in 1901, from Trinidad.)* As that sort of school, it may have been successful. The girls may have got what they needed – but we didn't. I have a feeling that the Miss F's, who by now had established themselves as two ladies who could be called upon by the surrounding gentry, were not paying their way, so they thought they would try day pupils as well. They collected a few of these, put in desks and hired two young women, one to teach French and German and the other to teach any subject under the sun that was demanded of her, poor soul.

I was always ready to get out of our house so, though unpunctual, I was in good time for school. Besides, my friends waited for me at the corner and I was in an urgent hurry to get to them and tell them of everything that had been happening since I parted from them the previous afternoon. We walked to school talking our heads off. We entered the strange towers of Camelot by a narrow passage, a public footpath *(Shepherd's Path)*, in the left wall of which was a door. When we got inside, we went very precipitately down steep steps. The house was all little steps up and down. Some winding, some straight. [A despairing house for a modern housewife, as no trolley could be used. Such things had not been heard of in those days.]

The two ladies swished from room to room. They, particularly Ellen, the tall one, wore very long dresses. They were tight fitting to her lean figure and then,

Shepherd's Path viewed from Lyndhurst Terrace; Bayford (now Old Conduit) House to the left

just below the knee, they burst forth into a cascade. It touched the ground in front but went pouring forth well on to the floor behind. Their dresses were always green. Ellen must have worn rustling silk beneath, as we could always hear her approaching by the sound of swishing skirts. Very useful for us as a warning.

This new school was all casual and haphazard. There were very few rules, practically none and no marks. No competition. Really it should have been wonderful. The idea was progressive. But nobody learnt anything. There were, no doubt, some exceptions. I learnt French and German. That was because I heard it spoken. I did not have to learn it. I came to me across the air. That was how my learning was done. I picked it up. Whereas at the first school everything was order and regimentation, here everything was the reverse.

A typical day would be this: having left our coats in the room downstairs, we came up and went into a book room, very small, where we each had a shelf for our books. We were supposed to collect all the books we would need until 11 o'clock, and not return to the book room. As we never did collect all the right books, we did return and nobody seemed to mind. In that strange house nearly all the rooms opened out of one another, sometimes with doors and sometimes merely with archways and curtains. I have no recollection of prayers. During the morning, the hours of work were arranged for us in this way: we might start off with an half hour's prep, followed by a history lesson of an half hour, followed by another half hour's prep. These half hours were interspersed among the lessons, so as to prevent any of us from straining our brains! I suppose it was really done so that the teachers could get the teaching done. We sat at desks in the main room. Very nice desks with chairs. The time table must have been a complicated affair as we were of such varying ages. *(The six boarders listed in the 1901 census were aged between 14 and 18.)*

We were supposed, when we did our prep, to prepare a lesson for next morning, but naturally what we did was – if we were having a history lesson at 10 – to learn it up from 9.30 to 10. This was not good for our memories, but it got us through the lessons. At 11 o'clock we went for a walk, having just consumed biscuits and milk. These had to be paid for as extras. My mother didn't like paying for extras so I alone had no milk or biscuits. But friends of mine used very kindly to supply me with biscuits which they brought from home. That was the sort of thing that made me ashamed and resentful. Perhaps if I had asked my mother for them, but no, I knew it would be no good and, I so hated arguments, I had learnt when not to speak.

We then went out for a walk for a quarter of an hour. Just up the road and down again, in a crocodile. I liked walking in a crocodile, though the others hated it, but I felt I was then like one of those lucky beings who went to a boarding school: my great ambition, which was never realised. On Mondays and Fridays a large part of the morning was given up to drawing. A visiting master came one of those days and on the other we worked alone. All our drawing consisted of drawing, in chalk or charcoal, plastic casts. Plums, apples and pears to start with, going on to heads and busts. These casts hung on the walls or stood about the rooms.

History, geography and literature were lectures delivered by Miss Ellen Farnell *(who also gave public lectures on these subjects)*. We were supposed to take notes but nobody seemed to mind if we didn't. At the age of 10 it is not easy to take notes. The history book we used was *(John Richard)* Green's '*(A Short)* History of the English People' *(Macmillan, 1874, which told the story not of kings or conquests, but of the people; he omitted the battles.)* The literature book was Stafford Brooke *(sic, probably Rev. Stopford Brooke's 'English Literature from A.D. 670 to A.D. 1832' (Macmillan, 1876))*. One strange thing was that these two ladies were liberals or radicals. How my parents ever sent me there I can't think, unless it was that I was taken at a very reduced fee. *(Phyllis' mother was doubtless also attracted by the riding, see advert.p 74)*.

As half of two mornings were taken up with drawing, and part of each of the others with prep, and I had a French lesson and a German lesson daily, there wasn't much time for anything else. Miss Farnell's lessons had a way of dissolving in thin air. She was always late for them and quite unaware of what she was going to discourse on. If her sister Ida was not available, it frequently happened that the maid would come in and ask Miss F to come and see the plumber, or something of the sort. I always thought Miss F was pleased at these interruptions. Then it was quite possible that she herself would break the lesson off. She would look about her in a vague way and then say that she must go and see about the meals or something. French and German, at least once daily, were taught by a Swiss governess with varying accents. *(The French teacher in 1901 was Hélène Michelbouch, a 31-year-old Belgian national born in Luxembourg.)* But Mrs Couton had grounded me and my accent was good, also I found languages a pleasant occupation, especially French. The rule was that we must always speak French to one another and we did. Doggerel French but it gave one confidence. I found as I grew up that I knew more French and German than girls I knew.

[When I had left school, a young woman *(Hilda Garnett, see p 163)*, who was always a very anxious for the well being of the souls of others, asked me to join a class to study French. A French lady was hired and we all met at a large house on the Heath. I was astounded. There were gathered the well to do young women of the neighbourhood. They had all been at expensive schools. To hear them slowly staggering through sentences and then stumblingly to translate them! It was a pathetic exhibition. I read through the chapters waiting for my turn to come. Much the same happened with German – the same young woman dragged me to Polytechnic classes. They were so elementary I couldn't bear them. And this girl, Hilda Garnett, had been at one of the most expensive schools in Hampstead.]

Otherwise what did I learn *(at Bayford House)*? Drawing. The two hours drawing on Monday and the 2 hour's prep for it on Friday were a joy to me. There wasn't much time left. Maths or arithmetic for half an hour a week, taught by a poor little woman who couldn't do sums herself. I was almost sorry for her. How she tried to open out busily doing nothing, when she couldn't do a problem, and her relief when the half hour had finished and her ignorance had, she hoped, not come to light. Poor little soul, so poor and so ineffectual. Every now and then we had a smattering of science – electricity and magnetism. Also we "did" some botany. These things were learnt jointly by the mistress and ourselves out of books. She knew no more than we did at the start. *(Ellen Farnell was a member of the Hampstead Scientific Society.)*

When I had been there some time 3 years or so *(1899)*, mother began to think I wasn't being properly educated and she went and demanded from Miss Farnell that I should learn algebra – then a little later on, Latin. The mornings didn't grow any longer and there was no school in the afternoon, so where were these things to be squeezed in? The obvious thing would have been to give all the mornings to lessons and have the prep done at home in the afternoons. But this didn't happen. I suppose there were such a variety of ages amongst the few pupils that it kept the teachers busy – I was sorry for the little woman who could not teach arithmetic, but I was sorrier still for the young woman who succeeded her, when she was suddenly told by Miss Farnell that she must teach me algebra, and then later on Latin. She was a nice young woman and together we wrestled over algebra, neither of us understanding much. Latin was a bit better, because by then she had got engaged and her young man wrote all the answers of tomorrow's exercise in the margin.

Our school was right against the little lane *(Shepherd's Path)*. One late evening Rosalind, the headmistress's niece leaned out of her bedroom, "Why must I be favourite one to go first?" A young man in the passage was gazing up at her. She was in her nightdress. In those days a nightdress was as unalluring as plate armour. They were engaged in talking nonsense. Rosalind's bedroom door opened and in walked Miss Millar, our nice English teacher. Rosalind was quick. All Miss Millar heard of the conversation was a sad, perplexed voice saying, "Oh, if only I could believe." Next day I heard the two sides to the situation. Rosalind was highly amused that she had had the wit to pretend she was wrestling with her own soul. Miss Millar most impressed: "I never thought Rosalind was such a deep thinking girl." *(Rosalind, about the same age as Phyllis, was a daughter of the Eastbourne-based Dr Henry Farnell. The 1901 census lists a 26-year-old "Jean E. Miller", an English teacher born in Bowes Park.)*

But at school I did no wrestling with texts. I slid along, the days passing, my only deep regret being that on fine sunny days I must spend the mornings indoors. I always was longing to be out.

(Ida Farnell had left Hampstead by 1900, to serve for six years as headmistress of St Michael's Hall, a girls' boarding school in Hove, Sussex. Her book, 'Spanish Prose and Poetry Old and New, with translated specimens' was published in 1920. She died in Hove in 1933 and was buried in Highgate Cemetery. By 1901 her widowed mother Harriette was living in Hampstead, at 5 Rudall Crescent with her unmarried eldest daughter Mary. By 1904 Ellen Farnell had left Bayford House, and in 1911 was the "principal" of a "student house" in Kensington, with one female student in residence. She died in Oxford in 1917 and was buried at nearby Wolvercote. Later interred there

with Ellen, in 1928, was Ida Marion Silver, a close friend of Ida Farnell. Cambridge University still administers a charitable Ellen Farnell Fund, founded under Miss Silver's will; it now endows both a medical fellowship and a bed in Addenbrooke's Hospital.)

My school friend, Gladys

At first I made a great friend. That is to say we, Gladys Townsend and I, made friends. She was, my eldest brother said, like a milkmaid, and he found her unattractive. Looking back I should say she was more like a barmaid. She was full of curves – her round cheeks were red and she had a full red mouth. I didn't really like her very much, but I thought she was terribly attractive and that seemed to me a most desirable quality. Her father was in India. Her mother had died. She lived with two very gentle old-fashioned ladies, her aunts, in Church Row. Gladys was certainly not like her aunts and they must have found her an awkward proposition. I had to be friends with someone and besides there was something dare devil and risky about Gladys that fascinated me. Mother naturally disapproved. I was told to ask her to tea. How I dreaded asking my friends to tea. I loved going out, but not the ordeal of my friends not behaving, or not looking as they ought, and mother's withering criticism afterwards. Gladys came. When she had gone, mother said "What dreadfully short skirts that girl was wearing, and such fat legs too – sitting on that low chair in the drawing room, she looked positively indecent". But mother knew the old aunts and they wanted Gladys and me to be friends.

It was through Gladys that I met my first love. It was probably because of her that I began to think of boys. The aunts took a furnished house at some place on the sea – I don't know where. The house we were in was semi-detached and its garden opened on to the esplanade. Up and down this esplanade Gladys and I gallivanted. I had discovered that one could drop down on to the shingle below without hurting oneself. It was quite a big drop and sand would have been painful. I used to walk along with Gladys and suddenly, as if by accident, walk over the edge and people would run to see if I was hurt. Soon Gladys had noted the time when a group of young lads would be passing daily. "Come on quick," she used to whisper to me. We would walk demurely along and, as we passed them, Gladys would giggle and bump into one of them. I was horrified. The boys liked it and would catcall after us and I thought it was all "very common", but also rather exciting. We also amused ourselves with skipping ropes. I was really good at that. Some children from the next house came out and we played with them and one day we used a rope for jumping over. Gladys and a small child were holding the rope for me to jump. I was no good at jumping, no good at all, but the rope was low and I ran at it quite confidently and jumped. As I did so, Gladys and the child suddenly raised the rope. This had been instigated by Gladys. I caught my foot and fell headlong on the pavement with all my weight on my arms. I was in agony. I got up onto my feet and, holding my arms against my chest, I walked slowly back into the house trying not to cry. In the sitting room I sat down gingerly on the edge of a sofa and allowed myself to cry. There was no one there. Gladys had said nothing and done nothing, she was either scared stiff or as hard as a rock. The pain was very bad and I sat quite miserable holding my arms against me. In came an aunt. She was much concerned and sent for the doctor. She asked me how it happened and I said I fell, but I did not say why. Meanwhile I could hear her berating Gladys for being so callous. The doctor said I had badly sprained both wrists but I must have the use of one arm. So one arm was bound up in sticky plaster up to the elbow and put in a sling and the other was plastered half way up to the elbow.

I was going home next day anyway and my general discomfort and misery were increased by strange happenings in my lower regions; I was rather frightened and couldn't think what was the matter. For once I was glad to get home. As soon as I saw the little maid, I begged her to wash my knickers so that mother wouldn't see them. She looked at me oddly. Then mother appeared - "she had not thought this would happen", she murmured, not yet, and so awkward being away, and she ought to have warned me and I must wear this and so embarrassed was she and so inarticulate that I felt quite sorry for her; I had no idea what it was all about. But next day I had so much pain that the idiot doctor was fetched and he said nothing enlightening. I still thought I had had a strange attack of diarrhoea. I was kept on a sofa in the drawing room and was in such pain I was glad to stay there. Hetty came to see me and I casually told her my symptoms. "It's your monthly", she said. "My what?" I almost shouted. "Your monthly – you get it once a month." "Oh no", I yelled – no, not that not once a month. No, no, I can't bear it. But I had to, and another trial was added to my headache, and my indigestion and I felt it was all unfair, as here was Hetty without a day's illness and not a pain in her body.

Considering how my friend Gladys had behaved to me, it seems to me odd that I continued to be her friend, but at school the choice was very limited. There were so few day girls and so few of one's own age. Besides, there was something dashing about Gladys that I admired. Oh yes, my father was furious and I think rightly so, when a bill came in from Miss Field, Gladys' aunt, for the doctor who had attended me. My father said it was all Gladys' fault. She had tripped me up. Her aunt ought to pay. But I reiterated that the aunt didn't know Gladys had tripped me up - I didn't feel a bit virtuous about this. It was just a thing one wouldn't do to a friend. It still seems to me odd that the two aunts should have sent the bill to my father, but heavens how odd people are about money.

Gladys and I arranged to meet in the afternoon for a walk. I only once was asked to her house; she, like me, liked to escape from her home. I was escorted on my walks by a scruffy orphan, but Gladys was freer and went alone. I used to let the orphan escort me as far as the Heath and I would then place her on a seat, meet Gladys and go off together. In this way we met Hubert Eisdell.

Hubert Eisdell

(Hubert Mortimer Eisdell, 1882-1948, was an English tenor who later settled in Canada, enjoying considerable success on the concert stage in both England and Canada. While his musical training and earliest performances took place in England,

Eisdell made several visits to Canada between 1907 and 1930. After taking up permanent residence in Ontario in 1933, he became involved in the Canadian music scene as a performer and teacher.)

He thrilled me. I didn't count, but I adored him. He was taken with Gladys. She had picked him up on the Spaniards Road. I think she got a boy at Highgate School to introduce her. I know I was impressed, as she said she couldn't speak to anyone if she hadn't been introduced. Hubert bicycled to and from Highgate daily. I will tell what I know of his wife later. The first time I met him I had planted the orphan on a bench and, tacking along behind Gladys, I met the Adonis near the water works. But Gladys had evidently arranged to meet. I stood silent after being duly introduced. He was very beautiful, very fair and very gentle in his speech and manners. We met several times in the same place. Gladys kept up a voluble flow of inanities and the whole thing fizzled out, partly because Hubert got a scholarship to Christ's College, Cambridge and partly because he and Gladys had nothing whatsoever in common. On the mantelpiece at school stood a plaster head of the young Augustus and I used to look at that and think it was very like Hubert. It wasn't; Hubert's forehead was not so wide and his face was not so strong.

Beside my bed I unwisely had a little diary and in it I wrote "Met H.E." One day the orphan loyally came running to me. Your mother and sister are in your bedroom and they're reading your diary. My heart stood still. What lies should I have to tell to extricate myself from that entry "Met H.E."? But nothing happened and, after much suspense, my life went on again.

[About 40 years later I met H.E.. I know something of his story. He was the only son of the organist of Christ Church, Hampstead. He had one sister, a very pretty girl. The father trained the choir, but it did not occur to him that his own son might have a voice. One day a friend came to stay. He heard an angel singing in the bathroom. So the boy was trained and succeeding in getting a musical scholarship to Cambridge. But there was no money about, when his time there was up, and no push or drive either. Giving up his music, he applied for a school master's job in Canada. He got it and arrived out at a one horse place where the Headmaster's wife, a delightful woman, told me of the first evening that Hubert arrived. It was the holidays and no one was in but herself. She gave the shy young man supper. After that she could not think of how to entertain him, but he asked modestly, "Would you mind if I played the piano?" so he amused himself happily and she enjoyed it. Then he said quietly, "Would you mind if I sang?" Not at all. And suddenly she heard an angel singing in heaven. He sang his way back to London, how exactly I can't tell. He sang his way to the Queen's Hall and he filled it to "capacity" as the papers say year after year. He was the star turn of the Ballad Concerts. My husband spent an evening in town and next morning reported to me that he had been at a smoking concert, the singer Hubert Eisdell. I still felt a pluck at my heart when he said that name. Yes, he was very nice looking, yes he sang charmingly. He became the idol of the Queen's Hall ladies.]

A few days after our arrival in Canada *(in 1934 Phyllis' husband, Sir Francis Floud, was made High Commissioner in Ottawa)* I was rung up. Would I and my daughter join the morning musical club which met on Thursday? Yes, delighted. We would come next Thursday. Who was performing? "A singer called Hubert Eisdell, perhaps I knew him." I was thrilled and yet slightly embarrassed at the thought of seeing him again. But anyway he was English and already I was longing for the sound of a pure English voice and a real English conversation. Before going to the concert, I told my daughter what I intended to do. I must not push forward, but if possible I must speak to him and there might be a remote chance of getting the great man to come to our house. The hall was well filled and he sang. His voice was clear and pure and sweet. There was no enthusiasm. The Canadians are entirely unmusical. They only go to concerts because they think they are cultural. I had expected the artist to be mobbed and invited out by a crowd. They boast of their hospitality, but then he wasn't a popular hero. He was not a Lord. He was merely a musician. Mollie *(Phyllis' daughter)* and I went round to the back and met him and his accompanist. He didn't remember me, but when I said I knew where he had lived etc., his rather reserved manner broke down and he came home and lunched and we were friends from then on. I heard, and this may be incorrect, that what had happened was this. At the top of his fame he became involved as co-respondent in a divorce suit. It was his ruin. He lost money and reputation. He went back to Canada trying to pick up a living teaching singing in Toronto. He probably got few pupils and he told me teaching Canadians to sing was a nightmare as they had no ear for sound, if they had, would they talk as they did? His old schoolmaster took pity on him. He went back to Lakefield *(Ontario)* as a music master. He had acquired a young Canadian wife. They were very poor. Once we got him to come and stay with us and sing after dinner, when Lord Tweedsmuir *(the author John Buchan, then Governor-General of Canada)* was dining with us in Ottawa. After a few drinks one evening, he burst forth, railing against his poverty: "You don't know how poor I am. I can't afford to buy another pair of trousers. Your butler is better off than I am." That I could well believe. I rang up the C.B.C. *(Canadian Broadcasting Corporation)* and asked if they could give him some work. They said his type of song was out of fashion. I spoke to the morning music secretary and asked if they would have him again. She said she was sorry but there had been complaints after the concert that he could not be heard at the back of the hall.

My first experience of a holiday on a lakeside was at the Eisdell shack on Stony Lake. It was also my first experience in having to help with household chores. My impression of the weekend we spent with them was of incessant drudgery. I never stopped working it seemed. The weather was hot and I expected, when I went to stay by a lake, that I would spend my time in the lake, or on it. There never

Hubert Eisdell

seemed to be time for this. I had perforce to help and I was quite unaccustomed to housework or working, so I was probably terribly slow and incompetent. Then they must needs give the inevitable cocktail party and that entailed preparing nicknacks for about 30 people. My poor little hostess never sat down. If I had had any sense or known the ropes, I would have appeared armed with a roast chicken, a large meat pie, tins of strawberries, etc, etc. But it unfortunately did not occur to me, so we slogged away all day in great heat and to me it was an eye-opener. Did running a shack really entail all this work? I tried not to believe it and decided that the whole thing was my hostess and I must be very slow and incapable. I did not learn my lesson till many years later, when we took our house in the country.]

From the time of my meeting Hubert Eisdell to the time when I was married, by far my most important occupation was boys and young men, I don't think I got much encouragement from them until I was 16, and then life became a giddy whirl.

Gladys Townsend suddenly disappeared out of my life. One of her old aunts died and she was bundled off to another at a place called Annerley *(Anerley, near Crystal Palace in south London)*. Gladys' mother had died, either at her birth or shortly afterwards, Gladys used to show me her photograph and was sentimental; Gladys was like her father, red faced and tough; Gladys would dream of the day when she would go to India with her father and be his house keeper. We talked of it frequently and she lived for that day, I remember Gladys reciting Tennyson to me declaiming 'Lady Vere de Vere' *(Alfred, Lord Tennyson's poem 'Lady Clara Vere de Vere'. It includes the line, "Kind hearts are more than coronets, and simple faith than Norman blood.")* Her father was in business, I think in India, and it was Gladys' ambition and expectation to join him, when she was 17, and live in India, keeping house for him: India was the Mecca of all young girls and to marry an I.C.S. *(member of the Indian Civil Service)*, the very summit of ambition.

We made our own amusements so much in those days. What I liked about going out to tea, not tea parties but just tea, was the talking and discussions. We would sit together chatting our heads off, sometimes knitting or sewing and I drawing. They were pleasant quiet afternoons. Or, if the weather was fine, we would be out of doors on our precious bicycles, having competitions, doing trick riding, which I always won. Later on, tennis. My mother had an idea that if two young girls got together, their conversation must inevitably be smutty. How little she knew. Our conversation would not have made a nun blush. Occasionally a girl companion was produced by my mother, "a nice girl whom you would like" and her conversation would be of the lavatory type which simply froze me. There were children's parties, which in the summer entailed sports, I was a lanky girl and a shocking bad runner, so these parties, though I loved the noise and chatter, were always a disappointment because I could not run.

But when it came to bicycling I could do anything. Then ping pong came in. We played it on the dining room table with battledores. Our dining room table was round and with leaves in, of course, retained its curved ends, but still it did. I began to come up in the world, as I proved to be a demon player and was asked to parties.

After Gladys' aunt died she left Hampstead, as I said, and I did not see her for several years, and, I suppose, she had not gone to India. Her father had married again and Gladys had met the woman. She was a "fast" sort of creature, I gather, and she and Gladys disliked one another at sight. Her father told Gladys that, if she knuckled under and would agree to be dominated by her stepmother, she could come to India, otherwise no. Gladys honestly said she could not possibly live with that woman, so she gave up her dream and stayed in England. Later I heard she had married a man in the Australian Navy. I never heard of her again. But I admired her honesty. I felt terribly sorry for her and wondered how I would have behaved. I think I would have pretended to knuckle under just in order to get to India, but then I hadn't met stepmother, so I can't say. She was "fast", a Victorian word we often used. Women were fast and men were cads.

Remember, remember ...

(Another of the children's parties given by the Woodds, see p 64, was) on the 5th November. I heard my mother say that the Woods regarded it as a sort of religious festival, the day on which England was saved from the Pope. That Guy Fawkes party was a great affair, full of dreadful fears. A servant girl took me and, as we walked the short distance down the hill, already, though it was only 4 o'clock, the road was getting crowded with people making their way to the Heath for the great bonfire to be lit on the Sandy Ring. We were never allowed near the Heath on that day, but on the following one we would go up and look at the smouldering coals. Getting back from the party was more alarming, as by that time the "roughs" had greatly increased and people were beginning to line the route of the procession; a very primitive affair of decorated carts and horse drawn vans. Already crackers and fireworks were banging away and there were boys with those terrible masks that always frightened me. So getting to and from the party was exciting enough – rather too much, I often found – but the actual party was "super", or "capital" as the children would now say. We watched the fireworks' magnificence and beautiful Katharine Wheels *(sic)* that really went round and glorious rockets breaking in the sky and dropping coloured necklaces. The whole scene was frightening but fascinating. The dark figures running and crouching and suddenly an explosion of light and they all appeared red and yellow for a moment and then dark and hardly visible. It was thrilling. The huge crowd of young children watched through the great french windows and sighed and oohed as the rockets went up.

(On another Guy Fawkes Day) The pain was excruciating. Twice I didn't get to the lavatory in time and I was sick against the Cathedral wall *(This will have been at St Paul's, probably after one of their many visits to the City Guildhall for Church Lads' Brigade events; see p 113)*. I had diarrhoea in my drawers and eventually we started for home. Poor mother. She did have to put up with something. Walking away from the crowds was a great relief. The blood began to circulate and the pain in my head got less and then I saw something that I have never seen before, or since, and am not likely to see again. I saw a gentleman having his watch stolen.

We were in a back street and were alone, except across the road on the other pavement walked a "stout party": a very flashily-dressed man, with a pale waistcoat that made his fat tummy look even fatter. He was rather short and round and his top hat shone. He was most spruce, clean and dapper. He was walking along cheerfully. He was going the same way as me, only on the other pavement. He had got just in front of us, when a down and out tramp in rags came towards him walking in the gutter. He shuffled along and then suddenly, quick as a knife, when he got to the stout party, he darted at him, wrenched the watch with the chain, which had been across the fat tummy of its owner, and turned and raced down the street again the way he had come. He got quite some way before the party could recover himself. Then he pursued, evidently not accustomed to running –.waving his stick and shouting "stop thief". People came from nowhere and all ran too, shouting "stop thief". I longed to go too. I longed for the thief to get away, but I was also sorry for the stout gentleman. Naturally mother didn't let me join the crowd and shout "stop thief", but I dearly wanted to know what happened at the end of the story.

We went home, how I don't know, and it was about 5 or 6 before we got back. By then I was finished completely. I was given a hot bath, and it wasn't Saturday, and no one grumbled about the state of my underclothes, which seemed to me very odd. And I was very glad to get into my bed. In spite of the hot sun, I had felt frozen cold all day. So ended my day and everyone else went onto the Heath to see the bonfires and I was to have gone too, even though it would have been way past my bed time.

From then on I was never told if I was going to have some special treat. I had to present a bouquet to the Lord Mayor on one occasion. I went with my parents to the Guildhall, but until the bouquet was thrust into my hands did not know what I was going to do.

We did not often have visitors to stay. Our house really wasn't run well enough, our little maids too incompetent. But on one occasion *(in 1899)*, our cousin Mabel *(Spottiswoode)*, the one who always said "Yes", was with us. Dinner was over – I was 13, so I don't know if I dined with my parents and Mabel or not – but, after the meal, they went into the drawing room and I stayed alone in the dining room. My young brother was out, because he had gone to a Guy Fawkes party. It was November 5th. My Guy Fawkes parties had ended long ago. Aubrey had been invited to fireworks over at West Hampstead. The people were related to our nice music mistress. I was reading, when, at about 9 o'clock, Aubrey barged in. He was very tired and rather cross and absolutely filthy. He said he'd go in and say "Good night" 'to mother and then go to bed."You can't go in there like that", I protested. "You simply can't; you must wash first". We argued as usual – but he was firm. He wasn't going to wash so he wouldn't go in and say "Good night", and he was going to bed. And he did.

This sort of thing had happened before. We had no one to look after us and were left a great deal to ourselves. Every day we had tea together in an awful room in the basement in which all the bicycles and junk were kept. One day mother came down and looked in on us and I got it hot and strong for letting Aubrey sit down to tea with dirty hands. I was expected to look after him, without being bossy. I wasn't bossy because I was really fond of him and he of me, but we sometimes let loose and threw boots at one another or pushed, on one occasion, one another through the french window.

So I was not going to bother to make him wash. He was too tired and so was I. Soon after, I put my book away and went to bed myself. And while I was asleep, this happened. At about 11 o'clock my parents and Mabel prepared to go upstairs to bed, when suddenly mother exclaimed that Aubrey was still out. He had not come home. He was to have come by train, only one station. *(One stop west from Hampstead Heath station – on the Hampstead Junction (aka North London) line – was Finchley Road & Frognal. West End Lane station, in central West Hampstead, would have been two stops away.)* Father must go at once to the station and make enquiries. He went off and not finding Aubrey at the station he walked as fast as he could to West Hampstead – quite a long way. The little villa was in darkness. There was some delay before he could get an answer to his knocking but at last Mr. X appeared in pyjamas. Aubrey had left them at 8.30! Mr. X hurriedly dressed and went to the station with father. There they made enquiries and the porter there had remembered Aubrey catching the train. Now father really got in a panic. A long tunnel ran between the two stations – Aubrey must have fallen out. *(The 'Hampstead Tunnel' is 1,166 yards long.)* As fast as he could he got back to mother anxiously waiting at home. He told her he was going down to the station and was going to get a search party to go along the tunnel with lanterns. Mother said she couldn't stay at home – she couldn't bear it. She must go with him. "I'll just run up and tell cook", she said. She shook the woman, who was in a dead sleep."We're going out, cook I and the master – Master Aubrey hasn't come home. Do you hear, cook?" Cook, in a sleepy voice: "Master Aubrey has been in his bed asleep this two hours, ma'am". My word! I didn't half get it in the morning.

Holidays before 1901

Summer holidays were the joy of my life. We went for six whole weeks and only twice did we go to the same place, so it was an enormous adventure each year. Father used to go off looking at houses and then they were discussed and settled on. I was too unimportant and young to join in these discussions. These holidays must have been a nightmare to Mother. Whether out of contrariness or not, Mother took the line of never wanting to go away anywhere. Father wanted to go anywhere all the time. He managed to go off on a business trip to India on one occasion, after which he always ate curry with a spoon. But the burden of everything fell upon Mother, and she did not take kindly to being orderly. We generally took two of our scrubby little servants with us. We also took silver and linen, all of which had to be packed up. Any silver we did not use had to be packed in tin boxes and taken to the bank. The servants had nothing to do with

this. Mother practically did it all. Father was hopeless. Occasionally Mother would ask him to do some sort of packing, but he always either got my sister *(Marjory)* to do it, or got one of the servants. He was quite useless with his hands. As my sister grew up she became the mainstay. She was capable, so things were parked on to her, but she was not over amiable, so one had to draw the line.
I personally would never have dreamt of asking her to do anything for me. On one occasion, she was going for a walk with a friend, Violet Crayie, later Jay. Mother asked her to take me too and she acquiesced. I was pleased and got dressed and we started up the road, and, looking down, I saw I was wearing one boot and one indoor shoe. I felt miserably that that was the end of my walk, but to my surprise Marjory graciously suggested that if I hurried up they would wait. I was quite overwhelmed at the unusual kindness. I think the presence of Violet Jay must have had a soothing influence. She didn't even say I was a silly little idiot.

Our holidays were on the whole in rented vicarages in the country, not too far from the sea. There had to be a pony trap to take the old and the very young, and the others had bicycles. We had three holidays or four near the East coast, two in a castle on the Welsh border, no sea there, which was a blow, certainly to me. Every day had much the same pattern, but each had outstanding features. The same pattern was the packing up. The house had a protector in our absence. A certain Miss Coburn, who crawled up the steep hill from the slum district of Fleet Road, like an insect up a wall. On one occasion when we returned, she reported to Mother with great importance that she had seen a mosquito, pronounced "moskita". She said it was her duty to report this.

On the morning we were to leave home, the house was full of trunks, holdalls and the oddest assortment of luggage. New luggage was never bought. Pieces of cord had to be found to tie some of the older items together. The main parts of us all was to go in two four wheelers *(4-wheeled cabs, often known as 'growlers')*. It would have been more convenient to have ordered conveyance from the livery stable. But more expensive. We never had dealings with the livery stable. A servant was sent to the cab rank at

The George, Haverstock Hill, 1908 (Camden Local Studies & Archives Centre)

The George *(Haverstock Hill)*, where it was hoped she would pick up either a four wheeler or, on some occasions, a *(2-wheeled)* hansom cab.

[Talking of the livery stable, I must mention here the romance that took place between our florid servant, the one who chided me for saying "You stink", and the eldest son of the livery stable. She herself told me about it. She had drifted to London at the age of 15 and had picked up a living in service. She came to us at 17, a jolly girl with a mass of fair curly hair. On a Sunday evening out she was wandering around not knowing what to do with herself, so she stood at the back of a crowd surrounding the Salvation Army band in the High Street at the top of Gayton Road. "I like a bit of music myself. That's the only thing I like about this house, you do sing, but your - the Missus doesn't like me singing. She stopped me the other day. Well as I was saying, I stopped behind the crowd and there were a lot of people there and then I felt someone staring at me and he came up and took off his hat and said "good evening, Miss", and I said good evening to him. He is ever so nice looking." And he was - a tall handsome fair young man. His father the owner of the biggest livery stables in Hampstead. They married shortly after. Mother was completely taken aback when Sally asked me to tell her.]

Sometimes, or perhaps always, we had two four wheelers and a cart for the luggage. The cart came earlier and started off before we did. Bicycles not being used could be put on the cart, and a pram. We were going to Wales one year, a very long journey, that – hours and hours. The cart for the luggage came late. That delayed us. In a frantic state (I, at least, was on the verge of hysterics), we rushed for the train. Our reserved carriage was found and in we tumbled. Safe, thank goodness, not left behind. The servants were safely in another carriage and my father, believe it or not, in another. A smoker, I believe. He never travelled with us. It can't have been much fun unless you liked that sort of thing. But Mother appeared to. We sang songs most lustily in parts for hours of the journey, also singing rounds. I was the one who couldn't keep a part and had to be tacked on to someone else, but I loved singing and we all had good clear voices, especially the brother 2 years older than me, Geoffrey, and later on the one younger than me, Aubrey. We all bundled into the train in a fever of excitement and off it started. And as it slowly drew out of the station, there on the platform Mother saw all our luggage. It wasn't until we had got well away that Mother suddenly said, "We've left all our lunch behind" – or she probably called it dinner. That was too dreadful – a real blow. Lunch on the train was always a thrill. Sandwiches and a hard boiled egg each. That was the peak, a hard boiled egg. On one occasion I slowly ate off the white, keeping the yolk as a bon *(bonne)* bouche. Just as I was going to put it in my mouth, it rolled out of my fingers onto the filthy floor. I retrieved it and intended to wipe it and eat it but no, Mother was firm and on that journey my lunch was a disappointment.

This time, no lunch basket, all the way to Wales! We had one piece of food with us. Aunt Frances had brought from abroad some French nougat. Mother, in the usual way, put it in a cupboard to hoard it. She had brought it on the journey.

Buns could have been bought and also a cup of tea certainly at one station on the way, but that would have been extravagant. Waste of money. The phrase used so often by my parents. Father had his lunch packed up in his pocket. The journey seemed endless and we got too thirsty to sing. At last mother produced the nougat. It appeared to be moving slightly. On closer examination she found it was covered on top with maggots. Never mind. We mustn't waste good food. Another slogan in our family. So the maggots were picked off, great amusement doing this, with a pen knife, and the nougat was eaten. There were no lavatories on the train in those days. There was generally one stop where we could get out. On one occasion we all got out, that is the children did, and the train started shunting and I thought we were left there forever.

The vicarages we went to were pleasant and spacious, the country around very lovely, though August is not the best month for it. One day I came home from school and said to my mother, "I've never seen fields yellow with cowslips". "Nor has anyone", said she. Cowslips hang their heads down, they couldn't make a field look yellow. I felt stupid. What had they been talking about at school? Fields yellow with primroses. Yes, primroses. "I meant primroses," I said. Mother: "Primroses don't grow in fields. They grow on banks and in woods." "Oh", I said. I never saw the country in the Spring until I was about 14, but six weeks in the country in the Summer was truly wonderful and I am eternally grateful for those holidays.

But the town child is rather lost in the country. I loved the feel of it and its smell, but I didn't know what to look at, or rather what to look for. One morning in Norfolk I decided to get up at the crack of dawn and wander out into the mist. I managed to make myself wake up, and I dressed and started wandering like the little girl in the book I was reading. I got very cold and very damp and cross. I didn't know what to do with myself till breakfast time. But I loved being in the country. And my passion for it and the sea was ever heated. My father did not like sand between his toes, so we never went to a sandy beach. We never bathed in shoes. We had to walk on the shingle bare foot without complaint. Also without complaint, I had to endure being carried by my Father out of my depth and then being ducked right under, in very cold water on the East coast. I screamed and yelled and struggled as my father seized me and carried me out the first time. I hated him and his hairy chest. He ducked me and laughed aloud and then carried me in. My mother told me if I ever made a noise again I should never be allowed to bathe anymore. Did I think my Father would drown me? I didn't answer. What was the use? We all learnt to swim early.

We went to the most dangerous beaches. The day began by a general exodus after breakfast. Pony cart for parents and youngest children. Others on bicycles. What a procession! Perhaps a boy would ride one way and drive the other. On the first day my Father had approached a farm near the sea asking permission to leave our tent there. The putting up of the tent was a great business. The boys left their bicycles at the farm and carried the tent down onto the shingle. That noise of the shingle when you walk on it! The tent had a centre pole and the canvas had pockets which had to be filled with stones to keep it down. In a wind it was quite a job to get the thing erected, and imagine that trouble daily in order that my sister and I should undress unobserved. Unobserved by whom? Nobody. Father and the boys removed themselves to a distance, so that they appeared specks and there was never a soul on the beach beside ourselves. Mother didn't bathe. She had never learnt to swim. My sister and I dressed and undressed in turns. We went to a beach two years running that was so steep and shelving that it was considered most dangerous. We all survived.

It seems so strange that we did all survive. No one really looked after us, and only accident was when Geoffrey fell over the banisters. To have survived Mother's doctoring must have meant we had iron constitutions. My sister did break her arm once and I sprained both my wrists. Carpentry tools were left about but no one cut themselves.

Those wonderful mornings. The drive in the pony trap. The bathe. The sun. The East coast air. Intoxicating. In the afternoons we explored or lazed about and, at Hempstead Vicarage the pond in the garden was a great joy. *(Hempstead is 5 miles from the coast at Weybourne, near Sheringham in north Norfolk.)* It was large enough to have an island in the middle and, oh joy, a boat on it. There were tadpoles and fishes. I caught a dozen or so tadpoles and put them in a tin basin. It never occurred to me to feed them. What puzzled me was that their number diminished rapidly, I thought the birds must be eating them, and then the few remaining ones turned a ghastly pale yellow colour and died. That upset me, badly. I used to be very strong minded when I got into bed, and not think about it. Also there was the case of the goldfish I caught. We fished in the pond and caught an occasional one the size of a sardine. We had been lent some beautiful rods. One day I left my rod on the bank and went into lunch. When I came out, the end of my rod had come out and was dashing round and round the pond. There was only a goldfish caught on the bait, but we had a great job to catch it. We got into the boat and pursued it and I felt so sick for that poor little goldfish.

My mother had been accustomed to horses all her life till she married. My Father hired one occasionally and went hacking on the Heath, before we economised. When we were away, Mother suffered greatly because Father liked driving. One afternoon they had been to call on someone. Father was driving the high dogcart. He and Mother sat in front and my little brother and I at the back, facing backwards. A strange way of balancing the cart one would say. About a mile from home, we came down a fairly steep hill. Father should have let the horse walk. He was an impatient man and he made it trot. Down it went on its knees. My father was hurled on to a hedge on the right. I saw him climbing out of it whip in hand. My mother went into the left hand ditch. The shafts broke and went onto the ground with the horse. The seat we were on went into the air. There we two sat, perched in the heavens it seemed. When I turned I saw the front seats empty and I thought it was time to do something so I began to cry. Then I saw Father emerging and, when I saw Mother was alive, I felt better. She came straight to us.

She could scarcely reach us, but she told me to run home as fast as I could and fetch the stable boy and tell him to bring help. Feeling that at last I was a heroine in a novel, I ran home and a party came out. The horse did not have to be shot, but its value was diminished and it was a subject that was never discussed in public.

Those six weeks of summer spent in the country mitigated to a great extent our suburban existence. We did all the things that children did in books. We had a donkey to ride, a donkey cart of our own to drive. What bliss! The people in the villages we went to were kindly. We seemed to quarrel less. There was a pony at Hempstead and Geoffrey went off riding by himself. He was always wanting to get away by himself. When we had a house, or rather castle, near the Wye, he got up early every morning to go out fishing. He never caught anything, but he did escape from his brothers. When he went off on this ride he had practically never been on a pony before, if ever. When he returned at lunch he was asked where he had been and he truthfully mentioned the name of a village about 2 miles away. Bursts of laughter from Mother. How could he have spent 4 hours getting there? Here all of us jeered. "I gave the pony long feeds by the way", he said meekly. This was greeted by more gusts of laughter from the whole family and "long feeds by the way" became a family slogan. He was never allowed to forget that pony ride.

I had read about milkmaids dabbling in the dew, and in one book a girl goes out to see the sunrise and registers her emotions. I tried it, but it was a flop, I wandered about wondering what to do next, I found it distinctly chilly and I got my shoes wet and I thought breakfast time would never come. Yet, without realizing it, I must all the same have noticed a great deal. I still can see the fields of poppies, the hazel copses, the woods which made me frightened of walking, the road through them. I remember everything. The church service was really entertaining. The school children were seated on low benches in front of the altar. They sat in a semi-circle facing a severe man with a long stick. He sat on a chair between the two front pews and during the service his long stick would reach out to touch the head of any offending chatter-box.

At Ludgershall *(Wiltshire)*, where we went when I was younger, there was a harmonium in a huge shed. We spent ages making noises on that. There were wonderful chestnut trees and I collected chestnuts. I loved them. A young girl who was looking after us, I don't know who, suggested I should make a bag to put them in. With some trouble I did. She must have helped me and I hung it on the end of my bed. When the day came to leave, I was sitting in the train on my miserable way home to Hampstead to face school and the winter. I suddenly remembered that I had left my most precious bag of chestnuts hanging on the end of the iron bed and my cup of sorrow was full. How could I have? I did love them so much. They were so beautiful and shiny and such a lovely colour. I'm not surprised Miss Olney said I was scatterbrained or something of the sort and my father called me a flibberty-jib.

Our castle holidays were good too, but rather frightening. A prison room with great deep windows and slits of windows, and the sad evidence of prisoners. Laboriously cut in the walls. "My glass is rom. It is time I was gone, For I have been a great space. And am weary of the place, Robin Belcher". "The day has come when thou shalt answer for it. For thou hast sworn against me." My sister and I slept in that room one year. It was a beautiful old castle and in those days rather dilapidated. One had to go out of doors from one turret to the other. One night my young brother, who was sleeping in the left turret, heard what he thought were footsteps above his head. He was all alone over there, poor child, and eventually arrived across in the other turret and threw himself into Mother's arms, trembling with fear. Mother was always very affectionate to that youngest child. The castle was a lovely rambling ruin, or half ruin when we were there. Our first exploit on arriving was to climb on to the great wide wall that encircled the garden. On one side was the garden, on the other the moat, right far down beneath us, empty of water. It must have been a very dangerous place, but there we sat until one of the boys jumped up yelling and nearly sent us all to our deaths down below. He ran along the wall yelling, and we soon followed as a cloud of wasps rose up around us. Only one of us was stung, strange to say, and the gardener said he knew there was a nest there. A few days later I was walking near the bee hives and to my horror felt a bee in my hair. I had masses of hair and it was buzzing like an engine, getting closer and closer to my head every moment. I ran and shouted and tore into the kitchen asking somebody to do something. But they none of them seemed at all keen and at last the wretched thing stung me and then died.

[A friend of mine, Dorothy Thornly, came home to her deaf old mother one evening after dining with friends. She wore a low evening dress. As she sat under the light, telling her mother about her party, a wasp which had been buzzing round the light fell down inside the front of Dorothy's dress. There it began to sting, and it went on, and Dodo was up and dancing around and trying to get the thing out, and Mrs. Thornly, quite deaf, thought she had taken leave of her senses.]

At the castle we had the usual pony trap, and also a donkey cart for us. How we loved that! I used to do the driving mostly. One day someone gave me 6d. A visitor, I think. That was a large sum and I liked acid drops. It seems impossible to have spent it all on acid drops but I think I did. Truly, one would have got a cwt. *(a hundredweight, or 50.8 kg)* for that in those days. Well anyway, I bought a bag of acid drops at the little village shop. How I loved those little shops with their delicious mixy smells and their kindly people serving in them. With my treasure in my hand, I ran into the stable boy. So I said, "Freddy, would you like a sweet?" The bag was slightly opened as I handed it to him. "Thank you, Miss," he said and collared the lot. I was too shy to remonstrate.

Return from holidays

I have said often enough that I hated coming home. The thing I detested was the "runners". Arrived at Victoria or Waterloo, my father would engage one or two four wheelers, bargaining about the price beforehand. As we left the station, a runner would attach himself to us, or possibly two or three. They were dressed in rags. The cast offs of the rich: torn old trench coats and battered top hats or bowlers. I watched one, whose sole of his boot was practically off, yet he managed to run with it flapping up every time he took a step. If two runners attached themselves, Mother would get very concerned and she would wave violently at the second man telling him to go, but generally he didn't. Two men might mean two sixpences and that would upset my parents. They ran, except up the steep bits, all the way, half-starved miseries, just trying to get enough for a few more tots of gin to put them into oblivion for a while. Having arrived at our house, one or two, they would get all the luggage down from the tops of the cabs, shoulder it and stagger with it up those steps, 14 of them, was it? And then up the stairs to the bedrooms. Their legs would tremble under them as they went. And all for sixpence. And inevitably a scene would ensue about the payment and also the payment of the cabby, who would protest that he had not known it would be so far. Those were the scenes that made me feel sick.

Riding on the buses

I have mentioned the poverty of the poor. There were parts of Hampstead where it existed, in rows of slummy roads. But on the top of the bus going into London, "going down to town" we always called it, one saw a good deal of the squalor of life in those days. I felt sick at the sight of the ill-fed, ill-clothed children and their drunken mothers and wizened grandmothers. They were in front of the gin palaces and there were plenty of those between Camden Town and Euston Road.

The bus started from a pub just below Flask Walk *(the Bird in Hand at 38-39 Hampstead High Street, whose yard was the terminus for the horse-buses of the London General Omnibus Company)*. The top of the bus had two long seats running from front to back divided by a wooden back. We sat back to back facing outwards. A Knife board. *(First introduced in 1875, knifeboard buses were so called because the back-to-back seating on the open upper deck resembled the boards used in Victorian kitchens to clean knives.)* The hills were very steep – going down them was quite exciting.

The coachmen were splendid to look at. Real characters. They dressed like the drivers of coaches and wore large, pale-coloured beaver top hats. There was a seat right up beside the driver and a passenger might sit there. I never did, but my brothers did occasionally. The drivers had a cockney wit, which they indulged in, to the amusement of the inside passengers. In those days the bus was supposed to stop whenever a passenger wished to get out. On a steep hill these stops entailed much hardship on the horses. You just told the conductor, he rang the bell and the bus stopped outside your door. If the conductor was not near the bell, he would stamp loudly with his feet. Reasonable people would get out when the bus stopped and walk a few yards, so as to save the horses. On one occasion the bus had just stopped on Haverstock Hill and started up and the bell rang again. The driver's voice rang out: "What you want is an omnibus to take you up your own front door steps, open the door and take you upstairs and put you to bed and tuck you up all pretty". Most of this was wasted on the back of the offending passenger, but it let off the

A Hampstead omnibus at the foot of Rosslyn Hill, 1887 (CLSAC). Note the third horse.

steam of the driver. At the bottom of Haverstock Hill was a 'Cock' horse. It was fastened on in front of the other two to go up the steep hills. *(The extra horse added on to horse transport to assist travel up hills is also called a trace horse).*

In town, one never could stand in crowds or watch the vulgar fun. I would so have liked to. An uncle of mine, an Archdeacon took me to London for a jaunt and the only thing I remember was that he would not let me stand and watch two women sitting close together in a little shop window, exhibiting their long hair. Advertising some stuff called Coed, I think – Coco for the hair. *(Rev. Ernest Austen Hammick MA, 1820-1920, was Vicar of Forrabury, near Boscastle, Cornwall, and then Archdeacon of Zululand from 1888 until after 1901. He went out to South Africa only 9 years after all the mission buildings had been razed to the ground in the Zulu wars.)*

More friends, the Hibberts

After Gladys departed, my friends at school were the Hibberts. *(Arthur Hibbert and his wife, Alice Holden Hibbert, lived in a house called Highcroft at 16 Lyndhurst Gardens with their daughters, Eva, Georgina, Marjorie and Amy. In 1901 they had 5 female servants.)* Four plain, very plain, sisters with a very handsome, debonair father and a very small, very plain, mother who was very rich. She was the daughter of Castile Soap. *(All four 'plain' sisters would still be unmarried in their late twenties. Their grandfather, Ambrose Knight, born in Whitechapel, was the manufacturer of 'Knight's*

The Very Rev. Ernest Austen Hammick, MA

Castile' luxury soap; the family soap- and candle-making firm had been founded by their great-grandfather, in Wapping in 1817.)

My mother said the father was a wonderfully handsome young man and he still was when I knew him; first class, but much too fond of the bottle. Mrs Hibbert had a very strong cockney accent, but the daughters had not. Mrs. Hibbert said she thought the school we were at was a good school, as it taught the girls to be ladies. That was the sort of remark that delighted my mother and I suffered from her jibes. I hated having my friends criticised and laughed at, though I knew quite well their faults and eccentricities. But I must have friends, that was essential; I couldn't live without friends and I had little or no choice. I cannot think why I was never bored but I wasn't. I only went to school in the mornings, and in the afternoons I was left to myself. Nothing was arranged for me, except that I was supposed to wander on the pavements with a badly dressed orphan. Gladys had alleviated my loneliness and now the Hibberts took her place, but they had none of the zest and fire and pure vulgarity of that young woman. They were very kind and my friend Marjorie Hibbert had a sense of humour. How we used to laugh! It was agonies to keep in our frantic laughter. My afternoons were now spent with them. They had a huge Willett house, vast rooms and a garden of about 2 acres; a great deal of money but no taste. Everything was very lavish.

Their staff consisted of 5 sisters; a most loyal and devoted family. When I married, I had one of their nieces *(Alice)* and she was with me 14 or 15 years. The Hibbert girls were entirely bought up and dressed by one of these women. Janie bought their clothes, Janie decided everything. Mrs Hibbert, when I knew her, was a weak-minded, querulous little woman – never able to decide anything. Conversation between her and her daughters was always a sort of game. "Well, what do you think?" "Well, really I don't know. What do you think?" "I don't know what to think, we'd better ask Eva *(the eldest daughter)* what she thinks." "Eva, what do you think?" and so on, and as there were 4 daughters this game could last all day and well

'Highcroft' No.16 Lyndhurst Gardens

into the evening. They were none of them blessed with brains. Margery *(Marjorie)* had the most and the one older than her could strum the piano with a touch of iron and read all the newest songs; I spent hours of my adolescence in their company. We sang songs by the hour, largely to please me. They bought all the newest ones. Always plenty of money. 'The Honeysuckle and the Bee', 'The Chorister', Gilbert and Sullivan, 'The Lost Chord'. I loved singing. I had a clear very high voice, rather like a boy's. At home on Sundays we all sang hymns, father playing, but no one ever noticed me. The boys had the beautiful voices. Here with the Hibberts I could shine. Gladys had always dominated me, but now I came on top. And they were so kind to me. For the first time in my life I met with affection and kindness.

Then came tennis. The passion of my young life. They had a grass court in their garden. The youngest one never played, so there we had a four and we played every hour of every afternoon in the summer, or so it seems to me now; I never remember it raining. We played the old fashioned, in fact now completely unknown, tennis, "standing" well behind the back line and driving long sweeping drives into the back line of the opponent. There was a wonderful thrill in this game and a steadiness and battling concentration, driving one's opponent into the corner relentlessly, keeping her there and then suddenly sweeping the ball over into the other corner. To us it was a very good game, though there was not net play; our long skirts would not permit quick activities and so one kept well behind the back line. We four would pound at one another incessantly and then all lie on our backs on the grass and eat cherries and talk.

I was the talker. A terrible chatterer but I don't think I talked at home. When I was out I let loose. We were very good-tempered and never a cross word passed between us. We used to laugh till it hurt, but what about heaven knows. But all this quite innocent pleasure was surreptitious: what I was supposed to be doing with myself on those sunny afternoons I do not know, but I was not supposed to be playing tennis with the Hibberts. Yet I feel mother must have known I was there. Her disapproval of my friends was quite obvious and I resented it. Admitted to myself that mother was right. They were plain girls, they had no social manners. When confronted in the street, they looked from side to side like frightened rabbits and would do anything to avoid catching the eye of their acquaintance. They were dressed by their maid and their clothes were often absurd. But on the other hand they were very kind and had no vices. "The Dearests." I think mother must have known I played tennis there, but daily I had to pretend I didn't. They had given me a spare racket and I kept a pair of gym shoes round there. They had tea early so that I could share it and then run home fast to have a very much duller tea at home. Mother was not usually in to tea, or she had it in the drawing room, and I had mine in the basement room with my young brother. It seems a pity I had to come home to tea. We could have got in some sets after tea. No mention at home was ever made of tennis or cherries or a "screaming funny joke"; they were completely a world apart.

At Guildford, before December 1902

My friends, the Hibberts, had a grandfather living in Guildford. He was a very wealthy man, being a manufacturer of soap. *(Ambrose Knight, 1828-1902, lived at Glenshee Lodge, Maori Road, Guildford at his death.)* He was a widower *(since 1878)* and lived in comfort and luxury, looked after by a staff of devoted maids. Going away anywhere to me was an enormous and very rare treat, and Marjorie Hibbert and I could always entertain ourselves. I doing most of the talking.

On Sunday morning we went to Church and sat in the old man's pew, the front pew, as he was deaf. Very soon after the service had begun, I became conscious, very conscious, of a young man in the choir. He was tall and good-looking and he fixed me with his eyes and never took them off me. This caused me a considerable thrill. It went on through prayers and the hymns and everything. After we got back to lunch, I told Marjorie about it and we decided in the afternoon to wander forth in search. I knew perfectly well that I was behaving, or hoping to behave, not at all like a lady. But Gladys Townsend had seemed to me to have a most dashing time when she stayed with her aunt, picking up stray young men – I'd see how I got on. And, when we arrived near the High Street, coming towards us was my young man and a very young friend – a nice-looking boy. We walked straight past them but were pleased to see, glancing behind, that they had turned and were following us. This was just as it should be and we went prancing along till we came to the Castle Grounds. There a highly exciting game of sort of hide and seek ensued, until we were cornered in an ivy covered shelter, on purpose, of course. So then we started chatting and they proposed a walk and we said yes.

I knew quite well that they were not gentlemen and I also knew only too well that I was behaving like a shop girl, and I liked it very much. I don't know where we went, but when we came to some fields, my young man put his arm round my waist, and so we walked. Behind us came the other two, but Marjorie told me afterwards that she had punched her boy in the stomach with her elbow when he tried to take liberties. We seemed to walk a very long way and I was glad when we came to stiles, as it was very uncomfortable walking like a crab. Before long we had completely finished all pretence at conversation and we trudged along in silence. I was greatly relieved when I realised we were nearing home and I stopped and said, "Goodbye" and the young man said, "Well all good things must come to an end" and we parted and never saw one another again.

I will later mention my day of hockey playing. *(Phyllis found this a miserable experience – see p 148.)* My day was not made any happier by the Captain of the team, a charming young woman, and a friend of our family, saying to me casually but also pointedly, "the last time I saw you was in Guildford Church. I was sitting just behind you." I blushed scarlet and spent the rest of the day wondering just how much she had seen, and praying that she wouldn't tell mother – but all was well, she did not.

Motoring to Henley

I had to depend for my amusements on other people. It wasn't the fault of my parents that they couldn't afford to provide them. My friends, the Hibberts, were taken to a matinee every Saturday. I went to the pit of a theatre once in the Christmas holidays, if I could manage to save up 2/6d. It didn't occur to me to feel aggrieved that I couldn't go more often and I enjoyed my rare treat more than I can say.

One of the highlights in the social world was, I gathered, Henley. I knew little about it but it was something enormously enjoyed by those who were lucky enough to go. One evening a sister of a friend of mine called to see my mother. It was quite late. She had come to ask if I might go with the party she and her sister were getting up for Henley. A girl had just fallen out and numbers must be equal. This family was very active in organising things. Their father was a well-to-do man and he had to be considering the number of his children. They weren't at all well arranged. First a son, then 6 daughters and then a son. The daughters were always up to something. Every year they got up a party for Henley and, marvellous to relate, they invited me. We met next morning early at the station and went by train. When we got to the river we hired two punts and two canoes and up the river, or down, we went. It was a lovely day and a charming spectacle. The boats with the spectators in were solid across the river from one bank to the other. None of us took the slightest notice of the racing. A wonderful lunch had been provided, which we ate sitting on the bank. When it began to get dark, entertainers in punts lit with fairy lights pushed their boats in among others and gave performances, I found everything enchanting. We returned home by train very late. And they invited me again next year.

My third visit to Henley Regatta was quite different but most thrilling. A Mr Pearce, who had an invalid wife and one daughter whom he adored, spent a lot of his money on trying to give her a good time. He was a rich man. Bessie was plain but very charming and a beautiful dancer. She was several years older than me. Mr Pearce used to make up a party of four and take us out to dinner and dance at some place in London. Two men and two girls, and I was lucky enough frequently to be the other girl. The two men were always perfect dancers. The evenings spent like this were for me a dream of joy. On one occasion, when I arrived home at about 1am, one of the men came up our steps with me to see me into my house. Mother was sitting up as usual and opened the door. When the young man had gone, Mother asked who he was. I told her and she said, "Oh, he looks more of the gentleman than he used to". I was amused and said to myself, "All right, you needn't worry, I'm not going to marry him".

Mother had never called on his parents because they were Unitarians. It always annoyed me, as they lived in one of the most delectable houses on the Heath and were noted for the wonderful dances they gave. Well, my third visit to Henley was all arranged and paid for by Mr Pearce and of all the exciting dashing things, almost unheard of, we drove there in motor cars. It was the first time that I had been in one of these new machines. Bessie and I discussed what clothes we should wear and particularly hats. Our hats perched on our heads at that time, on top of our hair. So we bought motor veils, voluminous pieces of tulle and tied our hats on with this. The motor cars, like our hats, were perched up high and had no roofs, so that we got all the winds which blew, and the dust. Mr Pearce had wisely arranged to go in one motor car with some elderly people and we young ones had another. Our vehicle had five punctures on the way there. Each puncture had to be mended which meant quite a lot of standing about by the roadside but it didn't worry us. The country was very pretty. At last we arrived.

The other motor car had got there first and we were all taken to Phyllis Court to wash and have lunch. *(Phyllis Court Private Members Club, by the Thames at Henley was established in 1906. It is, and was, luxuriously exclusive.)* We were doing everything in style. But poor Bessie, she unwisely washed her face. Well we were thick with dust. But she had red hair and a very sensitive skin, covered with freckles. Washing it was a tragedy. She became scarlet as a lobster and remained so all day, poor girl, her face like a furnace. It was a blazing day and I, as usual, enjoyed every moment. I don't know why but we didn't have any punctures at all going home and it was a wonderful experience to drive in the dark and to see how strange the trees looked, and beautiful in the lights.

By this time orphans no longer dogged my footsteps. I was growing up. I was winning prizes at very amateur ping pong. But wherever I went and whatever I did, I was entirely convinced of my own failure and stupidity. When about 14 I was invited to a young people's dance at the Champneys'. *(The architect Basil Champneys (1842-1935), who designed John Rylands Library, Manchester, several Oxbridge colleges and St Luke's Church, Kidderpore Avenue, lived in Hall Oak, his self-built house in Frognal Lane.)* They had a lovely old house and were one of *the* families, but I don't think I knew anyone there except by sight, I found myself in the garden with a boy. We sat down in an alcove. He put his arm round my waist, I said "I think we had better go in," and we did. That was the end of that.

I puzzled and puzzled afterwards on how I ought to have behaved and was thrilled. I would have loved to have gone on to have been kissed and fondled. It would have made me feel pretty and attractive. That would have been so wonderful to feel attractive. I didn't know. I couldn't solve it. A sort of moral poker ran through my spine. Some things were done, some weren't. Kissing in alcoves weren't. All very difficult. I envied the courting couples I saw in the streets at dusk. Lucky free people not hedged in by rules, I consoled myself by thinking I couldn't be too awful or the boy wouldn't have put his arm round my waist. That puritanical poker persisted through my life.

Holiday near Bexhill, 1902

About the time of the boy putting his arm round my waist, we went to stay at Bexhill. It was a makeshift holiday, really a rotten affair. By this time my family were out in the world, or nearly. Father had to be in 'Camp' on the cliffs outside Bexhill and Mother, Aubrey and I went to rooms. I think it was my first experience of lodgings. What I disliked was being told to come in, I could stay in the sea almost forever, but the voice of the attendant calling, "Time to come in please" would awaken me from my dreams as I floated on the waves. I don't remember disliking Bexhill. Anywhere with sea was heaven.

I found my brother a dull companion but I was devoted to him. Mother felt he was a chaperone and so we could go out where and when we wished. One afternoon we were sitting on the beach, just looking at the sea.

Everard Ford with the Bishop of London in Camp at Bexhill, 1902

By way of conversation I had just said to Aubrey, "Do you like high or low Church best?" The Hibberts were rabid Anglo Catholics and I was interested. Aubrey "cared for none of these things" rather naturally *(he was 11 years old)* and after some hesitation said, "Do you mean as high as that pier?" And I, being a little beast, laughed. I had just started explaining, when I became conscious of two young men, boys really. They were fooling about near the edge of the sea in front of us and quite obviously trying to get my attention, I drew in my horns and pretended to be wrapt up in my conversation with Aubrey. The fooling persisted and then, fully dressed, a wave caught the elder one and he sat down in the sand. That was really good fun, the sort of joke I liked and Aubrey and I laughed unashamedly. The ice was broken, they laughed back. We still were a little standoffish. They approached and stood close to us and the wet boy got out a hanky and tried to mop himself, Aubrey had a towel and offered it and I wondered if that was not a little forward. After a good deal of to and froing, they sat down near us and a chat ensued. It transpired that there was to be a display of fireworks that night. Weren't we coming?

On our way back to tea I drummed into Aubrey that he must say nothing about the two boys. I felt very very wicked to teach him to be deceitful but it really was necessary, just this once. To my surprise we got permission from mother to go out to see the fireworks. She realised, I think, that this was a dull holiday for us, almost as dull as it was for her.

I was in a state of agonising excitement. I was terrified Aubrey would give me away before we got out of the house and I was also terrified we shouldn't meet the boys – terrified that we should, and how to behave? And the whole situation was so agonising and so thrilling it was hardly bearable. At last I was seeing life. This was life. All the time I knew that I was being very common. I knew that the boys would be considered common by my mother but I didn't care. They had asked me to meet them. They had picked me up, though certainly I didn't use that phrase in those days. I had done nothing, absolutely nothing to get hold of them. It all seemed to me so strange, so unlikely. Why had they? I wasn't pretty. I hadn't curly hair. I was too tall and had enormous feet. They said they had seen me in the morning, after I had been bathing, so they had given me the once over before getting in touch. Very strange and rather flattering. I knew that they weren't out of the top drawer, but they nearly were, and the younger, about my age, was charmingly handsome. Dark curly hair and a bright face. The elder one I didn't like. He was heavy and too like my eldest brother.

We met shyly and walked alone together till the crowds got thick and we had to stop and then, all cosily pressed together, the youngest one took my hand. By now it was dark. I thrilled. Then he put my hand with his in his jacket pocket and I was swimming with ecstasy. So we spent the evening, talking a little, but not much, and wedged in the crowd. My hand held tight, electric shocks running up and down my spine at the pressure of his fingers. Next day their holiday was over and they left with their family. But they had made a rendezvous with me. Rather to my dismay I learned they lived in Finchley. They would bicycle up to the Whitestone Pond and meet me a week hence, and we fixed the time. I very dubious and worried. This sort of thing near home was different. We met and we walked about and sat on a bench. In broad daylight there was no hand holding. Conversation lagged rather, I was worried lest I should see or rather be seen by anyone I knew. The boys were going back to school so there was no time to arrange another meeting.

Months later Hetty *(Dalton)* and I were bicycling slowly up Bishops Avenue *(which connects Hampstead Lane, near Kenwood, with East Finchley)*. Down it on the other side coasted two boys. My friends. They saw me. I was suddenly panic stricken. I didn't want to see them, I didn't want Hetty to meet them, I felt terribly embarrassed. I urged Hetty on and we got to the top of the hill and I turned and saw they had turned and were following us. But we were well ahead. I begged Hetty to ride as fast as she could and we sped along the Spaniards *(Road)*, giving them the slip. I never saw them again. I just told Hetty that two boys I didn't like were following us and she asked no questions. She was a good friend, absolutely trustworthy.

There were other families whom we knew beside the Hibberts. I knew them but my family did not. They merely referred to the Hibberts as the "Dearests" and made slighting remarks about them. Once, this elicited a compliment from my mother. Goaded beyond endurance about the foolish stupidity of my friends by one of my brothers, I turned upon him in rage with my fists, crying at the same time. The worm had turned, to my brother Geoffrey's surprise. Mother said, "You can 'bully rag' Phyl forever about herself and she doesn't mind, but she certainly does stand up for her friends".

Of course I minded, I minded desperately. It is not amusing to feel always that you are less than the dust. Occasionally I would emerge slightly, push my head up through and feel I was the cat's whiskers. Not for long but how wonderful while it lasted. I had no reason to be proud of myself. I was not clever or kind.

Victorian and Edwardian fathers

We have just had a friend staying here, Keith Hicks. He lives in Toronto, but was bought up in England. His description of his father, of his father's rages, was just like what I experienced. Keith Hicks' father not only was violently religious, but he also had so many children so close together that his wife became an invalid and eventually died leaving him to wreak his vengeance on these daughters who never married, largely because of him.

Those autocratic fathers of the Victorian or Edwardian era made themselves into Gods. They were Gods to themselves and their children and households. The children trembled, the servants shook and the mother wept, when the God was angry. In our case this is an exaggeration. Strange. They were quite ordinary young men when they married but the obedience and slavish admiration began then and turned their heads. And the more ordinary they were, the more their heads were turned. They grew beards which assisted in the illusion that they were Gods. No doubt some of them were severely frustrated. They married young women who had no idea what marriage was. This terrible ordeal had to be gone through and it reduced the ignorant woman to the status of a mere chattel. To vast numbers of women, the whole marriage act was something unspeakably awful, which had to be endured and even to begin to think of getting pleasure from it for the woman would have been a sin. My mother, by the time I was married, hadn't heard of birth control and knew nothing about it. She told me that she and my father decided not to have a child more than every two years. Therefore there were stretches of months at a time when it was not safe for them to "marry". The strain must have been considerable, and perhaps the cause of the occasional violent ebullitions of temper from my father. One can't know. Of all of us six children, one inherited that temper, the rest of us were very easy going.

Discussing our respective fathers with Keith Hicks, I was amused that he was greatly shocked to hear my father kept a posse of canes in a drawer in his dressing room, but his father did beat him; though he seemed to think it was much better to beat with hands and fists, which is what his father did. Yes it was much better, when you think of it. That sort of beating was a sudden ebullition, a loss of control. My father's canes in the drawer were sinister. The thought of them still makes me feel sick. One was a very solid but beautifully made object. It looked like rosewood, very highly polished, and it had a ribbon in a loop at one end and the other end had a band of ivory on it. A fop's cane, probably inherited and never used for castigation. These parents no doubt entirely believed in 'spare the rod and spoil the child'. Religion.

They also believed in heaven and hell. They must at all costs keep their child out of hell. They were beginning to be a little wobbly about these things. That rather dreadful Mr Darwin had upset things considerably. It was really quite difficult to know what to believe and what not. But one thing was certain and that was, if you were a member of the Church of England, you believed what that Church ordered, like it or not. I said that economy was the ruling spirit of our household, I should have coupled with it religion. It appears to have been a very usual phenomenon at that date.

Sundays and Church

I have mentioned before that the word Christian had no part in our life. It was always Church. We had all been baptised, of course, and at about 14 years old we were each of us confirmed. After that, we had to go to early service *(Communion)* once a fortnight at 8am, like it or not. There was no question about it. My eldest brother, out late on Saturday night or rather home in the small hours of Sunday morning, must perforce be at early service at 8am. I, who at that time was very fervent, having just been confirmed, would kneel in Church, waiting to hear my brother come creeping in unshaven and slip into the end of our pew. Always late. The second boy, in the Navy, home on leave, would find he was expected to be out at Church at 8am. No one of us would have dared question it. I knew that the boys, none of them, believed a thing and I used to worry a bit over their partaking of the sacrament in that state of mind. But the fact that we all turned up there at 8am or thereabouts, like it or not, typified the whole set up of our household. We all submitted without a murmur, except to one another. Not only on Church matters but on everything, though my father was more dogmatic on those than any other grounds. Dissenters, which term I suppose embarrassed his own parents, were beyond the pale. There were many eminent Unitarians in Hampstead. We must not know them. As father could never discuss, but only tell you, he would not have got on very well with these learned, thoughtful people. No doubt he realised this and kept clear of them.

One day the young people in the house next door to us managed to talk to my brothers over the rather high garden wall. *(Various members of the Martineau family lived at 3 Eldon Road in 1901 and 1911. They were Mary Ellen b.1834, Gertrude b.1837, Basil b.1839, and Edith Martineau b.1842, the watercolourist, the children of Prof. James Martineau, religious philosopher, whose sister, Harriet Martineau (1802-1876) was the most famous member of this prominent Unitarian family. The 'young people' may have been visiting.)* My brothers were taken aback. They knew

that they were not supposed to know these children. The said young people, related to the distinguished family of Martineau, said, "We know why you mayn't speak to us. It's because we are dissenters". They may not have used the word dissenters, nonconformists I should think. Dr. Horton *(Dr Robert Forman Horton, 1855-1934, the Pastor of Lyndhurst Road Congregational Church)* was the great congregational light. We passed his "Chapel" on our way to Church.
(They were going to St Stephen's on Rosslyn Hill, almost opposite the Congregational Church. Samuel Teulon's 'mighty church', as he called it, was built to provide an additional place of worship for the increased population of the Parish of St John caused by the building of new streets between Belsize Park and Hampstead such as Lyndhurst and Thurlow Roads.

Lyndhurst Road Congregational Church (CLSAC)

When in 1864 it was decided to erect a new church, the job of architect ultimately fell to Samuel Teulon after Ewan Christian, architect to the Church Commissioners declined the post. The estimated cost of the church was £7,500 and the money was raised entirely by subscriptions and large donations from local people, its prospective congregation.)

My brother Bernard, Mother's favourite and therefore allowed some latitude, on our way to Church, seeing the crowds going in to Dr. Horton's said, "Shall I spit, Mother, shall I spit?" "You naughty boy," said mother laughing. She always enjoyed a joke.

After early service we came home to breakfast. Stiff porridge and salt, coffee, bread and butter, thick slices for Sunday, and boiled egg. That was to me

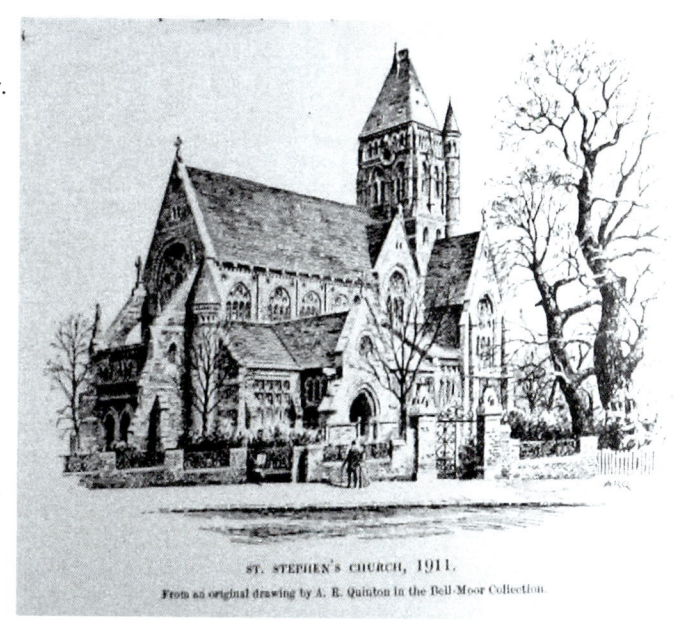

St Stephen's Church, 1911, drawn by A E Quinton (Bell Moor Collection, CLSAC)

a treat, but it sometimes turned out badly. That is, the eggs were often doubtful. Then an argument would ensue between my parents. Father saying, "Nonsense it wasn't bad – give it to me and I'll eat it," and mother, who never could stand eggs anyway, saying, "no-one should eat a bad egg."

After that meal was over, we learned the Collect for the Sunday. After the first year, I knew all the collects, so rarely had to look and see which one it was. I could now repeat most of them, if started off, and I love their beautiful language. I am always glad that I learned them and also that I am familiar with so much of the Bible. A friend of mine said to me one day that he could find a quotation in T.S. Elliott's *(sic)* poems to suit most occasions. I feel like that with the Bible. Bits of the Psalms come into my mind while I dig in the garden, to give me much satisfaction. [The other day, after our son Bernard's children left, I said to my husband: "They grow in wisdom and stature, and I hope in favour with God and man". What a wonderful description and what a piece of pure English.]

Having learnt our collects and the breakfast having been cleared away by the maid, we then sat down. Father on one side of the fire and the eldest of us present in the other arm chair, and the others drawn up close to receive a Bible lesson. We first said our collects and then Father expounded the Bible. I don't remember a thing about it. I don't think he could have been a very good teacher. I don't remember being bored, so I think I was probably able to think about interesting things while he carried on. There was one morning I remember. It was when he came to the judgement of Solomon. I had never heard the story, nor of course had Aubrey. Father was most embarrassed. It was not very suitable to read at a more-or-less tête à tête with an innocent daughter. So he said, "Shut your Bible, I'll tell you the story". He at first could not believe we had not heard it. But I took care afterwards to look it up in my Bible and find out what really did happen. The Bible bought forth quite a lot of useful information, if studied factfully. After this Bible lesson, we put on coats and hats to go to Church. There was never any time allowed even for going to the lavatory. It was fitted in if possible on occasions.

Church made for me a welcome interlude in an otherwise interminable and deadly dull day. One saw other people. One sang. Sometimes one talked to people after Church and there was a feeling of bustle and life. After Church – a walk. That walk was absolutely stereotyped. We would have felt we were breaking the Commandments if we had deviated from it. It was quite a pleasant round, as pleasant as any walking on pavements flanked by ugly houses can be. Up Lyndhurst Road, turn right *(Lyndhurst Terrace)* and then left down the narrow lane *(Shepherd's Path)* that goes past Bayford House, my school. Up the next turning of the lane *(Spring Path)* and just into Fitzjohn's Avenue. Only just in and out again. F.A. was to be avoided, though I would have rather liked to watch the parade going on. The rich and overdressed went up and down it. We just poked our noses into it and then turned into another lane, on the right *(presumably Shepherd's Walk, leading back to Rosslyn Hill)*. That Sunday walk was quite an ordinary affair. Father and mother walking ahead, stopping occasionally if they met friends, to have a short talk. The six of us straggled behind, probably quarrelling. One day they met Mrs Pooley, a great friend. She walked along with mother. They were just in front of me in the lane and just where it emerged into Fitzjohn's Avenue, Mother half stopped and I heard her say, "and it always seems to be the favourite one who must go first". I was of course not supposed to hear. Mother spoke so bitterly and so sadly. Then I realised. It was Bernard she was talking about, Bernard was going off abroad on his first sea voyage in the Royal Navy. If mother had known what that first voyage would lead to, she would indeed have been bitter and desperately sad. All that came later in an overwhelming mass.

After our Sunday walk, home to roast sirloin followed by fruit tart, or in the winter fruit pudding made with a suet crust. As soon as "dinner" was over, or very soon after, we went off with mother to afternoon church somewhere. It was rather noble of her, as she was longing to go to sleep. Sitting at the lunch table she would say, "Let me just have forty winks", and she would thereupon be asleep. She searched around for an interesting children's service. For some time we went to Christchurch *(up in Hampstead Square)* but very low form, then we shot up to the heights *(down)* at St Mary's, Primrose Hill.

We got back to tea, and I have an impression that we had tea, I mean the children did, in the drawing room on a Sunday. My parents always had drawing room tea every day. So to have it in the dining room would have been most second rate. When I was still small, there were strange little treats allowed only on church festivals such as Easter and Whitsun. At lunch on Sunday, but not on weekdays, we always had finger bowls. They were glass, good glass, and, if you wet your finger and put it gently along the top of the rim, it produced a bell like sound. On festivals we were allowed to do this. By altering the amount of water in the bowl you could alter the note. Therefore you could play in thirds, or in fact up the scale. Each bowl being a different note. This amused us and evidently mother liked it. But, though Father was the musical one, he took no interest in it at all, and just sat there looking aloof; I suppose you can't have it both ways. You can't be god almighty and at the same time chummy with your children. Poor father, he must have had a very unhappy life. He must have felt unloved. Occasionally he would burst forth in a gush of heartiness or humour that would nearly embarrass us.

This afternoon service business. My mother combed the churches to find a suitable service. I imagine she would have found one at Dr. Horton's. Now, surely the most important thing, if you are a clergyman, is to educate the children. But I find that in the country there is no church Sunday school or regular children's service in many of the villages. My brother-in-law is a parson *(Harold Arthur Floud, 1878-1966, Vicar of Effingham, near Leatherhead, Surrey)* and, when his daughter left home, he gave up having a Sunday school. He couldn't get any other young women to do it for him. Then why couldn't he do it himself? His wife *(Marion)* would say that he is worn out by the strenuous effort of a three-quarter hour service at 8 o'clock, for perhaps 10 communicants, followed by a service at 11, including a read sermon out of his archives. He must have a rest in the afternoon after such hard work, and another service in the evening. This for a man who can and does play 18 holes of golf 3 days a week. The only other work he does is once a month to write a letter for the Parish Magazine. Staying in his house, you become conscious of the date when the letter will be required. His wife reminds him and again reminds him and at last, in a sort of crescendo, the letter gets put in to the post, the very last post before publication. A terribly strenuous life. But give him his due. He visits – he knows all his parishioners and they love and respect him, though they certainly think parson gets his house and money easily.

Rev. Harold Arthur Floud

Mother's searches for church teaching led us eventually to St Mary's, Primrose Hill. A very long dull walk, as I have mentioned before. But quite worth it when you got there. It was called a catechism class. At first the parents of the well to do were anxious lest their children should catch fleas and diseases from the other children, because in their church there were no sheep and goats. No one paid rent for their pews and then turned strangers out who sat in them. There weren't any pews, it was all chairs. The catechism class mixed us all up. Granted it was not a slum area, that would have been more difficult. This service was treated with as much importance by the staff as the sung Eucharist. The Vicar, and two curates, Mr Newland Smith and another, were always there.

(Percy Dearmer, Vicar 1901-15, was an avowed socialist, serving as secretary of the Christian Social Union from 1891 to 1912. He worked with Ralph Vaughan Williams and Martin Shaw in 1906 to compile The English Hymnal. Dearmer wrote 'The Parson's

St Mary the Virgin, Primrose Hill

Handbook', concerned with general principles of ritual and ceremonial, but emphasising art and beauty in worship. He aims to "remedy the lamentable confusion, lawlessness, and vulgarity which are conspicuous in the Church at this time", expressing his ideas on how liturgy can be conducted in a proper Catholic and English manner.)

It was a church with very high church ideas. The services were arranged to be instructive and entertaining. I loved them all and, as my friends the Hibberts went to a similar one, we had much to compare. I wouldn't have missed it for anything and we went for years. The only thing is I can't remember giving it up. All the time mother realised that we were getting definite church teaching, but at the same time she disapproved of the socialism and also of the processions. On our way home she would argue against some of the teaching we had had, but I had already swallowed it hook line and sinker and was digesting it. Later I became a very inefficient secretary of a small branch of the Christian Social Union, but I am and was no organiser.

The weary walk home I have talked about, then tea in the drawing room and, if it was a special Sunday, we had out the china toys and ornaments kept in an appalling chiffonier *(popular Victorian small sideboard)*, if that's the name. There were 3 of these objects in the drawing room, a great long room heated by one small fire in a small grate surrounded by brass work. Above the fireplace was an overmantel on which, going almost to the ceiling, were jutting out little shelves on which stood objet d'arts *(sic)*. This particular chiffonier *(containing the china)* stood against the wall at the other end of the room from the fireplace. Have I mentioned that at the garden side of the room, the long side, were two huge French windows, which made the room colder? On days when the sun crept round at about 3 o'clock in the afternoon, heavy curtains were drawn with a thing called a 'long arm', a pole with a hook on the end, so as to prevent any of the furnishings from getting faded. The chiffonier was a wedding present to father from the church society of which he was secretary. The money was collected and he chose this object himself. Its glory was that in it were incorporated almost every wood that grows upon this earth. Naturally, as you may imagine, the result was awful. Ebony, satin wood, mahogany, walnut, etc. etc. It was quite instructive. In its cupboards were treasures. Books in the centre and china in the sides, and we were allowed on special days to have them out. Falstaff in china, a little house and, what I liked far best, a tea set of pink and white china, brought by my Aunt Frances from the Paris Exhibition 1851*(sic)*. Over it sat a golden stand, with the red plush and there was a glass dome.

[I have it here beside me now but the dome is not there. These little bits and pieces are not valuable, but I liked them very much as a child. There was also a Chinese Mandarin who, when wound up, nodded his head and fanned himself, but he is gone long ago and I am not sorry. I never liked anything Chinese. Their faces frightened me. I said I had these little objects beside me as I write, but that is not so. I write in bed after a fairly early breakfast. But the little tea set and co. have a little alcove in the drawing room all to themselves, with a light underneath to light them up at night. There is amongst them a large mug, very pleasantly decorated with flowers and my great grandfather's initials and his wife's; I am told it was probably a silver wedding cup. My mother had a large accumulation of china and silver as so many families had in those days. These little bits and pieces came to me as an afterthought; I had nothing else of my parents' things left to me.]

I got as far as the tea and china on Sunday. Sometimes people came to tea. Solitary men, but there were not many of them. There was a Mr Fry, an artist, wearing a huge beard. We all though him a terrible bore, but he had a sort of romantic admiration for mother, so she was rather amused by him. He was a widower with one daughter. He took a piece of land at the top of a very steep hill and there he built himself a house. When the little house was finished, he found he had forgotten to put a staircase into it. He hadn't even left room for one. So they used a glorified ladder. Any visitors, who might be with us, joined with us in hymn singing after tea. That was a part of the day that I loved, though my brothers always got praised for their lovely singing. Not Stephen, but all the others, especially Geoffrey.

1904?

One more incident in the little lane *(Shepherd's Path)* but this one I dread to report. I made such a fool of myself, thereby involving other people, that I still never think of it if I can possibly help it. But here goes. And I must get it done quickly. Very soon after my coming-out dance *(p 148)*, I went to another at the Drill Hall *(The Hampstead Drill Hall and Assembly Rooms in Holly Bush Vale, built in the 1888 for the Hampstead Rifle Volunteers, were transformed in 1920 into the Everyman Theatre.)* There I met a young man. He liked me and we danced together a great deal and also sat out and talked because he was a thoughtful person with a good brain. Fair, that to my mind was an essential ingredient, tall, quite nice looking and a gentleman. That was on a Saturday evening. On Sunday mother and I were walking together and we came to the lane and we had just entered it when, behold to my delight and surprise, here was the young man coming straight up the lane towards us. I was thrilled.

My conduct needs some explanation. The Hibberts had been given a book on "etiquette", either by one of their maids or someone. I don't know. Anyhow, we had pored over it with the deepest interest and I must have thoroughly absorbed it. One paragraph said "If you are introduced to a lady or gentleman at a party there is no need to recognise them when you meet them again. It is wiser always to wait for a second introduction before acknowledging the person." This book must have been very Victorian. I suddenly remembered the gipsies' warning and I walked straight past the young man, ignoring the fact that he was trying to take his hat off to me, and the passage was so narrow we practically brushed against one another as we met. It took some doing, I can tell you. Then, quite rightly, mother came down on me like a ton of bricks. Her great grievance was that the young man would think mother had told me to cut him. Well, I worried myself sick about it when mother explained how monstrous I had been. I hated hurting people. I think I can say with truth I never hurt anyone on purpose. I had liked the young man. If I had known his name I think I would have written, but, strange to say, I had not remembered it, even if I had ever heard it. I had an idea from his conversation that he was a nonconformist of some sort, Unitarian I think. I did not see him again till years later. I was then married and we went to stay in a hotel in Keswick and I saw him there. I practically never forget a face, I think he recognised me. He was, I think, on his honeymoon. I am not sure. I found out in the hotel his name was Bolton.

Living near us was a friend called Matheson and we saw a lot of him especially later on when he had divorced his wife. Matheson was always talking about his friend Bolton. Very rich in Lloyds I think. That was my Bolton, I never saw him again but I always regret having hurt him. He went on a cruise with our friend and died on board and was buried in the Mediterranean. I have a very similar story, only in reverse, which I will tell later. I was young. Young and very self conscious. So anxious to be grown up and correct. I thought my mother was terribly Bohemian. She didn't seem to mind.
In a year or so, I was as casual as she was.

Holiday in Scotland (c.1905?)

When my sister Marjory was quite grown up, she and father very often did not see eye to eye. We were having a dismal holiday up in Scotland. The whole holiday was a mistake. My sister and my young brother and I. What a party! After some of the summer holidays we had had, this was too awful. I picked up two young men at the tennis club but even they did not compensate for the lodgings and the rain. We bicycled to Braemar for the Gathering; damp and dreary we stood about and no doubt looked the picture of misery; at that moment father thought he would start being hearty and told me to cheer up and smile. Marjory looked at him with the utterest scorn and that provoked father: "Come on old girl," he said, "put on the sweet smile you keep for the parents at school". Now M. was a school mistress and, though mother had determined we should not let her get schoolmistressy in her manner, it had gradually crept into her and now we were too frightened of her to tell her. She had the schoolmistress's smile that is clicked on and off like an electric light. It isn't only school mistresses but many public speakers, especially Women's Institute, who have this. "I don't see anything to smile at," said M scornfully. "Can't you take a joke?" said father despairingly. He was worried by now; he had tried to be funny. "Your sense of humour is so abysmal", answered M.

I had never heard her be as rude as that. I shivered. That was too much for father. "I would have you know, young woman, that my sense of humour is just as good as yours any day". He was shouting by now and people were looking at us; I wanted to die. "Hush, hush, dear", my mother intervened. A furious silence ensued and persisted all day and that is how we enjoyed the Braemar games.

Mary Marjory Ford

Church Lads' Brigade

One dominant feature of life at home was father's constant activity with his Brigade. When I was at school I had occasion to speak of the "Brigade" with a great sense of pride. I was then taken aback as my school friends had never heard of it. The mistress said, "Do you mean the "shoe black's brigade?" Apparently, there was one. *(There were a dozen or so in London, established in the mid-19th century to provide accommodation and employment for destitute boys)*. And then some girl suggested I must mean the boys' brigade. This was very muddling. I thought the Brigade would be world famous. I asked mother and she said its proper name was the London Diocesan Church Lads' Brigade. Well that was too long; also it contained that contentious word church, and I never knew what Diocesan meant.

Everard Ford in Brigade uniform. Photo: CLCGB Historical Group

My father lived for his creation. It had started as a "Seaside Camp for London Working Boys" *(in 1888)* and then father, feeling that the boys went back to London and were lost in the slums, had the idea of starting a Brigade with a Company in every parish. *(The London Diocesan Church Lads' Brigade was founded in 1891 by Everard Ford and the Bishop of London, Rt Rev. Frederick Temple, whose normal working day at this time was one of 14 or 15 hours. Many of his clergy and candidates for ordination thought him a rather terrifying person, enforcing almost impossible standards of diligence, accuracy and preaching efficiency, but his*

In Camp at Worthing, 1917. Photo: CLCGB Historical Group

manifest devotion to his work and his zeal for the good of the people won him general confidence. In London he continued as a tireless temperance worker, and the working class instinctively recognised him as their friend.)

The Brigade throve and I believe still goes on. It preceded the Boy Scouts. Its idea, largely, was discipline. The boys marched, drilled, played games etc. under direction. It was good for their physique and also for their morale. In those days nothing was done for them, no recreation grounds, nothing. My father had a navy blue uniform and so did the officers, who were largely clergymen, curates. The whole movement absorbed my father completely. The organisation was immense and he lived in it and for it. As a child I looked forward with the utmost pleasure to the big rallies. The inspection in Hatfield Park or some such place. My father, who had a very fine figure and a military moustache, taking the salute at the march past, or some big military officer coming to inspect. There were continual entertainments in connection with the Brigade, swimming galas, sports, etc., to all of which we went. It seems so odd that father, who never had two words to say to his own sons, should have taken such an interest in other people's. When he was old, about 70 I suppose, a young man would love to come and sit with him in the evenings. Mother had grown impatient of the whole thing by then. I think she disliked her husband posing as a Colonel. He was actually made an Hon. Col. after the first war. *(When Everard died in 1928 his funeral was held in St Stephen's, Rosslyn Hill with an honour guard from the Church Lads' Brigade.)*

Mother found the officers very common young men and as I grew up so did I. I thoroughly enjoyed the Annual outings and the big evening performance at the Guildhall *(in the City of London)*. The building containing *(statues of the legendary giants)* Gog and Magog became quite familiar to me. (When I was 16, I began to present prizes at swimming galas etc. My father, standing beside me in the Holborn baths *(in Endell Street and since replaced by The Oasis)* on the first occasion, whispered to me "Look straight in his eyes", and I did. It was a useful hint. Early on I got accustomed to it and it came in useful later on.

[Years later, when I was going to present the prizes at again the Holborn baths, the final item programmed before the prize-giving was a polo match between the Police and the Civil Service. We sat half way along the side of the bath and

Colonel and Mrs Everard Ford on their golden wedding day, 1927

I, of course, all dressed up. Suddenly a policeman in the water, intending to throw the ball to the opposing team, instead threw it straight at me. It was a hard wet football. It hit me plum on the cheek, which stung like blazes. My chair rocked but I didn't quite go into the water. It would make a better story if I had. I was sorry for the man. Most awkward for him.] Father never wished to have young men engaged in his Brigade work who were of the sort mother and I wished to have to entertain. Once he made me take one to a dance. I never did it again.

I always had terrible misgivings when my parents asked anyone to the house and I was generally justified. They really did behave in an odd way. They didn't seem to think it at all necessary that they should both be in the drawing room to receive their guests. One would do. Usually father was the one to be ready. But at one dinner party neither was ready, and both were under the impression that the other one was down. When they did appear they were treated with great coolness by their guests. At big dinners I think the food was probably tolerable but at small ones it was not. Mother got the cook to try out experiments. One of her favourite sweets was a piece of sponge cake, a slice, and on it a half apricot surrounded by whipped cream. The effect, a poached egg. She enjoyed stopping her guests from putting salt on it.

Amy Moorgate

We did spend one awful evening. My mother heard that a daughter of a very old friend of hers was staying in London. Father said he had two very nice young men coming up to spend the evening with him, so mother had better ask the young woman and the friend she was staying with. Telegrams went back and forth and it was arranged that Amy Moorgate and her friend, Ivy Dean, should come to dinner. As I had quite expected, the two men weren't very young, nor were the women. All about 27. The two men were impossible. They were not at home and they tried to appear as if they were. I have little recollection of the meal but in despair afterwards mother suggested we play some game with counters. I never could find them. Amy was the daughter of a parson, and her friend lived in Lancaster Gate; both of them were very much out of the top drawer. Well, the men weren't and, while playing, one of them thought he would liven up the party by being a bit skittish and he kept stealing Amy's counters. At first she tried to take them back, but that led to his squeezing her hand, which made things worse. She got furious and he continued with complete satisfaction, no doubt feeling he was being a great success. He was very unattractive and wore a pince nez half way down his thin nose. Suddenly Amy got up and said they must go. Would we have a car sent for and we had to wait about till it came. When they said goodbye the man put his hand out to shake Amy's but she ignored it and walked straight past him.

I knew the storm would break when all of them had gone. I felt furious with father but also sorry for him. He could not see, or would not. He had not played with us. Mother began the attack on father, who asked what the man's crime had been. "Well. what is the matter with that?" We had too high and mighty notions by far, we couldn't enjoy a little joke. Probably, Amy, who father thought to be "a confirmed old spinster," and her friend too, "had not had such a jolly evening for years".

Amy Moorgate put me in the way of playing tennis in tournaments. But that I will speak of later. I did not see much of her. She was so much older than I, at least I felt so. I admired her capacity: a good pianist, cellist, singer, cook and tennis player. All the things I wasn't, but at the age of 25 or 26 she was unmarried, and another sister coming on. I stayed with her family once or twice in their snug country vicarage in Devon. Oh, yes. Amy led the bell ringers and was an expert. My young brother and I stayed there only for a night or two. It was one of those visits wished on our hosts by my mother. She would write to the most unlikely people and ask if we might stay with them. I could perfectly well sense the annoyance, when I arrived, of some of these unwilling hosts, I could feel it quite well when we had gone on our first visit to the Moorgates *(1902)*.

I was sixteen and Aubrey eleven. Not only did I feel responsible for my own behaviour, which was liable to get out of hand, but also for Aubrey's. Our first morning there was like this. We arrived down in the dining room in time for breakfast and were given chairs for prayers. Down we sat. On the table was a huge ham, their own home-cured; Aubrey glanced at me and then at the ham. He was very tiresome about food, the only one of our family who was. All of us ate anything but he, the youngest, was fussy. He never ate ham or bacon. I gently nodded and frowned and made it quite obvious to him that he must eat ham. This went on during the interminable prayers. Not only a Bible reading, but a droning exposition of the same by old Mr Moorgate *(the Vicar)*, who looked like Moses. After the sermon, a long time on our knees during which Moses told God that he, God, knew everything, but he, Moses, could give him some hints on his correct behaviour for the day. How did the wives, daughters and servants tolerate this, day after day? These people had one son, who wouldn't. He was a regular rascal, my mother said, and had been shipped off to South Africa.

When I stayed there, a very pleasant quiet woman appeared at meals. We were not introduced and no one spoke to her directly. She was a lady, over 30 I should say. In a roundabout way I found that this was the brother's wife. He had been ill in Africa and had married the woman who nursed him. He had no money and had raised enough to send her to his people, as she was pregnant. There she was in that Christian household. Her only sin was that she, a good responsible woman, had married their ne'er-do-well son and in that Christian family she was treated as an outcast. Not only did Aubrey have to eat ham, but he also had to swallow coffee, a thing he had never done before.

To return to Amy Moorgate, I stayed in the Vicarage a few years later. Amy was very occupied getting together clothes for a trip to Ceylon. I went with her to her little dressmaker, living in. The spinster was putting pins in the bodice; and also had many in her mouth. When she had finished, she looked at Amy archly and asked, "Going abroad to find Mr Right?" It was a bit discomforting to Amy who, though remarkably hard-boiled, flushed scarlet. I realised the sally had some truth in it. She must have been about 26 then. To Ceylon she went and met Mr Right, whose name was Jock Campbell. They married and shortly after, she found she had quite unknowingly married not a delightful man, but a millionaire. I met her again some years later. They had bought a house in Southampton, a bit outside. I came to the conclusion then that she had landed in Southampton, gone to the agent and bought the first enormous house she had seen. It was hideous and vast. They had a motor car, one of those new exciting toys. She would take us out in it. But we would need warm coats. Her clothes seemed to be just as limited as they were when she was a penniless parson's daughter. Her search to find me an overcoat amused me. Rooms furnished with vast and hideous wardrobes, all empty.

[The last occasion I saw her was when my brother and I went there to lunch. My brother Aubrey made me enraged by telling Amy, as a great joke, merely to ingratiate himself with me, "Do you know, her husband's a radical?" Roars of laughter from them both, I furious but impotent. I could hardly point out that my husband had more brains in his little finger than they both had in their two heads; that my husband's political views were the result of careful thought and study and not merely of class prejudice. Well, I never saw her again.]

The Patriotic League

I was saying that the Brigade entirely absorbed my father. [My husband who knew him on committees told me that he was a very autocratic person, that he must and did have his own way in everything]. Besides the (Church Lads) Brigade my father was also on local committees. One was for the glorification of our country. I think it was called the Patriotic League. To it belonged all the eminent local Conservatives. I also joined. I was at the age when to join anything was exciting. I only remember one meeting of the League. It had been advertised about the place and a prize was offered for the best essay on "Patriotism". I liked trying for prizes, even if I knew nothing of the subject. A Church Bazaar had offered a prize for the best iced cake. I knew nothing about cooking and the cook we had knew little about cake making. I made something which looked quite like a cake, but I don't know what its inside was like. I did not win a prize but I did win a prize for my essay. Chiefly because, I suppose, mine was the only entry. Also, the secretary of the League was in love with me, to say nothing of my father being the Chairman. In the essay I traced the development of man as a part of the family, and the tribe and I found that, to be logical, one must hope that man would come through the national patriotic loyalties and become truly international. It was probably the first time that I had seriously considered the question and I suddenly found myself realising that patriotism could not be an end in itself. It was the beginning of my breaking away from the surrounding Conservatism. In consequence of the views expressed, the essay was not printed as advertised, or perhaps because it just wasn't good enough. It was probably very immature. But I got £7, I think it was. £10 if it had been printed. It was a wonderful sum of money for me. I had not told anyone, not a soul, that I had entered for the competition, so I much enjoyed my parents' surprised pleasure. We went to the Conservatoire for the meeting and my sister came home to go with us and, as we hadn't told her, it was amusing to give her a surprise too. At that age and, in fact, for years to come, one of my chief desires in life was that my parents and my sister should acknowledge that I existed.

With part of the money I bought 2 bracelets, gold, one with rubies. Both were later on sold to send money to keep the Republican Army in Spain. With the rest of the money, I took my father out to a meal and a good seat at one of the Gilbert and Sullivan plays. My father had a passion for Gilbert and Sullivan and so had I. A very natural proclivity for the young, but I think one should grow out of it. To go on being "dotty" about G and S all one's life does seem to me to be rather undeveloped. It was an odd thing for one to do to take father out, as I expect we were both very embarrassed during the meal. We were not accustomed to talking together. My motives were probably mixed. I longed to go to a play and sit in something better than the pit; to eat a meal in a restaurant was a terrific thing and I also wanted, I am sure, to make my parents fond of me, to make them take notice of me.

[That is probably at the back of my generosity, even now. I am, as my daughter-in-law *(probably Jean Floud, Peter's wife)* said, ridiculously generous (quite pathological). I love to give presents. I am so bad at choosing little 'gifts'. I have a sister-in-law who excels in it, buying all through the year little objects to please everyone. I hate shopping and I can't be bothered, but what I like to do is to give something really wanted by someone. A grand piano or a bicycle. Not wasted money but a valuable possession, and then how I enjoy giving it. It's a great pleasure and quite selfish, as I love to hear the surprised delight of the recipient.]

The evening *(with father)* went off quite satisfactorily, except that I noticed at the theatre that my feet were as cold as stones. The Gipsy's warning. I then began to have an attack of indigestion, not very bad. I sat there saying nothing to my father but I realised that I was again doomed to another spell in bed.

Cycle trip, 1902

We visited the Moorgates when we were bicycling, Aubrey and I, from Torquay to Hampstead. It was strenuous going. Worked out by mother at 50 miles a day, with two days at each stop. I loved bicycling; it was to me like flying and it gave one a sense of power and freedom. The only thing about long rides was the saddle; I suppose they were not very good in those days. Clothes were a bother, as one could only take a small basket on the back of the machine. Our reception at our places of call varied. The Moorgates were freezing to start with but thawed.

Our Aunts at Salisbury were kind, but were completely obliterated *(sic)* by two selfish, pretty 'part' nieces, our cousins *(Georgina Mary Hammick, 1880-1965, and Jane Alexandra, 1881-1974)*. They were aged about 20 and 21and made no bones about the fact that we bored them. They lived in a whirl of girl friends and boy friends. They were very rich and very spoilt and lived in a superb house in the Close. We were supposed to have one day's rest before we set off again for another 50 miles and our cousins proposed, in fact, ordered, us to go on our bicycles to Stonehenge. So we did. On those saddles.

Poor Aubrey at the Close, Salisbury, at lunch. He said politely to his aunt, "Shall I pass you the milk"? She answered, "I should like the cream please". How those sort of things hurt. Fifty years has not obliterated that from his mind. Aunt Bar was a kindly, muddly old thing and wouldn't have hurt a flea. She couldn't have meant to put him in his place. She wasn't really any relation of ours.

(Two 'aunts' – Barbara S Townsend, b.1843, and her sister Gertrude E C Townsend, b.1846 – lived in The Close, Salisbury, Wiltshire, with Phyllis' uncle, William Maxwell Hammick JP, 1848-1915, her mother Rachel's brother. Widowed in 1882, he had three children, Georgina b.1880, Jane b.1881 and Robert b.1882.)

They *(the 'aunts')* were characters in Salisbury. Everybody called them Aunty Bar and Aunty Ger. They were both small women, Aunty Bar petite. She had neat, clean-cut features and bright blue eyes. She was like a robin or a wren. When I knew her, she dressed like this: silk and lace dresses, very full skirts and her hat fastened on top of a head of short curly hair. There was a vogue for short hair some time in Victorian days. Hers she kept short and she had some difficulty about hats. Hats at that time were pinned with enormous hat pins on top of the hair. She hadn't much hair, when I knew her, not on top and so she pinned a hair pad on to the top of her head. On that she planted the hat, a small hat, and then, to be quite sure, a veil was swathed all round so as to keep everything in place, I forgot to say

Women cyclists, 1899

she also wore a hairnet over her head. I cannot remember her ever without the hat, though I feel she probably wore a cap, a lace cap in the evening, yes, I think she did. But the hat was worn all day indoors and out. She was a water colour artist. A real artist, not just a painter. She was far ahead of her time in her style. Mother thought her painting quite bad and we were brought up to think that Aunty Bar was a great joke. She was in Torquay once when we were there and her sketch book was always in her hand. Gentle quick sketches, But the painting of hers we had at home was one of mother's jokes: "You didn't know which way up it went". It was not until later on when I again stayed in the Close that I realised how beautiful Aunty Bar's paintings were and how great her talent.

The other sister, Aunty Ger, was quite unattractive, not at all like a twittering bird. She dressed in black, with masses and masses of petticoats, and tight fitting bodice. Her face was red and blowsy and she looked as if she had been crying, a swollen nose. The fact is I didn't like her face, so I never looked at her, so I had better stop trying to describe her.

[One day I was looking in Debrett at our family record and I noticed something. My eldest Uncle *(Col. Sir St Vincent Alexander Hammick Bart, 1838-1927)* was married and had 3 children in 3 years, 2 girls and a boy; and his wife *(Penelope Sarah Blanche Beauclerk, 1847-86)* died young *(at the age of 39)*. This other *(Salisbury)* uncle *(William M Hammick)* was the same. Both men had quite charming wives and their pictures in the album tell me so. *(My)* father and mother had six children, but they did space them with some regard to mother's health.]

At our next port of call, Shere *(Surrey)*, we were supposed to stay with a Spottiswoode relation whom we had never seen. We got there late owing to punctures, and it was getting dark. We had some trouble in finding the house. Country houses don't have names on them and, when we got the front door answered, a housekeeper said Miss S could not accommodate us in the house but had arranged for us to go to the Inn. So off we went to the Inn. These experiences were good for one, and made one independent.

Stephen Ford

How my eldest brother tolerated life at home I don't know. He had got a scholarship at Winchester but there he did no good. Sir Humphrey Milford *(1877–1952, who became head of the London operations of Oxford University, and)* who had been there with him, said Stephen had made bad friends there. He would. He was bad himself, in a way, but easy going and good tempered as well. He could not go into the Army or the Navy because of his

Stephen Everard Ford in 1903

eyes. Nor did he wish to go into the church. Those were the three respectable professions in those days. None of mother's relations had gone into business. It was always Army or Navy or church. Stephen was to be a chartered accountant and, while he was learning and doing his exams, he lived at home. I suppose he had to because he had no money. Getting him out of bed in the morning seemed to need a great effort. But as father continually said, "you can't burn the candle at both ends". His evenings he spent, I believe, with his friends in pubs playing billiards. One morning, I was told by Bernard, Father had found Stephen in bed with his boots on. I was deeply shocked. He must have had a brain, though he never seemed to use it. He gave the impression of a 'silly fool'. Eyeglass in one eye, opera hat on the tilt, cane under his arm, he would go off to see Edna May in 'the Merry Widow', for the 20th time. He would turn at the door and, imitating some popular comedian, would wave his hand affectedly to mother and say, "ta ta". She would laugh adoringly. Father couldn't clamp down on his pursuits, but if he lived at home he must conform to father's passion for the Brigade.

So Stephen, cursing and swearing to me, would appear in his navy blue uniform to run some boys' club in West Hampstead: "I try not to see anyone when I'm dressed in this convict's rig", he said. "Look what a fool I'd feel if I met a pretty girl I knew and I dressed like this". I did feel sympathetic, though I must say I always thought he looked a fool. He had to go away to the seaside camp, like it or not. But, though he went, he was a thorn in the flesh to his father. The Colonel's son played the fool, though not viciously. He simply was out to "show off". That was his role in life, 'showing off and playing the fool'. He was a very fine swimmer, but insisted on bathing in a large panama hat and an eye glass. Father let loose to me on the subject. Yet what good brains he must have had. I never heard him make an intelligent remark. He appeared to do no work. He was out on the tiles night after night. But he passed all his exams first go. His holidays, beyond the seaside camp, he spent in boating on the Broads with his two or three friends. His Saturdays off, he told me, he spent in the company of a barmaid at Elstree. He had a passion for bicycling and did absurd things like riding from Norfolk home in record time with no food.

Enough. I will not talk of several years later, I wonder whether to write of it now, I wince inside – a piece of me just below the ribs contracts at some of my thoughts and I prefer to crush them away and never to think of them again.

Edna May (1878-1948), American actress and singer, and popular 'postcard beauty'

When Stephen had passed his exams he looked for a job. He had been articled to Jackson, Hussey, Dicksley *(accountants)*. Later on we knew the sons of Jackson very well. I do not know why he took a job abroad. It may have been the lure of better pay, or the desire to get clear of his father; I have a feeling that father urged it. That is my impression. And he went to South Africa, to Salisbury, Rhodesia. Perhaps Stephen was attracted by the name of Salisbury, for the last 3 or 4 years he had been going bicycling down to Salisbury to stay at the Close with the cousins I have described. They were just up his street. One day he was sitting at our breakfast table reading a letter. I may have mentioned it but I have the eyes of a vulture, I can see anything anywhere. But it wouldn't have taken much seeing to read in large printed letters, bright red, over the corner of the note paper ROSIE; I put Rose down in my mind as not out of the top drawer, which I later found out to be true. [I knew a woman slightly, years later, her sons played tennis with ours. She told me that my brother Stephen had been in love with her sister Rose.] If Rosie had been like her, I am glad he escaped, but I cannot honestly say that. He, I think, was desperately in love with her. I waited my chance and, when Stephen had done or said something particularly unpleasant, I asked, "How's dear Rosie?" Heavens, I thought he would have knocked me down, I never saw him so enraged. He really had a most equable temper. "You've been reading my letters," he shouted. Poor dear, he needn't have worried. All I knew was Rosie and I wasn't very interested.

He went to Salisbury, Rhodesia *(now Harare, Zimbabwe)*; I don't remember his leaving home at all *(he went in 1903 when Phyllis was 17)*; Father talked about the large salary he was going out to. Mother didn't talk at all. Her favourite son had gone some years ago, and now her second favourite. Those two were the only two she really loved and how she missed this one. Stephen avoided father as much as he could, but he and mother managed to see quite a lot of one another.

His bedroom mustn't be changed at all, said mother. Everything must be just as it is when he comes back in a few years. She never said that sort of thing. I had a pang. I felt sure he would not come back. He would never want to. Mother must have missed him terribly. Our family was now reduced to me *(Aubrey away at school)*. It seems strange I don't remember his going but I remember nothing of it. His salary was $700, I believe, and in those days it sounded a lot, but we none of us knew how expensive living was out there. I have no clear picture of his life in Salisbury, nor had mother, I think. At first a trickle of letters came. The post from South Africa came after lunch on Saturdays; waiting for a letter, Mother was tense all through lunch. If a letter came, she was overjoyed, though it was a wretched, short, typewritten thing. She would read a bit of it out and try and get father to talk about it, but no, father never would speak of him. Mother talked to a blank wall. No response from father and I'm afraid I wasn't much better. After a very short time one realised that Stephen's name was not to be mentioned in the house.

My brother Bernard gave me some explanation of this. Stephen told him that in 5 years, he had received one letter from father and that it was a demand for money. Father said that he had spent large sums on Stephen's education – [as Stephen got a scholarship to Winchester, I didn't see why] – and now that he was earning such a princely salary, it was time he returned the money. Stephen did not answer this and gradually his letters home lapsed altogether. Then Saturday's lunch became unbearable – week after week mother in a state of agonising tension. Every time the servant came into the room the quick look of expectancy on her face and then the quick fading out.

Then father had a report from a friend of his. This so called friend was a clergyman [and incidentally my Godfather]. He had been in South Africa and had stayed in Rhodesia. He had made enquiries about Stephen: "They were far from satisfactory". He was not leading a Godly life. This parson would, I think, have thought any form of amusement ungodly: card playing, dancing, etc.
Not that I am able to stand up for Stephen or his morals, but I do think it was an indefensible thing to come and report to father and then for father to tell it all to mother. From then on Stephen's name was never mentioned at home.

One day *(in 1912)* – I was then living with my husband and twin babies in Surrey – I heard that mother had had bad news of Stephen. He had been abroad 9 years. Now a telegram had come from someone unknown to say he was seriously ill. I went up at once and found mother in a terrible state. She was like one demented. Up and down the drawing room like a tormented soul, I had never seen mother like this and my heart ached for her, but at the same time I felt irritated that she should be in such a state about such a worthless young man. As she moved about she talked or rather ejaculated, "If only he had come home this would never have happened". Over and over again. "He was like your little Peter. He was such a lovely baby boy. ... He could have come home". I had to say something, so I said I supposed he hadn't come home because he couldn't afford it. "Your cousin Mabel offered to pay for him. She would have paid his fare home. She was his Godmother, you know." At hearing that, I felt annoyed. He hadn't come home to see mother even when he could have come back free. "Mother," I said, "You must not worry so much that he didn't come home, I expect he had work that kept him there. Anyway you must not blame yourself. He had the chance." "No, oh no, he didn't; that's just it, he didn't", Mother was crying and almost screaming. "He didn't have the chance. He never knew about Mabel's offer. He never knew; your father wouldn't let me tell him. Your father said it would have unsettled him. Your father thought it better he should stay out there."

My God, I thought, My God, and I was filled with a raging resentment against my father. How could he have been so cruelly selfish? How could he? Then I knew, as I had always known, my father had always been jealous of Stephen. He was born after *(mother's)* long months of poor health. My mother had had to lie on a sofa, and the birth was difficult. When he was born, a great fat boy, my mother at last had something to love, really to love, and she loved this beautiful baby with her whole heart. And father had never forgiven the child. I could find nothing to say to my mother. Not only did I rage inwardly against my father, but also against her. How could she have meekly acquiesced, or anyway acquiesced meekly or not? How could she have? I suppose it was this prevalent idea at that time that onlymen understood about business. Father probably stressed that Stephen's business would suffer. But father knew, just as I know or better guessed, that Stephen had no business. The people who sent the telegram to my mother thought they were being kind.

You see, mother wasn't a weak-kneed woman; she had far more guts than father, more brains, more initiative. How could she have allowed him to boss her around? But perhaps mother felt that the strain of having Stephen home, out of a job, and the bickering that would ensue would not be worth it.

On that day she talked and talked when we were waiting for further news. One thing she clung to. She kept on returning to it: Edie Munro, an acquaintance of our family, had married and gone to South Africa. She was in Salisbury one Sunday and she met Stephen coming out of church on Sunday morning. How mother clung to that straw of comfort. The parson, Mr Blaxland, had said Stephen was leading a bad life; that could not be true, as Edie Munro had seen him coming out of church on Sunday, so the day went on. I don't think my father appeared at all; I saw him when I arrived but not again until he came in carrying the second inevitable telegram: Stephen was dead. Whether mother believed in hell or not I am not sure, but I think she did. I did, until years later when my husband exorcised this demon from me, along with many others.

I heard little of Stephen's death. I went away after that terrible day. He seems to have left no belongings and no property at all. A kindly letter came from some woman saying that he had been a friend of her and her husband, that he had such a kindly nature, but he never seemed to have grown up. From somewhere else, I don't know where, they heard that he had gone to hospital, that the doctor had diagnosed a clot on the brain. The doctor had said he could operate but it might mean insanity. Stephen had refused, he probably had not money to pay for it anyway. He had walked away from the hospital and gone to the railway station. At the station he died. I can never bear to think of that. The diagnosis from the doctor. The hopeless despair, the complete loneliness and to die at a Railway Station, that was all I ever heard. He was 32. I suppose he must have thrown himself under a train.

"He was such a sweet boy" said mother to me, when we heard he had died. "At school *(Lynam's Prep School in Oxford, now The Dragon School)*, the house matron told me, I remember so well", she said. "She told me Stephen had been one of the best influences in the school she had ever had. At the time he was there, there were a lot of very undesirable boys, and Stephen used all his influence for good." I sat in my mother's drawing room, looking at her lined face full of sorrow for the loss of her wonderful boy. "You're telling me" I said to myself. I could feel nothing but pity for mother.

Then she told me why she was on the Sailors' Orphans Committee. I merely wish to state here that mother sat on a committee of the Sailors' Daughters Home *(suppliers of the Fords' 'orphan' servants, see p 65)* because, as she once told me, she would have died of boredom if she hadn't had something to do outside the house. Sitting on a committee in those days took up quite a bit of time and also gave the members who had no carriages quite a lot of exercise. We lived about a quarter of an hour *(on foot)* from the scene of mother's activities, and that and shopping "up the town" gave her all the exercise she had. She did nothing at all in the house.

The Sailors' Orphan Girls School & Home, Fitzjohn's Avenue (CLSAC)

Leaving school

My days at school passed agreeably enough; I learnt practically nothing but French, German and drawing, these being the only subjects which were decently taught. We played no games at school *(despite the advertised tennis and riding)*, but I got my tennis with the Hibberts in the summer and occasionally skating and tobogganing in the winter, Also ping pong. I enjoyed everything with a tremendous zest if it was outside my own home.

I had no regrets at leaving school. My only regret was that I could not be sorry, I felt this was an important event in my life and I ought to feel its importance but I couldn't. I was only too ready to be up and out in the world. No one asked me what I wanted to do, if they had, I would have said without hesitation, "Let me go to the Slade". *(The Slade School of Fine Art at University College, London was founded in 1871. Two of its most important periods were immediately before, and immediately after, the turn of the 20th century, described by Henry Tonks as its two 'crises of brilliance.' The first period included the students Augustus John, William Orpen and Percy Wyndham Lewis; the second included the students Dora Carrington, Mark Gertler, Paul Nash, C R W Nevinson and Sir Stanley Spencer. Phyllis did eventually attend the Slade after she was married.)* That was the only definite thing I knew. But in our household the name of the Slade could not be mentioned. How I knew this I do not know, but I did know it. I suppose my parents talked over my future. Oh yes, I know they did. Apparently, Father had on some occasion turned upon my sister in wrath and carped at her for not getting married.

Bedford College, 1902

(The Bedford College for Women was founded, as the Ladies' College, in Bedford Square, Bloomsbury in 1849, and renamed ten years later. In 1874 it moved to occupy two adjoining houses at 8 & 9 York Place, later renumbered as part of Baker Street. From 1878 women were able to sit the degree examinations of the University of London, of which Bedford College became a constituent part in 1900. Only in 1908, after Phyllis' time, did it move to its best-known location on the Inner Circle in Regent's Park. The college merged with Royal Holloway in 1985.)

I was informed by my mother that I was to go to Bedford College in London, daily. She did not even consult me as to what subjects I should take. Her ignorance about it all was pathetic. And my meekness in accepting her ridiculous curriculum was also pathetic. Mother must have taken some trouble to work it out. She had never learnt Latin herself, so the fact that I learnt it was important – "I must go on with my Latin". She did not know that my Latin, taught by a young woman who knew none herself was practically non-existent. When my mother decided that I must go to Bedford College, she also decided that maths and Latin must be two of my subjects, because I had had individual teaching and it would be a pity to waste it. I floundered helplessly over both. Even the elementary maths was beyond me, but I struggled hard; unfortunately Latin was being taught the new way at College and I couldn't make head or tail of it. How I wrestled with Caesar, 1st book *(The Gallic Wars)* and how little I understood. Science mother knew nothing of. She was impressed by the idea, "I must go on with my science". The same young woman had tried to teach us Elementary Science out of a book, also "Electricity and Magnetism". Algebra was in the same category. When it came to the point I knew nothing about any of them.

The subjects I knew something of were Drawing, French, German, which I did not like, and Literature and Botany – chiefly because I loved drawing flowers. Mother, without consulting me, went off to see the head of the college. The head said mother had chosen rather odd subjects, that I had better take Modern or Classical – but mother wouldn't be persuaded. I mustn't waste my Latin or my Science. Mother also thought that I must work for some course – I had better take Matric *(matriculation, the examination taken after one year which was essential to progress to a degree)*. I had never worked at anything before except drawing – I did concentrate on that and sometimes really worked but I had never worked on anything else.

Now I found myself in a new world and I suddenly wanted to learn. I wanted to know everything desperately. I felt my terrible ignorance and I also felt the glow and glory of mastering something new. I worked – I worked desperately, agonisingly and despairingly because I realised that I had no grounding in any subject and I should never catch up. Maths and algebra completely baffled me. I had loved Euclid at school – I had never measured an angle, but I knew all the books of Euclid by heart, simply because he intrigued me. But algebra I found almost incomprehensible.

Yet, though this was a ladies' college I was at, the teaching in the algebra class was very elementary. Miss Leigh, a PhD and no doubt a brilliant mathematician, had to teach us. She was to us a comic character and we would laugh at her scruffy appearance, clothes rather like a tramp, and a beard. But she had a sense of humour. One day she was explaining that you cannot add a to b. "You can't add tables and chairs. If you have 3 tables and 2 chairs, you must say 3 tables and 2 chairs."

"Oh no, Miss Leigh", said a girl called Wooldridge, "you would say 5 pieces of furniture". Miss Leigh snorted and laughed. "Oh very well, Miss Wooldridge, let us take another example - 3 tables and 2 elephants". Miss Wooldridge quickly retorted, "5 quadrupeds". The whole class burst out laughing, including Miss Leigh who much enjoyed the joke.

The classes I really liked were English Literature with a mild little man, Dr. Lawrence. On one occasion we were given a description of a garden. It just stated bald fact. The garden was long, hollyhocks on one side, etc. We were told to re-write. I did. I certainly took no trouble over it – I just wrote as I always do, straight away. Next lecture, Dr. Lawrence reported on the papers he had had. "I want to read one aloud to you because it could not be bettered. It is a very beautiful piece of English writing."

As he was reading it I began to have a faint recollection, and then I realised it was mine. I was so unaccustomed to do anything well that I nearly burst into tears. When he had finished, he read it beautifully, he asked "Who is Miss Ford?" He was surprised when I put up my hand – I was very young and an awful chatterbox and I think he was disappointed, but he again congratulated me very shyly and said he hoped to see a lot more of my work. Funny, I never even mentioned this to my mother when I got home. In my year at Bedford College that was the only time I was commended – and when it came to Matric, I think that *(English)* was the only subject I passed in.

I enjoyed my time there but it was strenuous. In the afternoons I sometimes went with the boating club to the Regents Park water – I enjoyed that. I don't know why I didn't join the tennis club. I think there must have been one. I could get lunch in College if I liked for 10d. I found it dull and so got my lunch out with a friend or two. Generally at the Dairy at Marble Arch, where it was possible to buy a mutton pie for 2d *(probably the Express Dairy at 554 Oxford Street)*. It wasn't very nice and we only bought it if we were very hard up.

I liked the freedom – the grown up-ness of my life. Shortly after I had joined, I had a letter from the head asking me to put my hair up, as Bedford College was not a girls' school – that was a blow and I was only 16 – not that I minded putting my hair up, but in those days when your hair went up your skirts inevitably went down, and mother wouldn't give me a new skirt. I therefore looked like a housemaid and I was very conscious of it. At weekends I let my hair down. I was coming back from Baker St. station on the terrible smoky underground one day *(the line was electrified only in 1905)*, when a friend of Stephen's, but a highly respectable one who lived with his parents and three sisters in a large house on the Heath, came up and spoke to me. I was dismayed when he got into my 3rd Class carriage as I knew he travelled 1st. All gentlemen did. I was even more confused when, after a silent journey through the noise and the smoke, he followed me out of the train at Swiss Cottage *(the original Metropolitan line station)*. "You ought to go on to Finchley Road surely?" said I. "Oh yes," he said, "but I wanted to walk with you". He was very old – 24 or 25, the age that, at that time, terrified me. I felt sure he was doing this just to annoy me, just to make me feel foolish. He must have noticed my short skirt – what did he want to walk an extra 2 miles for? *(A great exaggeration: the two stations were only 600 yards apart.)* I can remember nothing of his conversation and, when we arrived at my turning, I quickly said goodbye and fled. I burst in on mother and let loose, and there was Stephen laughing his head off at my embarrassment. That was the end of a foolish incident and it shows how absurdly unprepared I was to cope with situations.

Metropolitan Railway station, Swiss Cottage (CLSAC)

1903

Well, the matric results came when I was staying at the Manor House with my dear Hetty *(Dalton)* and her parents. Her mother did not like me and I was most unlikeable at that age. One Sunday a large party of distinguished people came to lunch and afterwards all but the elderly went for a long walk. Among these people was Lord Buckmaster, years older than I, but handsome and attractive; in fact, I suppose, he was the lion of the party. *(Stanley Owen Buckmaster, 1861-1934, was a lawyer and Liberal Party politician, later to be Lord Chancellor and made a Viscount.)* He paired himself off with me. He was a wonderful talker and he knew everything in the world, it seemed to me. All the things I had never heard talked about – the beginning of the world, evolution and then every plant, tree and bird. He knew the names of everything we saw and he made me see them. As we walked, I was entirely enthralled – I quite forgot to think about myself and I walked beside him eagerly listening to every word.

I greatly admired the man and his conversation was dazzling. He was responsible for our coming home to tea at least an hour late. Our hostess didn't like it at all – quite naturally. She didn't expect her attractive visitor to go wandering off with a gawky girl of 17 and, if he did, he should have chosen his hostess' daughter, who was the same age and much more attractive.

When the matric results came I felt rather awful. I had expected something of the sort but at the same time had hoped *(for better)*. But mother's letter, which came at the same time, was certainly depressing. She wrote that I must be unique – no one else could have failed in as many subjects as I. A long while after, I said I really did think she need not have been so damning. Surprised, she said she had written like that as a joke to make me laugh. But life was too gloriously full of everything at that moment to make me mind too much about the silly old exam. Life seemed to be opening out before me in most unexpected ways.

Stanley Owen Buckmaster

After that one year at college I stopped. I was never told why but I suppose money. Meanwhile, my friend Hetty went to Girton. *(Educated in Hampstead at Threave House School, 7 Heath Drive, founded in 1886 by the Misses McMillan, Catherine Esther Anne ('Hetty') Dalton studied maths at Girton College, Cambridge in 1905-08, getting a 3rd class in the Tripos. In 1928 she was awarded a 'titular' MA. Cambridge formally awarded degrees to women only in 1948. Hetty became a teacher. In 1921, in Bombay (Mumbai) she married Alfred Hale-White (1888-1939), an engineer. In her widowhood she lived for at least 20 years in Oxford, where her war work was testing small munitions and selling at the local Red Cross gift shop. Hetty died in 1972 in Westchester, NY, USA.)*

I envied Hetty in a way but yet, though I thought it would be wonderful to go away from home, I didn't think I would like to live for 3 years among nothing but women. Young men were becoming more interesting to me daily.

My parents now decided that I must get cracking. It was time I earned my living. At that date it was not the done thing. Young ladies did not earn their livings. My sister was the only woman I knew who was gainfully employed. Large numbers of them had taken

Henrietta (Hetty) Dalton

to slumming – that was very fashionable; all the best people did it. Quite a number from our neighbourhood went once a week to Bethnal Green. They talked of the sweating of the girl making buttonholes for boots all day long. They thought they would try to rescue some of them by bringing them into "service" in Hampstead, out of the frying-pan into the fire. Two girls were brought to a house in Prince Arthur Road. The clean beds were something new to them but, when it came to getting out of them in the morning, they just wouldn't. After two days they ran away back to their squalor and sweated labour, preferring it to the slavery of domestic service.

No doubt it was father who decided that I should follow in Marjory's footsteps, but I had no qualifications. I was a complete failure as a money raiser. My sister later on confided in me that, after she started earning, my father was always borrowing off her and never paying it back, saying she would get it when he died. She also had to go abroad with him for holidays, paying all her own expenses.

A secretarial course was decided on by my parents for me. How I should have loathed it. I had never got over my huge desire to be out of doors when the sun shone. My mother and sister couldn't understand it. They would both sit indoors all day. I got to bursting point and had to go out. Anyway, secretarial work wasn't my line. I only wanted to draw and paint. Practising for hours I could not do. One hour, two hours but no more – then I would run round to my friends the Hibberts, feeling furious with myself. Never would I be good at anything I never really stuck to anything. I had little talent. I was ready to try the secretarial course, anything once. I should get away from home.

So, not having asked my feelings on the subject, off went my mother and I to a Miss I don't know what – but she had *the* secretarial school in London. It was all very new and exciting. No government office employed a woman and, in fact, no one did except a few. She was rather nice, Miss so-and-so. I had a great desire to earn some money. She looked me up and down. "Too young", she said. "She's like a young colt. Give the girl her hand for a bit. Let her run loose, she's too young. If she wants to come back in a few years' time, I'll take her."

Teaching Betty Burnett, c.1905-1908

After I had been turned down by the Secretarial College, because I was too young, I lived aimlessly at home for a short time. I never remember being faintly bored, but I wanted to do something regular, and above all I was longing to earn a little money. So, when I was asked by a friend of my mother's, or rather an acquaintance of my mother, to give lessons to her small daughter *(aged about 6; solicitor Harry Cleather Burnett lived with his wife Elizabeth at 17 Lyndhurst Gardens; their daughter Elizabeth had been aged 19 months in 1901.)* I jumped at it. Already a daily governess had been tried but had failed. Betty had disliked her, and had spent the first morning sitting under the table and the second pursuing the governess round the table with a stick. Betty sounds rather an attractive character, but she wasn't. She started at a disadvantage with me. She had known me for some time and, encouraged by her mother, she adored me. Even so, our first morning was not very propitious. We were sitting together at the dining room table, when Betty suddenly slid down off her chair and disappeared. I thought, "Here goes." I was nervous and apprehensive. I sat and continued to read aloud the history we had been doing. Alfred and the cakes or some such.

When I had finished it, I just sat. Presently a feeble voice from under the table said, "If you say, 'Come out', I'll come". No answer from me. Long pause. The same repeated. Another long pause. Then a crest-fallen little girl crept out from under the table cloth. Her two enormous stone teeth protruding and her face in a fixed foolish grin. I felt very sorry for her but extremely relieved myself. I quietly started on an amusing lesson as if nothing had happened.

Later on we went into the drawing room for a piano lesson and here again Betty played the same game. She hid behind the sofa, saying pathetically after a while, "If you say 'come out' I'll come'.' I sat at the piano playing and hoping very much that her mother, a foolish creature, wouldn't come in. After that, we had no worries or troubles. She was a dull, plodding child. I did everything I could to make my teaching entertaining. I think successfully. Arthur Mee was just bringing out his first Children's Encyclopaedia (1908). It was of the greatest help. After a term or two, we were joined by Betty's cousin, Monica. Pretty and whimsy, with a very quick intelligence, as quick as Betty was slow. It was not easy to teach them together. Betty could be so easily lost, as her like adoration for me persisted. I found it an extremely pleasing occupation. I only worked in the mornings and I found it absorbingly interesting.

It transpired that Betty had curvature of the spine, or something of the sort, and she was sent by her own doctor to a man, who I suppose was a Dr., who had remedial classes. The usual treatment for curvature in those days was to make the unfortunate child lie for hours per day on a back board. This was therefore something revolutionary. I used to take Betty to these classes in London. The children who attended usually had crooked spines, short legs or some such thing. There was one little hunchback girl. She could never be cured. One day the Dr told the child to bring him over a tool. At once her Governess jumped up to fetch it. The Dr. was down on her like a ton of bricks: "Let the child bring it herself. Let her be independent. Heaven knows she'll need it, to be able to get through the world, poor child." He appeared to be a fierce man but he was very kindly to the children.

Betty was sitting astride on a wooden horse. He stood behind her and jerked her body, then her head and neck, just like a modern osteopath. Then I heard he was talking to her and his voice came out hot and strong to me, "Why did Betty only have an orange for breakfast? Is it true?" I said I didn't know, I didn't have breakfast with her. He fussed and fumed. "Tell her mother from me that she's to have what she wants for breakfast." Then to Betty, "Do you like eggs?" "Yes, well give her eggs. Tell her mother to give her eggs. Do you like bacon? Yes, well tell her mother to give her bacon." I felt this would not be very acceptable at Betty's home. There was plenty of money, but mother was a stupid woman and given to crazes. The latest was that children over ate, that everyone over ate. In those days they probably did. That is, the people of our class. Betty's mother was trying to introduce fruit instead of the greasy heavy diet people were accustomed to.

I longed to tell the Dr. about Betty's dress. On the first day that Betty went to him, he said to Mrs B, who took her there, "This child's dress is too tight. It is constricting her shoulders. She can't move freely." Mrs B told me how annoyed she was. Betty had plenty of nice dresses and she must wear them out before she had new ones. But to humour the Dr. she had made one blue serge dress and this Betty wore daily to the classes, but I had strict instructions that, as soon as we returned home, she must change at once into one of her tight dresses, which she would wear for the rest of the day. It was so preposterous that I longed to protest, but she was my employer and I couldn't. Luckily, in spite of this the curvature was corrected. Betty's mother ended in an asylum.

The Mays of West Heath Road

My mother got an invitation card from a friend, a Mrs. May, who lived on the Heath: "At Home in the garden". My first real garden party, for I was invited too. I don't think I have mentioned the Mays and especially Nelly May before, perhaps because the thought of her always gives me a pain inside. *(Peter Wilson May was a Foreign Merchant from Dublin, married to Eliza; she was widowed in 1902.)* The Mays lived in a very large new house in a new road called West Heath Road *(St Margaret's, 84 West Heath Road, now a Care Home)*. Every house had a drive, a conservatory and stables, and about 3 or 4 acres of garden with sweeping lawns, and near the house beds of odd shapes filled with bedding out plants. Servants were 10 a penny in those days, so there were plenty of them, quiet and orderly, indoors and in the garden. *(In 1891 the Mays had 9 live-in servants, including a coachman; the gardeners must have lived out.)* Mr. May was on the Stock Exchange. I think he was almost the only man there we knew.
We had always been brought up to think of the Stock Exchange as of the devil, so it was odd to find one's parents suddenly hobnobbing with them. Mr. May was a very large, handsome man with a big beard. His wife *(born in South Lambeth)* came from I know not where, but she had just the same *('Cockney')* accent and behaviour as Mrs. Hibbert. Both women seemed lost in a world of rides, and were feebly trying to keep their heads above water.

Mrs. May had produced a very fine family. She was a tiny, peevish little thing, but her four sons were all six foot and the daughter, who was the same age as my sister, was a lovely woman *(Charlotte, b.1880)*. Then after a considerable gap there was another girl. She was exactly my age *(Mary Eleanor May, known as Nelly, b.1886)*. She was always considered very delicate and she was exquisite, like china – a perfect oval face, blue eyes and dark, fluttering eyelashes, dark hair. When I was very young, I suffered considerably from her. Her mother would arrive at our house in the brougham and carry me off to be the plaything of the prettiest and most spoilt little devil in existence. It was like in a story book – the little poor girl and the little rich girl. I dreaded those visits as well as I might. I was unaccustomed to large houses and a lot of servants. I felt strange and awkward and Nelly thoroughly enjoyed my misery. She had a Governess, Miss Gray, who never dared to rebuke her. So Nelly could laugh at my clothes with only the feeblest protests from poor "Gray". Mrs. May had great 'at home' days. In spite of her violent cockney accent, people called. The Mays were rich.

On one 'at home' day, Nelly and I were dressed to go down to the drawing room. It happened that our warm, best dresses were the same colour. It was very fashionable for young girls at that time, a deep, rich red. I never had more than one "Sunday dress", one that is for winter and one for summer. I put on my red dress and Nelly then objected. I couldn't wear the same colour as her. I said it was my only "Sunday dress". She was very put out. She wanted to wear hers. Mine was a very plain dress and probably very badly made, as it was one of my mother's productions. Nelly's was very smart with straps and bands of black velvet on it. "Who made yours?" asked Nelly with infinite disgust. "My mother," I said. "Oh mine was made by …" – she said a fashionable dressmaker's name. We went downstairs and waited in the dining room and then were ushered into the packed drawing room.

Mrs. May was sitting there. Nelly rushed up to her, calling in her high shrill child's voice – "Mother, mother, look at Phyllis". She dragged me along. "Do you know her mother made that dress she has on?" Everyone in the room turned our way to see what this interruption was. In their circle mothers did not make their daughters' dresses.

One day we were skipping – I loved it, I was very good at it. Nelly and I were skipping together and somehow the rope flicked her eye. No doubt it was painful. But the scene! "Phyllis has blinded me". She rushed round the house to the kitchen to Miss Gray, to her mother. Running, shrieking, "I am blinded." I following in abject turn. What had I done, how dreadful! Well it was nothing. But I admit it probably had hurt her. My visits there were short, only for a few days, when Nelly had nothing better to do.

A coach drive to Victoria Station

One day *(evidently before Peter May's death in 1902)*, it was suggested, as a great treat for me, that I be allowed to drive to Victoria Station with Mr. May in the morning. Nelly would not go. She could not endure the motion of the brougham, she said. She emphasised what a treat it would be for me, the little poor girl who never went for drives. I looked forward to it, but next morning woke with "one of my headaches". I didn't like to say anything and make a fuss, so I ate some breakfast and went. I sat beside Mr. May, a great big man. I looked at the backs of the coachman and footman and began to feel sick. Then I felt very sick. I felt dreadfully sick. What could I do? If I ever got to Victoria Station, I must get out and be sick. I knew little about stations, but I thought perhaps I could find a lavatory. But what to say to the footman, one didn't mention lavatories in those days. Anyway should I ever get there – oh dear – agony, misery. The carriage slowed down and stopped,

Mr. May got out; the carriage went on and was on its way back. I had no time to stop anyway. Also I felt too ill to speak. Oh heavens, the carriage drove on through the park. I could bear it no more but I couldn't be sick out of the window in Hyde Park – and carriages passing. I spread my hanky on my lap. It was a large one and I was sick and sick. Then what to do? I took it quickly by the corners – I had already let down the window, and as we approached Marble Arch I got ready. As we went through I hurled this horrible bag of sickness out of the window against the inside of the Arch. I never see Marble Arch without remembering that, though one has not driven through it for years. I sat in abject wretchedness, my head splitting, until the carriage stopped and I walked out holding my head very erect as I did when I had a headache. A grey glazed look on my face and my neck rigid.

Nelly came to meet me and took one look; she gave a loud shriek and rushed round the house screaming that I was ill and she thought I'd been sick. By that time, no doubt, the footman had already spread the news, as I can't imagine that I didn't do some damage to the carpet or upholstery. While Miss Gray attended to my wants, my chief need was to be left in peace. Nelly reiterated over and over, "I knew the motion of the brougham would upset her, it always upsets me."

Tennis, 1903

I was never asked to stay there again. Now, after many years, came this invitation. My mother handed the card across to me at the breakfast table. "Oh, tennis!" I said, looking at the writing in the corner. The card was printed "At Home in the garden", and then in ink across the bottom left corner, "Tennis". "How lovely!" I said. "You can't possibly play tennis there", said my mother rather naturally. "To start with, you can't play and even if you did you wouldn't be good enough for them. They are very good you know. They have two courts" and, she repeated, "They are very good."

"I shall take my racquet," I said defiantly. I felt quite determined about this – the heavens had suddenly opened and I was not going to have the door banged shut in my face. And I took my racquet; short of seizing it from me, mother couldn't prevent it. But she argued as we walked. "You had better put your racquet down somewhere, and not let it be seen." But I didn't answer. My dress? Yes, rather unsuitable for running about on a tennis court but that is how we played in those days. Young ladies, who must have their dresses on the ground with a slight train behind, dresses generally made of muslin with frilly petticoats, walked on to the tennis courts and, so attired, played tennis. Playing with the Hibberts, I had not been so hampered, as my skirts had not come down by then. But now I was 17 and my hair was permanently up, at least supposed to be, so my dress must be long. We walked to the Mays.

It was a long walk but the last part was beautiful. I suppose it was about one and a half miles. We arrived; we went straight into the garden directed by the footman. There was a crowd of people; they were walking about the lawns but mostly they were sitting in rows and rows of chairs, watching the tennis. Mother and I said "How do you do?" to Mrs. May and we sat down.

Then I watched tennis for the first time in my life. This was wonderful, so quick, and the men took the ball on the volley and they stood quite close to the net. I watched breathless. The set ended. Fred May, the second son, came up and said "How do you do?" and asked me to come and play. I found myself in a state of terrific exaltation. The court was perfect, the balls were new, the pace was thrilling. I drove from the back line; I swept my back handers across the court. Besides having played with the Hibberts, on Saturdays, I had played singles with Hetty in Gainsborough Gardens on a very soggy court. *(J B Priestley is said to have played on these courts in the 1930s.)* We arranged to improve our backhanders and would steadily play to the other's back hand the whole afternoon. My father, who played a good game for his age, never took a back hand stroke. He always changed the racquet into his left hand, which shows that the pace was not very fast. To be able to take a back hander properly was considered an achievement.

This mixed four was to me dazzling. I had never played with men before, and so the game was infinitely faster than what I was accustomed to but I knew I was playing well. I was annoyed to feel my hair coming down. I had had it up such a short time that I really had not mastered the technique of keeping it up. As it unwound down my back I remembered my wickedness. The method of hairdressing was first to tie it with a narrow piece of brown ribbon, failing that a shoe lace. But I had been failing both of those and so had tied mine with a piece of white tape! I could imagine how cross mother would feel, quite naturally, at her daughter's deplorable untidiness.

[Talking of that makes me think of an old album with pictures of past actresses, etc. which we were looking at the other day and my daughter-in-law *(Jean probably)* said, "How untidy their hair was then", and, looking at them, we noticed Edna May for instance, all ready for the camera, but with wisps of hair about the place. There were no perms in those days to keep the hair in soft but tidy waves. The only thing was an iron wave and I don't suppose that would have kept in in the heat - so we were untidy.]

But the tennis was all important and what I looked like didn't matter much, I felt. I ought to mention that, besides the muslin dress, I was also wearing a straw hat, so to be able to hit a ball at all must have taken some concentration. At the end of the set, Fred ushered me off the court and I walked with him radiant, though dishevelled. He went straight up to my mother and said, "Where did Phyllis learn her forehand drive?" "I'm sure I don't know," said my mother looking a little awkward. "I didn't know she played."

Then Fred went on to ask what club I belonged to. He was astonished when he heard I didn't belong to one and he put it hot and strong to mother that I must join one, preferably the Cumberland *(in Alvanley Gardens, West Hampstead)*. So to my joy, I was allowed to join a club, but not the Cumberland. My parents would like a club where all the young people were nice. The tennis to them was just a social entertainment. The standard of tennis didn't matter as long as they were nice. The Cumberland was not a club like that. There I should have got first class tennis and found a high subscription I suppose. I should have been very shy, so I didn't really mind that I was put into a gentle little tennis club playing within a fenced piece of land in a remote part of the Heath. My friend Hetty joined too and so my tennis didn't get much of a chance, as she and I continued to play singles daily and the men who belonged had not much idea of the game. But I didn't ask much, and I now began to be invited out to tennis parties and there I shone. And so I began to get a little confidence and did not feel all the time that I was too awful for words.

New directions

Life was opening out in many directions. I had suddenly realised the joy of reading, Jane Austen, Thackeray, but I was not allowed the Brontes. Dickens I found sickening. When I was a child, mother, who didn't like him herself, started reading Oliver Twist to me. She must have been hard up for a book, I think. She stopped when she found me sitting listening with tears pouring down my face and that night I couldn't sleep. So Dickens was taken off the list.

Now I was naturally reading for myself and I devoured all I could find, poetry too but in very small quantities. I was allowed to read my brother Stephen's books and most of them were good. Stephenson and Conan Doyle – but I couldn't do with Sherlock Holmes stories or the few murder stories he had. They gave me fits and I didn't dare go to bed. But Sherlock Holmes gripped me so that I couldn't put him down however much I wanted to. When I was about 12, no younger, Jack the Ripper was in the headlines. I used to hear our servants talking behind my back in whispers and my blood froze. *(Phyllis had been only 2 years old in 1888 at the time of the Whitechapel Murders. A decade later, on 31 December 1898, Joseph Vacher, a serial killer dubbed 'The French Ripper', was guillotined for the horrific murders in rural France of one woman and ten teenage girls and boys. The case would doubtless have been headline news in the popular British press.)*

Now that I was 17, I found the world full of things I wanted to do. Mother suddenly announced one day that she had seen advertisements in the paper of Art Classes at the Conservatory. *(The Hampstead Conservatoire of Music & School of Art was at 62-64 Eton Avenue, Swiss Cottage; Cecil Sharp, the folk-music promoter, was its principal until 1905; it declined in the 1920s and its (1888) building became the Embassy Theatre; it is now occupied by the Royal Central School of Speech & Drama.)* We might walk down and see about them. As she spoke my inside turned right over with excitement. At last real Art Classes – not the Slade, but perhaps quite good. Life was wonderful and I walked on air beside her. The building stands back slightly and has a red brick wall along by the pavement. Steps lead up to the main door. As we approached I saw large posters on the walls and I was frozen stiff with dismay. Life Classes said the posters. Oh, perhaps mother wouldn't see.

Oh, perhaps she didn't know what life meant. I was very vague myself but I knew it was something not very nice. I didn't know until years later, when I went to the Slade, that men wore singlets. I prayed violently as we walked up the first steps. As we reached the doors at the top mother turned to me and said, "I think we will arrange singing lessons, not drawing lessons". So it had happened and my world fell to pieces. I said nothing, I couldn't agree about drawing naked people. The thought had always scared me rather. If I had made a song and dance mother would have said, "I will give you some pictures to copy when we get home; that will do just as well."

I was miserable and resentful. Mother went on to say that I might as well have the cheapest singing mistress as she would be just as good as an expensive one. I wasn't interested then. But I loved singing and was very glad later on to have had lessons, even cheap ones, as they made all the difference to me in years to come. How strange that I apparently acquiesced meekly. The power of parents in those days was terrific.

A friend of mine whom I have not yet mentioned, one of those friends that one doesn't like but one goes on being friends from circumstances or habit, was asked about this time to go out to the Black Forest to spend the winter, as companion to a German girl. She didn't want to go – she wouldn't. She was a stuffy creature, but I jumped at it and rushed home to ask permission. Mother seemed quite pleased, and there was only my father to be got round and he slowly accepted the idea. I went to bed in a trance of delight, surrounded by snow-covered Christmas trees. Next morning father suddenly announces that "Your mother and I have decided you cannot go to Germany. You might get ill there." No more to be said. Parents are so drastic.

The Band of Hope in Lisson Grove, 1903-09

I went on with my weekly piano lessons. I wasn't much good but I very much liked my music mistress, Miss Stuart. She wasn't more than a year or two older than I myself. A gay bubbling person, extremely sensitive and shy. One day she came to give me the usual lesson and she began talking about a concert she had been playing at. It had been a concert given in a slum parish in a place called Lisson Grove *(in Marylebone, near the then recently opened Great Central Railway station)*. She had never seen anything like it before. The people didn't look human. They were in rags and they sat there gnawing bones out of newspapers. The clergyman of this parish was trying to do something for these people. He was getting up these concerts but what he wanted above all was to do something for the children. He wanted someone to come and have a drilling class for the children in connection with a Band of Hope.

(One of the first responses to the problems of excessive drinking in the 1800s was the formation of temperance societies. The Band of Hope was one of the first Children's Temperance Societies to be formed and became one of the most well-known. It was established by Ann Jane Carlile and the Reverend Jabez Tunniclif in 1847 in Leeds, and

by 1889 there were over two million members in the UK. The Band of Hope spread throughout the English-speaking world. Many Bands of Hope were associated with Churches and temperance classes were often run in conjunction with Sunday School. The Band of Hope targeted children of parents who wanted their children to be educated and have a secure future. It was seen by many adults as a way to develop self-reliant working men who could use temperance as a route to self improvement. To encourage children to join and remain members, groups held annual outings, tea meetings, offered music lessons, established orchestras and produced newspapers whose content promoted temperance. Meetings began with a temperance hymn, prayers and the chairman's speech, this was followed by music, recitations, readings and pledge signing.)

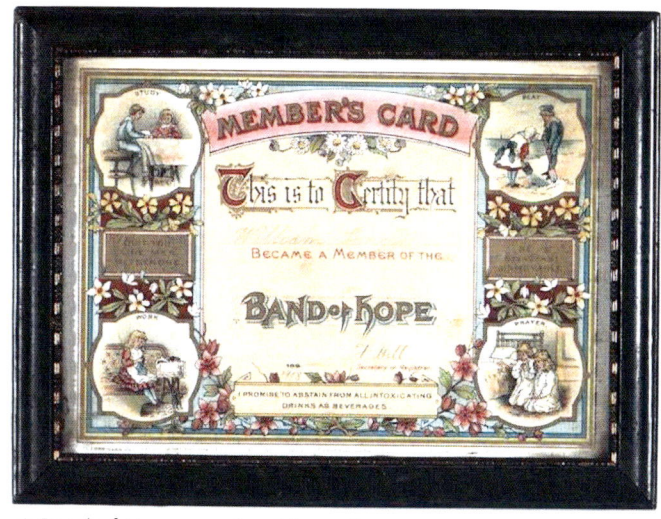

A Band of Hope membership card

Miss Stuart had at once thought of me. If I would do it, she would play the piano for me. I was appalled but interested in the idea and I went down to see this slum parish. It was all that Miss Stuart had said. It was a warren of decaying houses in the midst of well-to-do surroundings. It was the refuge of thieves and prostitutes. Later on, when I saw, it at night it was truly sinister – open shops with no fronts, benches in them, girls chopping wood, lit by great flares. Round the doorways boys lounging, waiting to get the girl's wages as soon as she had earned enough. Drunks galore, the streets filthy and ill lit.

I went down in daylight to see the deaconess of the parish. A little woman in some sort of uniform – she met me in the hall. An awkward square room with pillars supporting the room above. I put on an act as though I was perfectly at my ease and then asked her how many children I should expect. "About 100 boys and girls", she said, "under 12". I tried not to flinch but this was more than I had bargained for. And so it began. I loved those evenings and I loved the children. I never missed a Tuesday. Miss Stuart, whose piano playing was enough to make everyone lift up their heart as well as their feet, soon had enough of it. She was like that. So I got Hetty and every week through the winter we slogged down there. *(How Hetty could have been in Lisson Grove every week is a mystery, since she was at Girton College, Cambridge from 1905-8.)* Train to Baker Street and then walk; or St John's Wood by bus and then walked. We walked "plenty" in those days.

And I could do it. I could teach and I loved it. I had always loved drilling, marching time and the rhythm of one's body. The Band of Hope produced

Lisson Grove (Edwardian postcard)

a curriculum, so we had one year to have dumb bells and another barbells. It was hard to afford these and also gym shoes for the children. Miss Stuart organised a little concert in mother's drawing room and we got a little money that way. The children poured in. Any who could afford a penny were allowed in. There was always a huge mob of them waiting outside, hoping to be let in for nothing. The room was terribly crowded but I managed.

    One evening as we were walking back to the bus, I said to Hetty that I thought it absurd that the deaconess should come to sit there every time – quite unnecessary. Next week, when we got there, we found that our hall was needed for something else and so would we please go up the stairs, which came into the street and to the hall above – a wretched place. The deaconess was not anywhere about. The children all wore heavy boots. We had not enough gym shoes to let them have them except for special occasions. The noise of the boots on the floor made a terrible din in this hall. It was like a sounding board. When the children marched or ran they could not hear the piano. There wasn't room for them all to drill at once and there was nowhere for the others to sit. One or two of the bigger boys started fooling. I felt things were getting out of hand. I sent them out and they sat on the stairs banging with their feet. At last pandemonium broke out. I said to Hetty it was no good; we must stop. I told them all to go. They didn't want to, but I insisted. At last I got them out but they wouldn't budge off the dark narrow staircase. We were just ready to leave, when a boy slipped back into the room and turned out the gas. We were in complete darkness and, when we groped our way to the door, we found it was locked on the outside. The children sat on the staircase yelling songs. We were stuck. Then I thought of my whistle.

My father had given it to me and I used it occasionally for calling the children together. He had not told me it was a police whistle. I hoped that the caretaker might hear it and come. I blew and blew and blew. I wished afterwards I could have seen the happenings outside. Police came running from all directions, crowds and crowds of people thronged and pressed in the narrow street. The children on the stairs escaped as quick as they could. The sight of one policeman was enough for them, and there were four. Oh! We did feel fools when they unlocked the door and came in. And we had to come down into the street and face those crowds, who were all hoping that at least one mangled corpse would be brought out. And the police would not leave us. They walked, two of them, with us to Baker St. and then put us into a train. I have found the truest proverb that I know is "Pride comes before a fall". Inevitably if you think you are the cat's whiskers for just a little while you get a good hard slap in the face. But one must have a certain amount of pride in one's achievements or one would never do anything.

I entered a team 3 or 4 years running *(1905-09)* for the Marylebone competitions. That was our borough. It was hard on us that we were the only slum parish in that neighbourhood. At once it was noticeable. The class of child was quite different. Their hair and their physique. The first year we could only manage to supply gym shoes for the team, so the children wore white pinnies and a scarlet sash. All the other teams had gym costumes. But we won! So we were then eligible to go to the Crystal Palace, and we went. *(Massive public events organised by the Band of Hope Union included annual rallies in the Crystal Palace at Sydenham, when massed children's choirs sang excerpts from well-known oratorios. At one of their Crystal Palace rallies (1886), the Band of Hope summoned 100,000 supporters together with 3 children's*

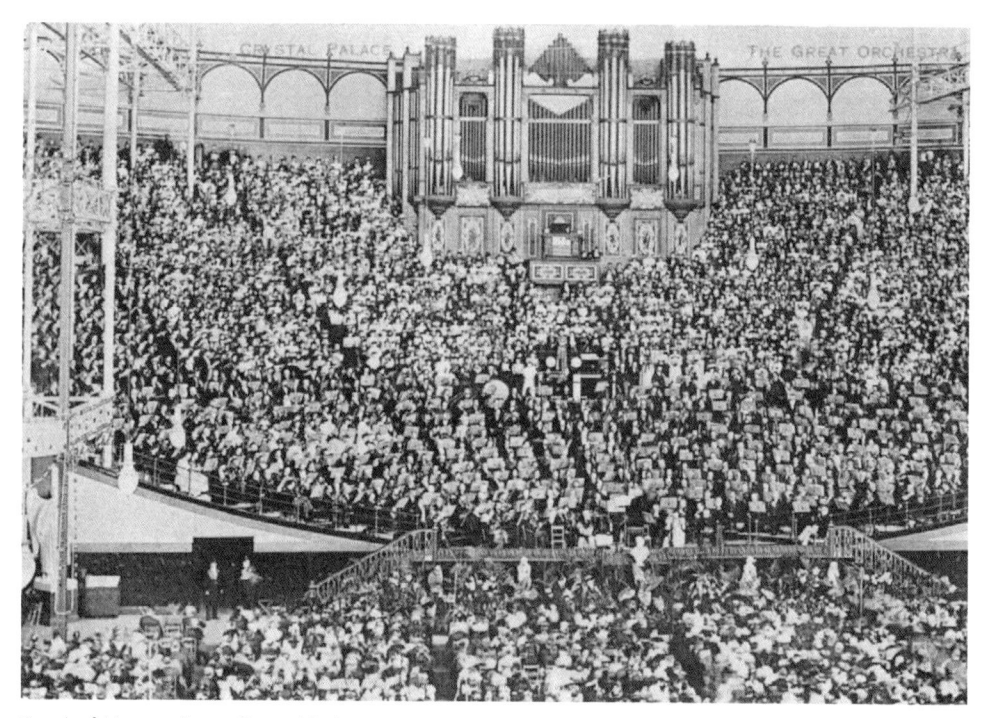

Band of Hope rally at Crystal Palace

choirs numbering 5,000.) What a day – we didn't disgrace ourselves even there. And each year we won and each year we won the Borough Competition too. Hetty stuck nobly by me and together we carried on.

The caretaker of the Lisson Grove hall was an ugly squat little man. He and his wife were very friendly to me and sometimes I would go and have a cup of hot liquid, called coffee, in their tiny parlour adjoining the hall. Their son Augustus, exactly like Father, wore on best occasions a full blown kilt, no doubt bought at Chas. Baker. For years there was a kilted dummy standing in their window *(at the north end of)* Tottenham Court Road. Did not my friend Gladys Griffith buy one for her son and take it back with her to the Middle West for her son to wear to Church? She really ought to have known better, having been brought up in Fitzjohns Avenue.

Chas. Baker & Co. advertisement

One day the old chap asked me to come into his parlour as he had acquired a new moth. That was his great hobby – butterflies, moths. His tiny room had framed specimens on every inch of the walls. One day he told me he had been a confirmed drunkard. One day a friend of his gave him some bananas. The children used to give me fried chips in newspaper as presents and sometimes a banana. Bananas often found their way into the homes of these people as some of the men worked in the docks. This special bunch of bananas had a chrysalis on it. Interested in something he had never seen before, he kept it and it hatched out into a huge beautiful moth. He set it and framed it. Soon he was always being brought chrysalids or moths from foreign parts. Life had changed for him. He gave up the booze and never touched a drop.

Nelly Dix sticks in my mind – her bright blue eyes – a drunken sodden mother. One evening a child came to me and said she had lost her purse. Then one or two started murmuring and I heard the name Nelly Dix. I liked the child and wondered what to do. So I said we'd turn all the lights out and they must all search and whoever found the purse – a little purse, not a handbag – they must put it on the floor in the middle of the room. Lights were put out and in 2 seconds I saw someone put something on the floor. It was Nelly Dix. Everyone knew that she had originally taken it but it saved her face a bit. One day some girls were talking together and one detached herself from the group and came up to me and said, "Please Miss, Gertie's farver came 'ome las' night and cut 'er muvver's throat".

I never was able to get anyone to take the class over when I left. It was very sad. A few young women, whom I thought would be suitable, said they didn't want to tie themselves. The last time I saw the children was on our wedding day, when we drove down and cut the cake we had provided.

I wrote to a godmother of mine, a very old lady, to thank her for a present. Mother said, "Tell her about Lisson Grove", so I did. I got back a letter saying that she, Mrs. Masterman, would rather hear about my going to dances and balls dressed in pretty clothes than the account I had given of going to a "frightfully poor parish." She must have sniffed signs of left wing political bias. Practically everybody we knew was conservative, until gradually mother found she must include some liberal young men, and even a Congregationalist was admitted to the house.

Entertaining: river party for my friends (?1904/05)

One of the worst efforts of the kind came when I was fairly launched and was being invited out a lot for tennis, ping pong and dances. I could feel the clouds gathering as mother murmured at intervals to my father "We must do something about all these people". Eventually it transpired that they had decided what it was to be. I was not consulted. I knew nothing about it till it was all arranged. In the days before I could remember, father had, I believe, spent a lot of his time rowing up and down the Thames. My parents therefore thought they would give a river picnic. Most of it I have forgotten. I could not think about it. After it was over, I pushed the thought of it away and did my best to forget it. Somehow we all arrived at the station. Both my parents came. My father handed out tickets to the dozen or so young people met there and I noticed then that the tickets were surreptitiously being examined

Boating party on the river Thames

and a good deal of amused comment was going on. Father had bought before the day cheap tickets for an excursion party.

We were only going a very short distance by train and most of the people in the party were accustomed to travelling 1st. Father always travelled 1st, but here we were taking these people 3rd and at excursion rates.

We arrived somewhere – Staines I think, anyway a part of the river not frequented by the gentry. I remember feeling completely detached as I stood silent on the muddy river bank, while father picked out the boats he had already chosen. This jollification, as mother called it, had made father quite busy. He had left nothing to chance. He had not only bought the railway tickets in advance, but had been to Staines to bargain with the boat men up and down the river to hire at the cheapest rate. I stood frozen while 3 rowing boats were brought to the fore, while our depressed party criticised or cursed quietly under their breath. "Good heavens, does he think we are going in rowing boats? Whatever next?" But none of them dared tell father out loud that rowing boats were not the thing – only cads went in rowing boats – cads in braces. Punts or canoes were the craft of gentlemen. I heard all their murmurs, not a thing escaped me, and I became more and more paralysed. The groans, very modified, of the young people told to go in my father's boat or in my mother's. Heavens, why couldn't father and mother go in the same boat? Anyway why had they come at all? Would the day ever be over? It did end, but not really, because it still went on at home.

"You weren't very helpful, I didn't think. People often tell me you are the life and soul of the party. I must say I didn't notice it". Then, when mother was safely out of the way, father began. "Young men like to be admired, that is, they like to feel that they know more than young women do. You should always take care not to appear cleverer than they. You didn't seem to me to be doing anything the other day to make yourself attractive."

So on and so forth, and my mother would continually harp on the wonderful meal she had provided. Poor dear: she had no idea of food and quite firmly thought that to make chicken patties with rabbit was "just as good". What an ungrateful creature I must have appeared to be. It certainly never occurred to me to say, "Thank you for the lovely picnic." But our family were not polite to one another in their home life. I think mother would have considered unnecessary politeness as "sloppy".

One other form of entertainment at that time, which I suppose was entirely suburban, was the whist drive. Mother gave one or two but I wasn't old enough to play. I merely appeared for a short time and heard about them after. For instance, I heard that the parents of my friends were there. Mother must have swallowed twice before asking them to the house. Mrs Hibbert won the first prize, but afterwards it was discovered that she could not possibly have honestly acquired all those little plays. I was covered with confusion when I heard this being discussed by the family later. To be common was no real crime, but to cheat. Oh dear!

Untidiness at Eldon Grove

Before these parties, dinner parties, etc., father would start a tidying up campaign. Mother was incredibly untidy and never seemed to notice dirt. Cushion covers might be and were grimy, small tables had confused rubbish on them, but, when father started on this clearance of the Augean stables, a furious controversy took place. Mother protesting that the house must look lived in and father retorting that it looked as if it was lived in by pigs. His final insult being to demand that mother clear out a wicker work table in the corner of the dining room next to her desk. "Will you please come and remove your dung heap?" he said. He was thoroughly enjoying himself and giggling quietly, but mother was furious simply furious - at the disgusting suggestion. I was shocked but amused. This didn't seem to me to be a very good prelude to a dinner party but it didn't seem to matter.

Holidays again

Our family summer holidays had by now come to an end. The family had broken up. Father could now go abroad accompanied by Marjory, who could now pay for herself. They went in a party generally. Marjory told me that father walked in the same way as he bicycled. He never looked to right or left. He plodded straight ahead. When he came home, he talked mostly of food but that is a usual habit of English people.

Our holidays took on a new pattern and for the next few years were very thrilling. We had one at Wellswood, when I was 15 *(1901)*, I should think. My mother took a house in Wellswood Park *(this suburb of Torquay was built by the Victorians and filled with large Italianate villas surrounded by pines and palms)*, up above Torquay towards Ansteys Cove and Babbacombe. There again we had masses of cousins and friends with us, a tremendous party. Bicycle rides, picnics, bathing at Ansteys Cove, which was a little fisherman's cove, run by Thomas who taught me, or tried, to dive. Up on his shed was painted a rhyme ending: "Thomas is the man who provides everything, and also teaches young people to swim". During that holiday, besides my cousins, I got to know other families. My aunt and my grandmother were well known there and I found many young people who were "great fun", as we said in those days.

Then we had the Val André holiday *(probably 1902)*. I had a large number of cousins and about 15 or more of us went to the Brittany coast together with mother, her sister Aunt Mary, and Aunt Constance *(Constance née Schneider, 1860-1937, wife of Stephen Hammick MA, of the Indian Civil Service)*, mother's sister-in-law *(who had five children)*. It was the gayest time.

We all had bicycles and in fact Aubrey and I rode *(348 miles)* on our own from Calais to Val André *(Pieneuf-Val-André, a seaside village in Brittany)*. We had a puncture and very little money. It was good for our French. We bathed in the sea daily and went for picnics. The blackberries were so profuse that I ate till I was sick. In the pension at night we danced. My cousin Dot and I shared the attention of a male cousin and his friend. *(Dorothea Constance Hammick was born in February 1886, the same month as Phyllis, and was the daughter of Sir Murray Hammick ICS.)* They were a little older than we and learning to be grown up. Luckily, the friend, Caledon Dolling *(b.1886 in Ireland, living in Tonbridge, Kent)* fell to my share. A very good looking boy, but I didn't really like him very much. He gave me a photo of himself when the holiday was over, unasked. I kept it about a week and then put it in the fire when I got home. My mother and the two others bickered a certain amount but enjoyed themselves.

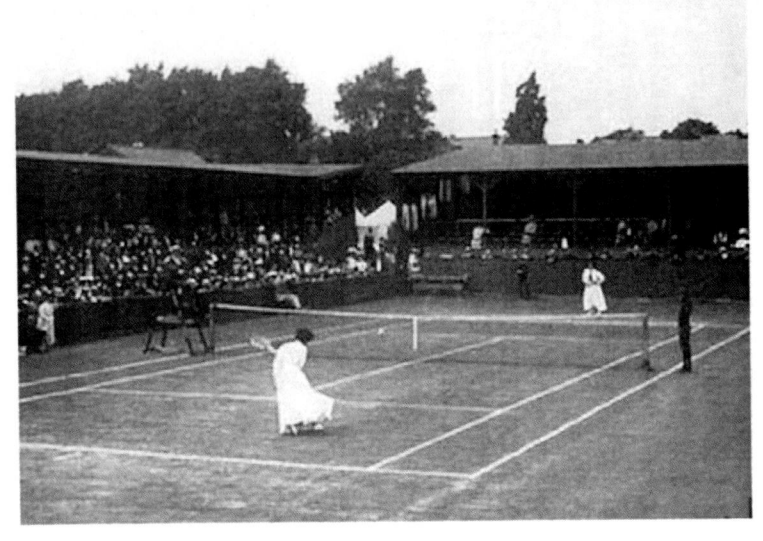

The little old Wimbledon by the railway line: final of ladies' lawn tennis singles tournament at the 1908 Olympics

Mother defended us stoutly against the criticisms of Aunt Mary, and mother in turn criticised Dot and Henry *(Henry Alexander Hammick, 1890-1968, Dot's brother)*, the two in charge of Aunt Mary. Their parents were in India and Aunt Mary brought them up. I had joined the little tennis club and enjoyed it. One day at tea Aunt Mary, who was really a dear, boasted that Dot had spent the afternoon making a blouse. Dot did wonderful needlework. Mother retorted that it seemed a silly way to spend a holiday, to sit indoors and sew, and a tense atmosphere pervaded for a short time. A small tennis tournament took place and I got into the finals. I had to play a Mrs. Cuthbert. I was having a practice game in the morning when I was suddenly smitten with pain inside. I'd had it before many times but this was bad. Since I was quite a child I had had attacks of indigestion as they were called. Mother would deal with them in varying ways. Now this time in Val André she dosed me with cascara but I had to abandon playing in the finals. As I knew I should be beaten, it didn't matter much.

(In 1903, another holiday at Torquay.) This time I was grown up – playing, and winning *(matches)* in my first proper tennis tournament and ready to go to dances. Amy *(Moorgate?)* was by now playing at Wimbledon. The little old Wimbledon by the railway line. She rather adopted me. She sent me a ticket and I felt very proud of my friend, dressed in white pique from neck to ground (1 inch

off) and a stiff man's collar and tie. She then asked me to play in the Torquay Tournament with her, which I did. She was a very good player and I was not. Some opponents soon found that out, so that I felt as if I was under fire from a machine gun, peppered and battered. But in the singles I held my own and got into the finals of the open event. I will not go on talking about tennis. To those who play it is a wonderful game. They know the exhilaration of it. It can be nothing to those who don't play. To watch can never come near the pleasure of playing.

I entered for the St. Marychurch and Babbacombe tournaments. My tennis partner, whom I was allotted, was a young man on his own in lodgings. He had a sailing boat. Against my mother's express wishes, I went out sailing with him alone and we got becalmed. Meanwhile, a much more attractive young man was playing tennis with me; he lived near me. He I approved of. There were parties, dances and then a final party for the last night of the regatta.

(This was the Torquay Royal Regatta. As well as organising top class sailing races, the event has included motor boat racing, rowing, running, water-skiing, swimming and diving. In 1847, Trewman's 'Exeter Flying Post' commented that the regatta attracted people who 'enjoy the donkey racing rather than the yacht racing'. The organising committee have always provided a range of social and recreational facilities for 'landlubbers' with a grand ball (since 1813), firework displays (since 1836), and funfairs (since 1841).)

Oh, the regatta! That was a terrible blow to me. Three of my best young men friends asked me to go out sailing with them to watch the regatta. Safety in numbers, mother felt, so I was allowed to go. It was a thoroughly choppy sea. We started out from Torquay quay. It soon became obvious that I was going to be sick and I was. I heard them say we'd better take her back, and they did. They landed me at the harbour. I never pass that seat without remembering the chagrin of that morning. Alone I sat and cursed my luck. But the evening made up for it. About a dozen of us went to the Regatta fair. The three of the sailing boat were most attentive. We went on horses and some went on swings. The noise and glamour of the fair were something I had never experienced before, and with several young men paying attention to me I was in seventh heaven.

I was very careful about not going on swings and only going on the roundabout with long pauses in between – I mustn't be sick again. I sat on a horse which went up and down and round; on the head sat one young man and on the rump another, and another on the next horse. I don't remember much about the rest of the party. We walked home in a bunch up the steep hill. All very happy, all talking our heads off, nothing taken but lemonade. We dawdled about and took ages to say good night and at 1 o'clock I was delivered at my door. Mother always sat up for anyone who was out. She sat up for me – I arrived in a state of blissful content to be greeted by a torrent of questions. What had I been doing? Where had I been? She seemed unbalanced. I could answer quite truthfully this time and at last I got to bed. A double bed which I had to share with mother, a thing I hated. I went bang off to sleep – one was never allowed to sleep on in our household. If

I was up to 5 a.m. dancing, I was called next morning and expected to be down at 8 a.m. for prayers. So I was awake when mother was doing her hair, with her back to me. She was looking in the glass but addressing me. A long, long preamble and then a sort of gypsy's warning, all muffled up and camouflaged like a doctor trying to tell a patient he has an incurable disease. Words and words.

At first, I didn't take much notice – vague hints about the dangers of staying out late at night. Then a description of what she had gone through and suffered the night before. Then, "You remember those two pretty twins who we saw here last year; they both had to be put away". Now, that I couldn't understand. Why were they put away? Had they been put in a lunatic asylum? My mind just touched on the possibility that they might have had babies, but I had been brought up never to think of such things. Thinking about those things was a sin. How often had we been told so? So I never seriously got down and considered these things. I wouldn't have dared. I never visualised what marriage was. I knew it was something indecent, that was all. I became very, very angry at mother's rigmarole. What was she hinting? Obviously she thought I was capable of some gross indecency with the men, nice clean young men I had gone out with. I grew very hot under the bedclothes but said nothing. That was very awkward. Mother must have suffered as, looking back, I think she thought that was a usual habit of the young.

One day on that thrilling holiday, I stretched my arms in the air and said, "Oh I'm happy, happy, happy." "This isn't happiness," said my mother. At such times, I literally hated my mother. "It is just that you feel you are a success." Very true, but it's a very nice feeling and one doesn't often get it in this wicked world. It brought its troubles too. I could not make up my mind or, in other words, I was not in love with anyone. I just loved any admiration I got; lapped it up but was very critical of the admirers. I found mother's attitude to young men was that if they were not in a position to marry, that is hadn't a fixed income, they were safe, as they would not propose.

It seemed the Victorian idea was that you should accept the first man who proposed, if he could keep you and if he was not infirm. I was quite determined to marry but not for the sake of marrying. Looking back, I can understand mother's worry and agitation. Mother had one daughter *(Marjory)* who, so far, had shown no signs of getting married. No one had asked her. (She had a chance later on but turned it down.) Her other daughter, who had no looks, and never had any money, turned down eligible admirers.

Health, again

At that time, life was very full of a great many new and thrilling things. But one thing which was a great hardship to me was my health. I think my parents were genuinely worried and I was dragged around to doctors. Now I would be taken to see some man about my headaches, then another about my attacks of indigestion. They none of them had anything to recommend beyond the "Let her take plenty of outdoor exercise". One more modern fashionable one said, "Let her go for motor car drives regularly". That annoyed mother, who retorted I could go on the top of a tram but she had not a motor car. Another one suggested Turkish baths; and mother got it all muddled up and so, when I had my next grumbling pains in my right side, she said, "The doctor recommended a Turkish bath. You had better go and have one." The Turkish bath had been for my headaches, not my internal pains. Mother said she would come too. She said the nearest one was Camden Town and the cheapest I am sure. *(Probably the Savoy Turkish Baths at 11a Kentish Town Road, which had a plunge pool and hot rooms facing Camden High Street; by 1914 they had closed.)*

After lunch we started forth. We walked to the George *(near the top of Haverstock Hill)*. The pain was getting rather bad. I described it as a knife turning round inside. We got a bus to Camden Town. We found the baths, which looked like slum lodgings. Dreadful. The woman in charge was also dreadful. Mother very nobly said she would have one too. She must have loathed it worse than I. I heard her say in a horrified whisper to the woman, "Must I take my clothes off?" The heat and the sitting were quite a relief to me but then came the rubbing. The pain was acute but I didn't say anything. After this drubbing, we lay in grey blankets, that made me feel sick, on divans. That was a relief. After about an hour, mother said we had better dress and go, and we had better walk instead of going by bus as I might catch a chill. I still remember every step of that walk. That evening the doctor was brought in. He never said anything before me.

This time was the first that I had been kept in bed by my pain. I had about 10 days of it. I was at the top of the house with no bell. I was allowed to eat almost nothing. I had to lie flat. I had no visitors. I don't know why, and I saw no one except mother who never sat down. She would rush into the room with a piece of blancmange or a cold cup of tea saying, "A nice cup of tea for you," and out again. One day in a rage, I said, "Why do you say it's a *nice* cup of tea? It's always stone cold!" One night mother found what she called father's hot water bag. *(Rubber hot water bottles had been invented only in 1903; previously they were ceramic.)* The only hot water bottle in the house. She brought it up and put it in my bed. At about 2 a.m. I woke. I was lying in a pond. I was not allowed to move. I banged the wall. The servants did not hear, so I lay until mother came up at breakfast time. "Oh dear," she said, "I *thought* the washer had gone."

I lay on the bed worrying over one thing. Would I be well enough to go to a dance at the town hall in a week's time? I asked the doctor. "Oh yes", he assured me. The silly fool. After a few days in bed I thought I might find my legs a bit weak, so when I was alone, I used to make myself get out of bed and do dance steps round the room. I felt very wobbly. Of course, on the day before the dance, the doctor said I would not be able to go, which was not a surprise to me, but a great disappointment. All my best partners would be there – oh misery. After that I would get attacks at intervals of 5 or 6 months and go to bed. The despair when I felt the pain – another bout of solitary confinement, missing everything.

One doctor had said I must play hockey. That was for headaches. The internal pain had not been mentioned. So mother approached a young woman who very kindly said I could play with a mixed club. This club included the May brothers and all the society young women of the neighbourhood, all years older than I. I knew nothing about hockey and I don't think I'd ever seen it played. I was given one of the boys' sticks and went off with the crowd to some country house. One thing which sticks in my mind was the absurdity of women's prudishness. The women were put in a large bedroom to change their skirts. I heard a lot of giggling. They wanted to go to the lavatory but didn't dare go and look for it! They then decided to use the one jerry under the bed. When it came to my turn I was nervous and couldn't do it, though I was dying to. I spent an agonising afternoon. I found hockey a damp cold game and I didn't know what to do, so I moved away when the ball came near me. On my way home in the cold train the pain in my side began. I never played hockey again.

Coming out dance (1903) and other dances

It was a New Year's party, my coming out dance. I enjoyed it enormously. It had few incidents. It was at the Wharncliffe Rooms and it was given by an Uncle and Aunt of my friends, the Hibberts. *(The Wharncliffe Rooms were the ballroom of the Great Central Hotel at Marylebone; opened in 1899, they were a fashionable venue.)* I didn't really look forward to it, but then I never do. Any party is still an agony, more or less to me, until I am in it and fairly launched. Arriving is always painful. This coming out dance was alarming. I had been invited and Mother had discussed it with Marjory, with my opinion not being asked, and it was at last decided that I should be allowed to accept. All I knew was that Mother highly disapproved of the whole thing, but as father would never afford a dance for me, and they never had for my sister, they must take what was offered. I had a white satin dress made for me by the dressmaker and I felt very indecent and thought it was terribly low, but didn't dare say so.

G. *(Georgina)* Hibbert, two years my senior, was also coming out. I think both she and I did together. They had white Japanese silk dresses, about the cheapest material one could buy, made by Jane, their nanny! Mother was very scornful and rightly so. That woman had clothed those four girls according to her own taste for years, making everything herself, and when they grew up she persisted. Then at last she left. None of the girls had ever brushed their own hair. [Jane cropped up again in my life later on. When she left the Hibberts, she went to India. Then she took a place in Epsom with some friends of hers who had two babies under 3, I think. She had sole charge – the parents were not interested, but the mother did object when she found the boy of 2 tied to the nursery table. In those days they had no play pens and Jane was old – too old to be looking after babies and I gather getting no sleep. The mother told me the little boy was given sleeping draughts. I didn't know. Jane's days of glory were passed, when she ruled

The Great Central Hotel, Marylebone

the nursery and the mistress at the Hibberts had had two sisters and 3 maids also working in the house.]

The Wharncliffe Rooms seemed to me like a fairy palace. I had been about very little. I had never had a meal in a hotel, much less stayed in one, when I was 17. It was so glamorous, so opulent looking. [I have been there since those days and either I or the Wharncliffe Rooms have changed. A scruffy looking place, I thought.] I had great luck at that first dance of mine. So many women have told me that their first dance was a flop. Such a fuss and to-do about it and then no fairy prince. Either boys their own age, or younger or old men. By old men I suppose I mean over 20. I went to the dance with the Hibberts. They had several four wheelers and I stood with the girls, nervous in my long white gloves and low cut neck; and a man, looking fair, clean and tall was brought up and introduced, and we danced practically the whole evening together. I liked him so much and he liked me, and I never saw him again, but I can still thank him in my heart for making my first dance such a happy success. He apparently knew as few people as I did. The Hibberts' boys, them I knew, but nobody else and I certainly remember only this young man. I feel though that I cannot have danced with him all the evening. If I had I would have been ticked off by someone and told I was "fast". But the evening afterwards I was told by Jane, the Hibberts' nurse, that my young man, whose name I don't think I ever knew, was working to be called to the Bar and that he had a great future before him. One and all, the grown up lookers-on were impressed and, I have no doubt, very surprised, that I had got off so well at my first dance. The young man and I were going in to supper together and I said that this was my first dance. He was taken aback. I stood still, apologising. He hadn't known; wouldn't I rather go in to supper with someone else and I said, no, I don't know anyone here and he was nicer than ever after that. Then we had champagne, gallons of it, and a marvellous sit-down supper at a huge long table, and at midnight we all stood in one chain and linked arms and sang Auld Lang Syne, and I climbed onto the table. But it was all fun and, even next day, no one ticked me off and so I can't have behaved too badly, but mother suddenly said that she had meant to warn me before the dance about drinking champagne. That I must be careful not to drink too much. "You're telling me", I thought, or the equivalent in the correct language of my time.

That dance was the first of innumerable others. I didn't go to as many as my rich friends did but I had enough to keep me going. At first they were all private ones, very often in people's houses, sometimes dancing on a stretched covering over the drawing room carpet, but subscription dances were just beginning to come in. At those, usual practice was for a hostess to invite a large party of young people to her house, give them dinner and send them on to the dancehall *(often in a hotel)*. Dances were therefore socially exciting. One did not know who one was going to meet and invariably met at least half a dozen new people during the evening. Naturally, not all one's partners were superb dancers but that had to be put up with. If they couldn't dance, perhaps they could talk, and anyway one only had to have one dance with them.

The programme was a sure defence. If an attractive looking young man was introduced, one probably launched him one's programme and hoped he would take several dances. If a 'weary Willy' type was brought up, one coyly said "I have number 3 free." "Oh thank you," he would reply and take it. You had not mentioned that you had number 3 and a dozen others free. Booking up was quite a science. The most important dance was supper. I would be a little anxious until it was gone. I didn't mind not being booked right up at the start, as it was possible that a new person might want another dance. What I liked to happen was to be introduced to a stranger. Possibly the stranger had asked to be introduced. He might have gone up to a friend and said, "Who's that tall girl in deep red? I wish you'd introduce me, old chap." He would then, if he was a good dancer and a man who knew his way about, take only one dance right at the beginning. He would find I was a good dancer and, when we sat out, I could make him laugh – at least I could talk. He would then take his programme out of his waistcoat pocket and say, "I wonder could you spare me another dance?" and I would hand him my programme. Possibly only one blank on it, but he would take any blanks there were. That meant a really successful evening for me. On the other hand, if he turned out to be uninteresting, one kept one's programme firmly out of sight, or brought it out and pretended to look it through, and said "I'm so sorry". But it was a tricky business, because if by chance you didn't get booked the only thing to do was to sit in the ladies cloakroom. The whole set up has gone now. I think it was Rose

Macaulay who really railed against it as an out and out marriage market. So it was, no doubt a very successful one, and also extremely enjoyable if one happened to be a success in a ballroom.

I had one terrible dance, all owing to my brother, Bernard. It was the only dance I went to when I failed to get a partner for every dance. It was all his fault. He would not dress in time. He was home on leave from the Navy. I called up the stairs I don't know how often. I was really in despair because at those suburban dances every one turned up early and started booking up their programmes. It was no good. He didn't see the urgency. He was accustomed to arriving at "hops", as he called them, hours late. He was such a dear, but I could have murdered him that night. We, or I, practically ran to the dance in the drill hall *(in Holly Bush Vale)* when he was at last ready. Just as I thought, everyone was booked up. Annoyed young men came up to me when they had stopped dancing. "Why are you so late?" "I'm quite booked up. I've kept one for you. We all thought you couldn't be coming." I merely said Bernard had been delayed and then sat down to the only dance, before I was married, that I really hated. The family joke was that every dance I went to was the most heavenly dance I had ever been to, and I meant it.

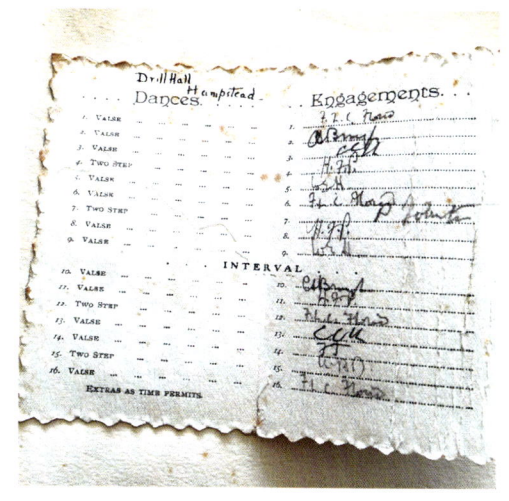

Programme for a dance at Hampstead Drill Hall

A few duds, who couldn't fill their cards, asked me to dance and I did. I went round the room with them but, what was truly unfortunate, was that at this dance was a man who wanted to marry me. He had proposed about half a dozen times and I had refused him. I never danced more than one with him at any dance and generally managed to avoid that, but this evening I was sunk. Each time the dancing began he made a bee line for me. I hadn't the face to try to book everything beforehand and, as I saw I should have to dance with him again and no help was forthcoming, I rose from my seat and quietly slipped away to the ladies' – and there I spent most of my evening, and there I listened to the dance music, and there I gnashed my teeth. The odd thing is I don't remember dancing with my brother. Bernard was duly sorry and apologised to me, but that couldn't make up for that ghastly evening. When we got home, mother as usual was sitting up for us. I said nothing of the miserable time I had had – but Bernard said, "Look here, mother. You'll have to push that fellow Weaver through the window, he did nothing but pester Phyl all the time." Mother, who was firmly hoping that I would relent and accept, was rather put out.

[There is a "continued in our next" to that episode. It was many years later. My husband and I drove to see our elder boy at school *(Peter Castle Floud, 1911-60)*.

It was speech day. As we got out of our car, our son greeted us and another boy spoke to him and then walked off. He was an odd looking youth, plain and odd. Who's that queer looking boy, I asked? I was taken aback when he said "That's Weaver." I know that the Weaver I knew had married a very nice wife whom I knew. A good deal older than myself, and I had heard vaguely that a son was at this school, but I'd forgotten. Then my son added with a tone of mixed contempt and peculiarity, "But have you seen his father?" How cruel the young can be. Really he wasn't as bad as all that. He was very kind and very healthy. I suddenly felt indignantly anxious to stand up for my old suitor and then to say, "Well, he might have been your father". But I held my peace. And my husband had a good laugh over it.]

Then that terrible evening with the Johnstons. A family of 3 sons and one daughter. The parents common, but nice, with a large house and garden and tennis court. Marjory was a little older than all of them, but I younger. I had played tennis with the sons a lot. Marjory made the usual fuss before we started, and I said she didn't want to go. Why on earth she went I couldn't make out. It spoilt the evening for me, and she was miserable, so why go? Arriving at the Johnstons' house, I was in the bedroom changing my shoes. We walked to all dances if we went on our own. A young woman a little older than myself was chatting to a friend. The friend said, "Aren't your sisters here?" and the girl answered, "Oh no – they're too old now for the Master Johnstons. They used to be asked but now it's my turn." How awful, I thought, Marjory will be much too old. We were having dinner. I was next to papa Johnston, a city man who tried to be funny. On this occasion I think he must have had too much to drink. "Whatever are you doing here?" he asked Marjory brutally, "I suppose you are going to be a wallflower?" Marjory blushed scarlet and for once was so discomposed she could not find a cutting retort. As we got ready to drive on to the dance, she whispered to me, "Did you hear what that brute said? He must have been drunk." But he was only too right and there she sat, a wallflower, most of the evening.

Mother came to a dance at the *(Hampstead)* Town Hall, not as a chaperone, but as a guest. Chaperones had practically gone when I came out, and I rarely had one. It was a very large dance and one room was arranged for whist. Mother's comment on the dance the next day surprised me. She said she had seen no signs of flirting. People sat round the room. There seemed to be no cosy sitting-out nookerys *(sic)* and, above all, none of the girls "flirted their fans". In Mother's day fans were used very skilfully, girls making eyes over the tops of them. I thought it all sounded very silly. Fans, and long white gloves, were on the way out in my day and in fact had nearly died the death by the time I was married. Long white gowns were still considered absolutely essential.

The son of our friend was one of my best partners. He was thin and little and with a beautiful face, so sad that he was asked by the artist to pose for the painting he did – one Chantry Bequest picture now in the Tate called 'Sentence'. A picture of a young man being told by a doctor he had only 2 weeks or months to live. The sort of picture everyone loved in those days, I adored them. 'Too Late' *(Windus)*.

I haven't seen it for years but a young lady (who looked to me old) staggering along in a garden, obviously just about to die and a gent in a top hat, coming over a stile to the rescue, but too late. 'The last day in the old home' *(Martineau)*. 'His first offence' – a pathetic little boy in the dock.

[Years later I was in the Tate. I was going to see the French pictures etc., which always delight me, and I was nearly swept off my feet by a crash tour. They swarmed though the gallery in close formation at great speed led by a conductor. They looked not to right nor left. I, intrigued, tagged on with them. The conductor made a bee line for the Chantry Bequest pictures and then suddenly came to an abrupt halt in front of a smallish picture. It was of a little girl sitting on a staircase crying – a well dressed little girl in very pitiable surroundings, and sitting on the stairs beside her was a bull terrier licking her face. The picture is called 'Sympathy'. The conductor stopped, the following mob all breathing hard after their chase also abruptly stopped and the conductor said, "To my mind there is only one picture worth looking at in this Gallery. This one. Pause. But then I always was partial to dogs. Now let's get a move on."]

My mother went with Hetty and me to Woolwich for a regimental ball there. Hetty had a cousin there and I also, but my cousin was a white rabbit of a creature with

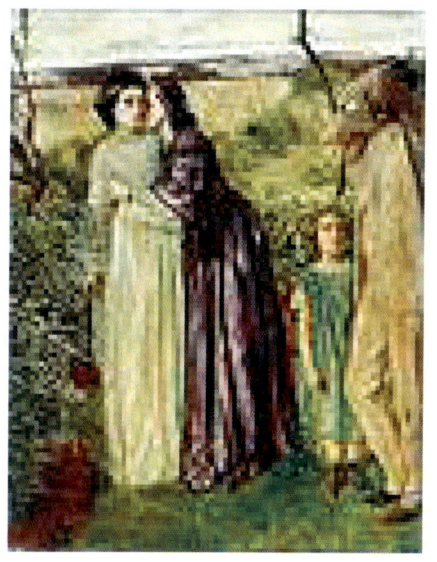

Too Late, by William Lindsay Windus, 1858

The Last Day in the Old Home, by Robert Braithwaite Martineau, 1862

whom I would have been ashamed to have been seen walking down the street. But an invitation to the *(ball?)* at Woolwich did not come every day and Hetty's mother was very keen that Hetty should go. To stay the night at Woolwich would have been the reasonable thing to do, but expensive. So mother had the idea of coming home by the milk train which we did, 5 a.m. I think. I have little recollection of the dance except that my hair would flop over my face and that mother sat wrestling to keep awake, not very successfully. My mother was given to falling asleep anywhere and any when. But Hetty swears that I never danced with my cousin. I don't remember, but if I didn't, I say it was his fault. Hetty says her cousin, a very nice young man, and his friends, crowded round us and were introduced, and our programmes were filled before the white rabbit got a chance. I know it was a dazzling affair, only marred by my hair, which didn't really matter, and we went home on the milk train and that same afternoon had a friendly game of hockey with Hetty's cousins and friends. I felt iller and iller, as I lopped about on a wet and chilly field and was down with a pain that night.

(On another occasion) I had been asked to join a party to the Wharncliffe Rooms to dance. The horse bus went round picking us up and, when all were collected and we were on our way to the Central Hotel, one young lady suddenly discovered she had two left gloves. Nothing would do but she must go back and get the right glove. We all raged inwardly and some said it was appalling but, on the whole, it was considered best to go back, although it made us late. I rather think that young lady never forgot that dance, as when we returned in the early morning hours, she was engaged to be married.

Programmes persisted and I think that when they went, the dance as a social event went too. The advantage of the programme was manifest. You could avoid unwanted partners and it gave you a sense of security. But they went when the new idea took over that a girl could ask a man to go to a dance with her, to form a party and then that the two should go to a dance together alone and dance together all the evening. That came in after my day and I think it must have been a great come-down after the thrilling parties I went to, when very possibly not all one's partners were good dancers, but there was variety and the interest of meeting new people and the pleasure of conversation.

To go back to my sister *(Marjory)*. The same people as gave that Town Hall dance gave a very small dance in their drawing room one night. The young man, Gerald, was two years older than I, but his two sisters must have been about the same age as my sister. One of them we always considered "fast". She liked to be modern and at this little dance she decided there should be no programmes. Everybody thought this rather smart. Halfway through I heard one of the sisters go up to old Mrs X, who sat there like a fat old market woman, and say, "You must do something, mother. She's been stuck with that old man for hours." I had a horrid feeling inside. Up to then I hadn't bothered about Marjory, I had been enjoying myself too much, and then I remembered seeing her sitting somewhere with a bearded "old" man, probably aged 40. A rescue party was arranged. 'The Lancers' was to be the next dance and every light was to be put out. Men on one side of the room, girls on the other. In the dark they were to choose their partners and dance one figure, also in the dark. I had got my sister's "beau", but it got her a dance, 'The Lancers' didn't really matter, as one met so many others. (After the lights went up I heard the fast daughter telling a friend that some man had put his hand into her bosom – screams of laughter.) How my sister "carried on", poor dear, about the dreadful men in the world! She was heading straight for the suffragettes.

Longman dinner

I was invited to a dinner in London by some relations of my mother. *(Rachel's brother Rear-Admiral Robert Frederick Hammick married Grace Longman, whose father, William Longman with his brother, Thomas, ran Longmans Publishers)*. I did not know at all what I was in for and I went in the usual trepidation. It turned out to be a dinner for girls, or young women, given by a young woman of about 23, I suppose. She had a nervous outward manner and I should think brains. As we sat at dinner, I thought that this girl's mother must have been in despair and decided on this form of entertainment so as to kill off a large number of girls without having to supply men. Mother then wisely withdrew to a restaurant and left her daughter to it. The young woman on my left asked me "Are you up for the Season?" I longed to say I was, but felt forced to admit that, "No, I live in Hampstead". Suburban! Labelled at once! All the others at the large dinner table were "Up for the Season". Conversation was spasmodic and patchy. I was sorry for our hostess. I felt very out of it all. Then some of them started talking about cooking classes they were going to. And chiefly about learning to skin a rabbit.

I couldn't even join in this as I had never cooked anything in my life. But I suddenly thought I had an opportunity. I never could keep quiet for long, not in those days. "Why do you want to learn to skin a rabbit?" I asked." They will always do it at the shop for you. I know Sainsbury's will." Complete silence round the table then I realised. These people didn't *buy* rabbits, they shot them on their estates. Suburban again. I had made them feel awkward. Now sit still, and for heaven's sake keep your mouth shut. Prolonged silence does not suit my temperament, but I did not open my mouth again. None of the young people there were unkind or snobbish. They just didn't know what to make of me as I so obviously didn't belong. The dinner ended. Our hostess, trying to be bright, pretended to smoke a cigarette with empty fingers. No cigarettes appeared, naturally. It was considered fast of a woman to smoke. We got up to go out of the room. Let's go out in couples, she said, and the men can all smoke. I give them permission. We went out arm in arm, some of the girls going through the motions of smoking. Silly fools, I thought. I was sulking. What an evening. Heavens, would it never end? Coffee in the drawing room, and then, "A lady is now here who will teach us some dancing" – Miss Marelli. Her pianist sat down and played a few chords. Miss Marelli started to work. She was an accomplished teacher and soon we were hard at it. Various steps, and then a concentration on the dance. All my sulks were gone and I was in seventh heaven, dancing with energy and delight, surprised to see how the others were. Surely these girls had all learnt dancing. If not, why not? They weren't short of money, but perhaps there weren't dancing mistresses in the country. Perhaps that was it. I did not realise then how essential it was to have a sense of rhythm and an ear for music. We had not been going for long, when the teacher called out, "Take your partners for the Waltz." Oh Lord, I thought. But before I could move she had come up to me and said "Will you be my partner?" All my woe was forgotten. She would stop every now and then and call out to the others to watch and she and I alone glided round the room. So it went on. "Where did you learn your dancing?" she asked. "I really haven't learnt much", I said. I had a few lessons with a Miss Valol. She must be a good teacher, she said. No more but enough. All the evening I was her partner. Occasionally she stopped and took on someone who was in difficulties but not for long. She then would call on me to demonstrate a step. The evening ended with a most violent Highland Scottish and I was soaked through the heat. I went onto the balcony, where it was cold, with the others and we drank lemonade.

Next day I was in bed with tonsillitis. Up, down, up! Such was life. Our friends on the whole were not wildly intelligent people. Just medium. As a family we considered ourselves second to none but we would never have thought of ourselves as intellectuals. To be an intellectual would be wrong. People mustn't be too clever: that made everyone uncomfortable. Then into our midst came a really brilliant family and they were all so odd that they were a never ending sources of entertainment to their neighbours. I met them at a dance at the Town Hall.

The Garnetts

Two very tall men, fine figures, plain faces but very striking looking. The elder one *(James Clerk Maxwell Garnett, 1880-1945)*, aged about 24, dark, and the second one *(William H S, 1882-1962)* fair. There was a younger one still *(Kenneth G, b.1893)*. A few days later to my surprise and confusion, Nelly *(May)* drove up in her dog cart to our humble abode. She looked very smart, perched up there with her groom. I was worried; what did she want? She had never before descended upon us in this way and I saw very little of her now we were grown up. At tennis parties at her house, we had little to do with one another, as she didn't play. She was announced and came fluttering into the room, the dining room as it was morning, and at present there was no fire in the drawing room. She mustn't stay a minute, but would I come with her to a small dance at her dear friends, the Garnetts? I was delighted and ran off to ask mother's permission. Yes, I could go. Neither she nor I knew at that time that the new comers were great supporters of the Congregational Church. As Nelly fluttered out she whispered to me in a very meaning way, "Wear your red dress", and with a simper she was gone. That was how I got to know this strange family.

(Dr William Garnett, 1850-1932, was a professor and educational adviser (to the LCC), specialising in maths and physics and with a particular interest in electric street lighting. He had previously lived in Hampstead at 3 Foley Avenue (Well Walk) and 50 Downshire Hill, and was later to live at 31 Willow Road; but by 1903 he was installed with his family in Redington Road.)

My red dress had done the trick apparently; they called me the 'red glass girl' because the silk looked just like a ruby glass. Mother *(Rebecca, née Samways)* a pretty, dainty, 'butterfly' woman, always wearing flowing drapettes and veils and very feminine, had fine delicate features and beautiful hands – this little woman ruled the family. She had a great eye for artistic furnishing and also for business. They had bought, or I don't know which, a new house on the Heath. *(The house at 66 Redington Road – near to the West Heath and to the Mays, and named 'The Wabe' – was designed and built for the Garnetts in 1902/03, in an eclectic mixture of styles, including Arts & Crafts, Art Nouveau and Scottish Baronial. The house's name was inspired by Lewis Carroll's poem 'Jabberwocky': "'Twas brillig, and the slithy toves did gyre and gimble in the wabe..."). In 1913 Dr Garnett sold the house to industrialist Harold Ellis and his suffragist wife Mina Benson Hubbard, the Canadian explorer; their guests at The Wabe included Emmeline Pankhurst, G B Shaw, Kipling and H G Wells. More recent occupants have been actor Tom Conti and footballer Thierry Henry.)*

I went to the Garnetts' with Nelly *(May)*, who for some strange reason had become greatly attached to this new family. This first dance was typical of many parties I went to there. There was an assembly of all classes. None of them people I knew. They were all dressed anyhow. The rugs in the seven-sided drawing room had been removed. Everyone was introduced by the sons and the two daughters *(Hilda, 1884-1968 and Dorothy, 1887-1956)*. Two moon-faced (only very red moons) young women, almost identical. They spoke with lisps and were not at all brainy. They were intense and made my spine creep. At the piano sat a miserable looking little man. It turned out he was an organist and he wanted to make a little money, so had put an advertisement in the local paper. Armed with an old book of dance music, he had come to play. Poor little man, it was so bad. No time, no rhythm, no tune. At last Mrs Garnett thrust him off his seat and sat there thumping a polka. That suited the family down to the ground. They had no idea of music. They could none of them dance, but they liked to bounce around, holding their partners at arms length. When they had had enough of that, everyone subsided on the floor and the elder sister, who had taken her glasses off for the occasion, and was therefore as blind as a bat, groped her way and stood at the end of the room. She was dressed in a Kate Greenaway sort of dress and had a blue ribbon in her curly hair and wore tiny mittens. She lisped as she talked. She would recite a poem. It was called a "Twagedy". She then lisped through two verses about a little girl who had "pwicked" herself with a pin. It was so unexpected it was quite effective. And she looked so childishly demure. In the midst of the party, father came home from work.

He was a very tall man with a beard and he walked with his head thrown back. He was also almost blind. *(Dr Garnett was later forced to retire through deafness.)* He came in, taking no notice of anyone. He wandered into the kitchen. We might all have been flies on the wall. He brought out a small tray of bread and jam and a glass of milk. He sat down at the nearest table, ate his supper and retired. The family dragged us out of the corners and made us play games. Very childish games, we all felt except them: 'pass in the corner' was one. They were determined simple lifers, but at the same time, having a tennis court, they liked to go the entertainments that other people gave. So they gave dances and tennis parties. Their dances were odd but their tennis parties were odder. Mrs Garnett arranged the fours with a view to matrimony. Dear Miss So and So, you must play with Mr So and So, you will find him so interesting. His mother has a most remarkable collection of seaweed. He himself is in a very good position. Oh, the others are waiting. The tennis didn't count. The grass was long and the side netting very holey, so that long, very long intervals were spent in looking for balls. The day I arrived I heard an altercation going on between Mrs G and her youngest son. He in a furious voice, "But we can't play with only 4 balls mother". She, "Well how many do you want then?"."We must have six." Well, ring up Barnes – a shop 2 miles away and tell them to send up 2 tennis balls. *(John Barnes' department store near Finchley Road Station was actually just over one mile away.)* When I got into the garden, I found everyone searching for one of the 4 which had now disappeared. The 3 remaining ones were black and sodden. Mrs Garnett dominated, but was not very tactful, in the conversation.She was most kind hearted but tactless. A little man came hopping into the drawing room on a crutch. "Let me introduce you to my poor cripple friend", she said to everyone and he hopped round the room after her. Nelly's sister was engaged to a very handsome man. They were invited to dinner by the Garnetts. This is how they were introduced by Mrs G: "This is my dear friend Lottie May. She is engaged to be married to Mr Lamaison, but they will not be married for a long while as his prospects are very poor!"

In introducing, she gave a life history of each person, though generally unrecognisable to the people themselves. The Garnett family went to the Congregational Church. If mother had been asked to call in the normal way, she would not have done so, but Nelly's method of whisking me off there had done the trick and I found them a most interesting crowd of people. [Many of them became famous - but many more of them were swept off the earth by the First World War. Thank heaven none of us knew what was coming. Nearly all the young men I knew were killed.]

Thoughts on importance of marrying young

When I said to her very firmly, "I'm not going to marry until I am in love," mother was indignant. What silly nonsense (that was a very usual expression of hers). Do you expect a fairy prince on a white horse to come along and ask you to marry him? Do you think I was in love with your father when I married him? (No I am sure you weren't, I thought). No, said mother, I honoured and esteemed him but love did not come till later. (no, never, I thought). At that age *(in 1906)*, I was twenty. I was quite sure of my own rightness; now looking back I am not sure. My mother knew then what I know now, that marriage is essential to every normal woman. That no profession takes its place. Also that the longer a woman delays getting married, the fewer chances will she have, and the more she feels this, the more unattractive does she become. She tries desperately to get a husband and the more desperate she is, the less likely is she to get one. It is no doubt a Victorian point of view, but I still believe it persists amongst most women, though they would not own to it.

In England there are so many unmarried women. During the war (*WW1*) a Belgian lady came to stay with us. She was working in the Censor's Office at Liverpool. She was very interested in her colleagues and she was so surprised to find the office full of spinsters, none of them, or rather few of them, ugly. In her country, she said, every woman married unless she was downright ugly or impossible. But really the spinsters in Belgium wouldn't be noticeable because they would be in convents. There must be a pretty large number of them. What I hate is to see the gradually diminishing attraction of a girl reaching the age of about 23. Like a flower at 17. One reason in our class for the extra female population is that they don't get going on getting married early enough. Village girls looked very young and frequently married at 17. Their marriages turn out well. I know that their environment helps that. They have a family young, so what a blessing that is. The right age for having children is before 25. In our class, continued education and going to the university certainly used to be an obstacle to marriage. It should not be, because a woman who goes to the university is able to mix with quantities of men. I am very muddled about the whole thing. The only strong definite point in my mind is that girls should all marry.

A girl I knew had her engagement broken off by the man. An elderly lady, trying to cheer her up, said, "My dear, it is probably all for the best. So much better to find out before marriage and avoid a tragedy." "I'd much rather have had a tragedy", said the girl, "than just nothing". The years from 17 to 23 slip by, and the girl has little feeling of urgency. She has a good time. She may possibly not bother to bring a young man up to the point of proposing. She slides along with Tom, Dick and Harry, all attached by very slender strings, until she finds they have all gently slipped away and left her.

As all women and all men in this world are different, it is impossible to generalise. Life with everything, that is with a good husband, with beloved children, life without poverty and with moderate good health, is difficult enough, at least so I have found. But how does the lonely spinster come through at all? Sometimes they have an invalid mother to whom they are attached. But how do they go on day by day and year by year? It simply isn't fair. It is a terrible thought that there are so many of them in this country. Polygamy has advantages.

My life was gay but worried. I *must* marry, that I was sure of in my bones. To be an old maid, no. But I must be in love, and I wasn't. I came to the conclusion I loved nobody, not even myself. There was one that I liked very much. He was very good looking, good at games, and a scholar – and he loved me. He told me so when were at Torquay. I told him I wasn't sure, I didn't know. As I knew he was a man any girl would have gone mad about, I felt I was being extremely foolish not to accept him with thankfulness, but I couldn't.

One day I went round to see a so-called friend of mine, the stodgy plain one, six years older than myself. Her pretty, enchanting mother greeted me. "Poor Kathie", she said "It's very, very hard on her. She is terribly upset. Her cousin John is engaged to be married. Poor Kathie." Kathie then came in and mother withdrew. Poor girl, she was entirely submerged – finished. I felt so sorry. "Mother would keep on making me go and stay there. I didn't want to because I loved him and I knew he didn't care for me. Oh, it's been so dreadful and now it's far, far worse." She sat there crying and I could do nothing, such terrible despair, poor woman. When she was leaving she said, "Phyllis, never, never let yourself fall in love with a man until you know he is in love with you".

Her words of wisdom had sunk in, but I felt impatient and miserable with myself that I had not fallen in love with that delightful young man, nor with anyone else. He was going to India and had passed well into the ICS *(Indian Civil Service)*. That was so maddening. I longed to go to India. He asked if he might come and see us and I passed it on to mother, who said certainly he could come and stay for a weekend. She did not know he wanted to marry me. I didn't at all want him to come and stay. I was always at my worst at home. I was ashamed of the untidiness, the bad food and also mother's continued criticism of myself. I went in to tell Kathie my news and she asked, "Do your parents approve?" My parents? They don't know of course. I haven't told them. Whereupon she gave me a long lecture on the wickedness of my ways and my deceit, and that I must certainly tell my mother this young man had proposed before he set foot in the house. I had not felt rather worried about it, so I went home, found mother alone and told her. Well, the whole weekend after that was a fiasco. Mother was determined I should not get engaged unless my fiancé was in a position to keep me. Anyway, a 3 year engagement would be a disaster. He would change his mind. In order to prevent any collusion, she arranged the weekend so that we could not get one word alone together. Aubrey was put on as a watchdog and sent after us right and left.

February 1907

I was getting on – nearly 21. My parents and I were invited to a tea party in the house opposite – a large house, not up a ladder, as this was, but stretching along the ground – and it had a large conservatory, the definite sign of opulence at that date. Mother had called, I suppose, urged by someone to do so, and now we were asked to a tea party. Mother was undecided about going. She did not like the people and they certainly were not out of the top drawer. As usual, mother wasn't ready in time and father insisted on waiting for her, but I was told to go by myself and say they were coming. I was quite grown up. I was introduced by the daughter of the house to a man – or rather he was brought up to me. He was like the hero, or perhaps the villain, in a woman's magazine. Tall, handsome, dark, flashing eyes, and the air of a man who had been about the world and was also rich. In the course of conversation I made him suddenly burst out laughing and at that moment my parents were shown into the room. He was obviously intrigued by me and we stood talking all the time. The daughter, her nose well out of joint, came up to us and said "Oh, Mr. Niven, why don't you go into the conservatory, that's the place for people to flirt in". I was absolutely horrified at her cheapness and also at her aspersions. Surely I was behaving quite nicely, but Mr. N. said jealously, "But flirting is so out of date nowadays, Miss".

We continued our amusing conversation. Miss X tried to intrude again, by asking Mr. N. something which led me to thinking he was connected either with concerts or the theatre. I felt sure he was someone. He looked so very distinguished and he had the manners of a man of the world – very unlike my suburban friends and very attractive too. He was rather old, about 27 or 28, but very kindly and amusing. "Where did I live? Where did I go to Church?" I told him.

When we got home mother, who was very intrigued, asked me what had made us laugh so heartily. "Just something silly," I answered. "He told me he had just come back from South Africa and I said, "Did you lose all your teeth there?"' "Good heavens, no!" he answered, showing a beautiful set of teeth, which were his own, "Why should I have?" "Well," I answered, "I have a brother living there and he says it's a terrible climate for teeth". No, I told my mother. I'm not sure of his name.

It was my 21st birthday *(10 February 1907)*. No fuss was made at home. I suppose I was given some presents but in our family a birthday cake was unknown. Certainly none of my brothers would have remembered the date, and my sister probably gave me a picture she had bought at a school sale of work. Families all vary as to the emphasis on such anniversaries. Mother played down birthdays and Christmas and such like, saying with a voice of great authority "I never give presents"; and she didn't.

Next Sunday, what a thrill! There I saw him in church as I walked up the aisle. But things did not work out as they should have. After breakfast that morning we proceeded to Church, and as we walked up the aisle to our seats, to my dismay and excited pleasure I saw Mr. N. sitting four pews behind ours. I am sure my back must have been sending out welcoming messages to him during the service. After Church we all went out as usual but then something out of the routine had happened. Outside the porch in the enclosed piece of Church ground, I was surrounded by all my friends young and old. My parents had walked on but I glanced about surreptitiously and caught sight of my friend loitering about outside the iron gates. Of course he didn't know it was my 21st birthday; he must just have thought that I was having a gay gossip and so was not anxious to come out and leave them, though he was waiting. I tried to detach myself *(from the group)* but simply couldn't. I was given presents and had perforce to open them and exclaim, while all the time I was inwardly cursing the lot of them. By the time I could get a move on, it was too late. As I got into the road accompanied by a few of my friends, "he" was well on his way up the hill. So that was the end of that, I felt sure. Oh dear – why did things always go wrong with me? Oh dear. But still he had obviously been to Church to see me. That was something, and he could come again. Why not? But he didn't. Life went on.

Weeks later, however, as I was returning from a singing lesson near Swiss Cottage, I was passing St. Peter's Church *(Belsize Square)* and I walked straight into him. He seemed delighted to see me and, after chatting a bit, he said he would like to call on my parents!!! I said they were always at home on Sundays at tea time, perhaps he could come next Sunday. He said he would be very pleased and we shook hands, and I hoped he didn't notice that a finger of my right hand was poking through a hole in my shabby woollen glove. Naturally, I was thrilled but also alarmed. What would he think of our dreary house? It would all be rather awful, but very exciting. I said goodbye and I walked home on air. Now what to do about it? To warn Mother or not? I would much, much rather not, but then how would they behave if the door opened and this man was announced – one never knew – parents were so odd; besides which, we might have a very mingy tea if unprepared. I suppose I must tell Mother. How hateful, what a bore – but Mother took it quite reasonably and made no comment. On Sunday afternoon I finished with my Sunday school boys and came home feeling very nervous. The twice we had met we had been so happy together; why not go on like that and have no contact with anyone else?

I decided I wouldn't be in the drawing room when he was announced. I would make my entry later. I wanted him to be shown into the drawing room and get over the "how to do's" to Mother and Father before I came in. At 4 o'clock I posted myself on the upstairs landing from which I could see and hear, and I waited there till I simply had to descend for tea. We began tea. We finished tea and he had not come – he never did. Sunday dragged its weary way out and no front door bell went. Next Sunday and the next came and went but I never saw Mr. N; I never saw him or heard from him again. Had he noticed the hole in the finger of my right glove when we shook hands and said goodbye, or had he stood outside the gloomy semidetached suburban residence and thought better of it? Father mumbled something about some young man of mine coming to tea but mother quickly headed him off. Mother was very decent about it. She knew a little of what I was feeling and she said nothing. She and I never mentioned the subject again. If only I hadn't told them to expect him, then I shouldn't have minded, at least I shouldn't have minded so much. But to be made a fool of! I consoled myself by thinking that at least it wasn't my fault.

being 8 years younger than her, marry a man of an age eminently suitable for her. *(Francis Floud was born in 1875 and Marjory in 1878. He was 33 when he married and Phyllis was 23.)*

My sister was a queer, inhibited person, and being a schoolmistress for years didn't help her at all. When she retired, she lived with mother. *(In fact, Marjorie was forced to give up her career as a senior mistress at Roedean and live with her mother as soon as her father died. She wrote in the school magazine a year later (1933), putting a brave face on her new empty life as her mother's companion; she shared the fate of many unmarried daughters of the time.)* But they appeared to get along, and then mother had a stroke. Now a strange thing occurred. Mother, after her stroke, talked just like my half mental cousin, Theo *(Theodora Spottiswoode)*. Geoffrey and Katya Ford had a share in the large house which mother and Marjory bought. *(Geoffrey Ford and his Russian wife, Katerina Gorkhover, married in India in 1915. Geoffrey had joined the Indian Army in 1902.)* They moved from Hampstead, mother and Marjory; I should have thought they would have wanted a change but no, after searching most of England, they buy a mid-Victorian house, hideous with a suburban garden and laurels, in St Marychurch *(on the outskirts of Torquay in Devon; the house, 'Summerlands', 19 Belgrave Road, St Marychurch is now a guesthouse.)* Almost as ugly as the one in Hampstead which they had left.

After marriage

We settled in Hampstead. Our house *(Rosemount, 75 Flask Walk)*, for which we paid £90 year rent, was in a slum, at least just on the edge of a slum *(New End)* on one side and just on the edge of one of the most elite roads *(Flask Walk)* on the other. A lovely little old house with much charm and many drawbacks. Lovely old iron balconies. Good square rooms, all facing due south *(the house is one room deep)* – a great advantage in winter but apt to be unendurable in a hot summer. A minute garden. A view from the top window to St. Paul's.

My father's activities kept him busy day and night. To my husband's surprise, shortly after we were married, my mother took me to task about my husband "wasting his time" in the evenings. He ought to be employed somehow, gainfully if possible. "Look at the Lathams" she said most scornfully, "They've never done anything for anybody. Now look at your father. He never has an evening at home. I tried this on my new husband but he wasn't at all forthcoming: "I wish to spend the evenings with you, I work very hard during the day."

But the tables were turned when I proposed going off on my own. I became a member of the Philharmonic Choir, which meant a rehearsal in London at least one a week. When mother heard, she talked as if this was the thin end of the wedge. As if divorce was in sight. How I argued with her. But mother said she and father had joined a choral society in Hampstead and that it had been very pleasant. "Well", I said, "I can't take my husband to the Philharmonic because he doesn't sing at all. Does that mean I am never to sing?" I was extremely proud of one had been born and where one had lived all one's life. I didn't care two hoots about leaving my home. I had always disliked it and nothing could give me more pleasure than to up and off. My father, much more reasonably, wanted the wedding to be in the new hall, which had just been built, next to the church *(St Stephen's Hall, Pond Street).* A church room, in fact. He had a tidy mind and this would make an orderly place for a reception. Our house was always in a mess, and it *would* be in a terrible mess if it had to receive I don't know how many guests. As usual mother won. There was a great deal of fuss. The most inadequate balcony had to have a wide staircase built down to the garden, so that guests need not rub against or touch the sooty balustrade. All these doings went on and I observed in a detached sort of way, thinking, how could mother imagine that I didn't want to leave my home? We were all supposed to love our home.

My father was insistent on a wedding settlement. I think it was mother's money. My husband had no wish to have it, but my father said no gentleman allowed his daughter to be married without settling money on her. Whether my sister felt I had swindled her out of something, I don't know, but she treated me in a more standoffish way even than before. I certainly did not realise at the time what a bitter blow it must have been to her that I should,

Phyllis and Frank on their engagement

The wedding of Phyllis and Frank

I tried it on him. He bore it patiently for a minute; he was always the best tempered boy on earth. Then he exploded, "Come off it for heavens' sake, have you gone batty? For the love of Mike, shut up, you silly. … Don't talk like that when you get home or I don't know what will happen." I took his advice and said no more, ever. A year later an invitation came for me to go to another retreat run by the same ladies, this time at an Oxford college in the vacation.

My religious interest had persisted, not helped by my brother Bernard, who amused himself by making great fun of the Old Testament, saying it was nothing but a book of fairy tales. I had had little contact with the Miss Hawkeys and really avoided them. I only went to Oxford because I wanted so badly to see the University City and the idea of staying in a college was irresistible. On my 3rd day there I received a message from the up-lift lady telling me to meet her in the hall at 1 o'clock and we would go for a walk together. I was appalled, but turned up at the time and together we sallied forth. Probed by her, I told her of my religious doubts, but her only response to that was that she would give me the name of a book I could read. She had just launched off onto the usual tack - about throwing myself into the arms of Jesus and being gathered into his bosom – when a cheerful voice broke in: "Hullo, Phyllis. What on earth are you doing here?" Standing in front of me was Fred May, looking so happy and jolly. Before I could introduce him, Miss Hawkey had walked straight on. I answered his question by asking what he was doing there. He was only in Oxford for the day on business. "Who's the sour old puss you're with? She didn't half give me a cutting look." "A family friend I'm staying with. I must go", and I ran after Miss Hawkey, but the thread of her discourse had been broken. The gay Fred was too real to be pushed on one side. "We will go in now," she said in a very disgruntled way.

Once I saw her years later. I never forget faces and I knew her at once. I was walking in a park in the country, a lovely park full of magnificent trees. As I walked along a path, I saw an odd figure coming towards me and old, wearing a coloured apron which she had gathered up in front of her; as she wandered along she picked up little bits of wood and put them in it. I stood back, watching .It was she, no doubt about that. She walked or ambled in an aimless fashion. Every now and then she would pick up a hand full of dried leaves and throw them up in the air and then wander on, picking up sticks, and all the time she was talking, talking and talking to herself.

My wedding, April 1909

When I was married there was a discussion between my parents on where the reception should take place. It seems odd I was not consulted. If I had been, I should not have been able to decide. I never could make up my mind at that age. If I did, I found I was wrong and was terribly upset. But my mother's argument about the wedding was that one must be married from one's own home. She spoke quite sentimentally – and she was not sentimental – about leaving the home where

[One of our most famous film actors is his son.] *(If Mr N was indeed William Edward Graham Niven, father of David Niven, his conduct is rather suspect – he had been married since 1899 and in 1907 his wife gave birth to their 3rd child. David Niven, the 4th was born in 1910. William was killed in action at Gallipoli in 1915.)*

Religion

Religion was a worry to me. I liked Church services, especially the High variety, but I found believing a very different matter and it worried me. Two well-to-do sisters of unimpeachable background decided, at the age of about 50, that their life's work was in the sphere of well-to-do girls and young women. They therefore rented a monastery for a week, while the monks were having a holiday, and invited the daughters of the rich to come and stay there free of charge for a retreat. An Aunt by marriage of mine recommended this for me to my mother, saying I should get plenty of tennis. Anything for a free holiday, though I was rather alarmed at the sound of it all and didn't believe about the tennis. So I took a suitcase which would take a tennis racquet, and no one would see it, which was as well as there wasn't any tennis. One Miss Hawkey was the spiritual leader of this effort and the other was the practical one who saw that people caught their trains, etc. She adored her younger sister. The spiritual one was just the same type as the elder Garnett sister *(Hilda)*. She had a moon face, untidy hair, couldn't pronounce her r's and lisped. She lectured the 40 young women who had come to stay, and what we all did with ourselves heaven knows. Talk, I think. They naturally talked about themselves. I listened and the abysmal dullness of their lives struck me. They were all well off, but they were all condemned to live with their parents. They obviously would not marry. They were all designed to be virtuous spiritualists living at home. They were all accepting that role though they didn't enjoy it, making it out to be their duty because, I thought, they hadn't the guts to do anything else. Better, thought I, to live in a suburb and get a job – far, far better to be poor. I had nothing in common with them. I was younger than they and their lives were far apart from mine. The Miss Hawkeys were really like their own guests, only 30 years older. Two sentimental women wanting to be adored by the younger ones. The only thing I remember of Miss Hawkey's "up lifts" was her constant reference to herself and us as the brides of Christ. Christ the bridegroom was continually referred to and the whole idea I found unpleasant, but continually stressed, I tried to be fervent. I played in my cell, which had the name Grace beautifully painted on a card hanging on it. Each of us was named after a virtue and I had drawn the very unsuitable name of Grace. We all called one another by these names, Courage, Glory, etc., thereby doing away with the stilted form of address, "Miss Levantine Peacock" or some such. A week was quite enough for me, I had no exercise and became constipated. When we left we were extolled to go forth into the world and tell everyone we met that we had found Jesus. We must be bold about it. My young brother came to meet me, I forget where and, as we travelled together in the train,

No.75 Flask Walk, 'Rosemount' (family photo, 23 July 1909)

having passed the test for the Philharmonic and I wouldn't have missed the weekly rehearsals for words, nor the magnificent concerts we gave in the Albert Hall, but mostly the Queen's Hall, conducted by all the leading conductors, our favourite being Sir Thomas Beecham.

My mother advised me now I was married to drop my friends. "Your husband has married you, not your friends", but we did not take any notice of that. I must have two servants, said my mother. "Who would open the door when my maidservant was having her afternoon off?" "I would," I said. "Unheard of", said my mother and we started with a living-in cook general and then got a daily girl as well.

Alice, the Cook General

She was the niece of the five servants who looked after my friends, the Hibberts. She would like to come to me. I must interview her. She came to my mother's house, as I was not yet married. She didn't look to me like anybody's niece. She looked much more like somebody's aunt. She was years older than me and I was rather frightened of her.

All I asked her was, "Can you make cakes?" and she said she could. She turned out a quite first class plain cook. She never made a mistake. My mother had given her the once over when she came to be interviewed. Her hair was untidy. You must tell her to do it properly, said she. What an awful thing to have to do I thought. It seems so rude, so I asked my friend Mabel Hibbert, whose house was supported by the five aunts of Alice. "I wouldn't say anything if I were you," said she, "I believe she had rheumatic fever and lost a lot of hair and perhaps she wears a wig." "It doesn't look like a wig", I said, but I was very relieved at not having to tackle the question, and when she wore a white cap all was well.

Having suffered from my mother's haphazard housekeeping, I was going to do the thing properly. I would buy in bulk. No running short of things and having to dash out to the shops, though as they were quite close it wouldn't have mattered. Alice was very dour and almost sour looking. Very plain, poor thing. Extremely efficient.

On the day that Harrods bought my orders, I was very thrilled, Harrods had a posh sound about it. Mother had never dealt there. I leant over the banisters, going down the staircase to the basement and watched unseen. The man tramped back and forth. Presently he stopped and said to Alice, "Seem fond of macaroni in this house". My stomach winced slightly. "Oh, she don't know nothing about anything", came the prompt reply. My stomach turned right over. I crept away and very quietly slipped on a hat and coat and, like a burglar, escaped from my own home, past the man from Harrods – and made for the Heath. Once there I started to run and I ran madly until I could run no more, and then I collapsed on a tree trunk. I felt a little bit better. After 1 o'clock that night, after Alice was safely in her room at the top of the house, F. *(Frank)* and I went down to the basement. It had two good rooms in it of equal size, one was kitchen, one was scullery. F. turned on the light. The scullery had a strange sort of erection in the middle of it. It looked like a haystack and it nearly reached the ceiling. Four years later we moved from that house and the haystack had to be moved too. F. never has liked macaroni very much.

A few years after my first housekeeping effort, I asked Alice if she would mind sharing her bedroom with a young girl who was coming up from the country to live in. Alice was aghast. After a day or so she came to me almost in tears. She had to confess something to me. She hoped I wouldn't be too angry, etc, etc. She sounded as if she had stolen my pearl necklace. After a good deal of paving the way the crime came out. She wore a wig, she said. She ought to have told me before, etc, etc. I, bent on trying to avoid giving up our only spare bedroom, said I was sure the young girl wouldn't mind. It was very unkind and selfish of me. I warned the girl and explained, but she did mind and when Alice sat up in bed wigless the girl started screaming. Poor Alice. I must admit she must have been an upsetting sight.

Appendicitis, 1909

I had suffered, as I have already said, from attacks of indigestion ever since I could remember. They and my continual headaches were the bane of my life. My mother had a strange belief in what it said on the bottle, and dosed me indiscriminately with anything and everything. On a few occasions a doctor was called in. Most embarrassing to the three of us – mother in a dither of nerves, the doctor not much better and I in a state of bewilderment, not understanding what they were talking about. Flatulence, constipation, what did they mean? I didn't know, so I said "No" firmly when the doctor asked me if I suffered from either of these or other complaints.

As I grew up the attacks increased in frequency and violence. I thought I had indigestion and that was all, but these prostrating attacks were warping my life, getting in the way of dances and tennis and all the things I wanted to do. Then one day, I was walking up the High Street and a young woman called Watson, older than I, greeted me and said, "I hear you have appendicitis too!" This was a revelation to me. At last something definite, though still almost unmentionable. One's inside was a subject which was absolutely taboo. Wasn't it about this time that Barry *(sic)* wrote that play foolishly called "Little Mary"? Little Mary being the way one referred to one's stomach if one wished to. My mother was evidently very intrigued by it. To her every position of one's anatomy was absolutely unmentionable and she thought Barry had been very daring to write such a play. *(J M Barrie's 'Little Mary' had premiered at Wyndham's Theatre in October 1903, and the humorous nickname for the stomach, deriving from the play, had entered popular usage soon after.)*

I, the younger generation, just thought it was silly. I also thought the same of a play in which Cyril Maude (really a gentleman, and church warden of St. Something's, *E(a)*ton Square) had a stammer. *(The renowned actor-manager Cyril Maude, 1862-1951, once noted for his stuttering roles; he was a grandson of Viscount Hawarden. The church in Eaton Square, Belgravia is St Peter's.)* He became completely tongue-tied unless he first ejaculated the word "damn" loudly. Therefore in order to propose, he had to say damn many times so as to get going. This was unheard of. Damn on the stage was not done. Damn was never spoken before ladies. Anyone who said damn in front of a lady was a cad. But dear Cyril Maude was such a gentleman he got away with it and all the ladies in the audience shivered and thrilled at the audacity of it. But I was the new generation and thought it silly.

Now the King had some illness and it appeared to be appendicitis *(1902)*; the word was just whispered about and then spoken aloud. And here was Maud Watson, the most proper young woman, mentioning it in the High Street. I was elated. At last I knew what was the matter with me. And this was curable – I could have an operation. As soon as I could find a propitious opportunity, I demanded of my father that I be operated on. He was extremely annoyed. Who had told me I had appendicitis? He fussed and bluffed and talked at length and suddenly he found an escape. He said he didn't approve of operations. He blustered about over that for a bit and then said they were against the will of God. This was a new one to me and also to mother, by the look on her face, and besides it was very second rate to mention the will of God at breakfast. We weren't Methodists or Dissenters. I knew, or rather felt, that the whole issue was money. Father didn't want the expense of an operation. "As soon as I get engaged," I said, "I will ask my fiancé to let me have an operation for appendicitis". (And that is what happened.) Soon after my marriage *(June 1909)*, I had to get in our family doctor as I had an attack. He told Frank that for years he had been recommending to my parents that I have an operation. How my father could have dared to refuse, I do not know. How my mother acquiesced is even more extraordinary.

We had married on £300 a year *(today worth £109,000)* and so had not got money to burn. All F.'s savings had been swallowed up by doctors a few years before we married. A friend of his offered to get my operation done by a first class surgeon for half price. I went to see him. To my dismay, he diagnosed my pain as due to a floating kidney. I had never had appendicitis. No quick cure, no operation. I must be fitted with a stiff corset. Misery. Surreptitiously I had always taken all the bones out of my stays; to wear a stiff corset would be awful, but I had to. Our own doctor sniffed and he knew it was appendicitis, but he couldn't say much when the great surgeon had given his opinion.

Our marriage meant a series of ladies calling, and dinner parties and tea parties. I was having tea at someone's house. I knew the daughters, as I played tennis there, when suddenly I was attacked by a vicious pain. I said goodbye politely and managed somehow to get home. It was about an hour's walk, but it seemed endless. I went to bed and awaited the arrival of Frank from London. No telephone in the house. When he got home, he sent Alice off about 20 minutes walk to our doctor. He telephoned the surgeon, who came up at once and had to agree with our doctor. Acute appendicitis and I might have to be operated on at once. But luckily that didn't happen, and I was able to wait until I was fairly fit again before I went into the Hampstead hospital. Here I was operated on, exactly six months *(Dec 1909)* after our marriage. This was a completely new world to me and I loathed it. To lose one's independence and to have to submit to being washed, etc.

It was about five years after the start of that, I was away with Nanny and the family and Nanny one morning came to me with a letter she had had from Alice, who was having her annual fortnightly holiday. A slight tragedy had befallen Alice. She had had to buy a new wig. "I never knew she wore a wig," said Nanny, "it never entered my head. I did think sometimes that it was odd that I never saw her wash her hair, but that was all." "Well, go on with the letter, what's the trouble?" The new wig isn't the same colour as the old and they won't change it and it's too expensive to buy a new one, so Alice felt she had better tell Nanny – which shows how sensitive she was about it, as the new wig was very little different from the old, only as if it had been washed in a rinse "to bring out the lights", as the hairdresser would say.

My children were very fond of Alice and I used to look on nervously sometimes when a rough and tumble was going on and one of the babies would clutch her wig. She stayed with us for 15 years and was absolutely devoted, though morose and gloomy. But she had something to put up with from me. As she said, I knew nothing. My only cooking experience had been a class on Saturday mornings for a few months. As I was teaching, I could only go to learn cooking on a Saturday. At this place the meals were the same every day of the week, that is Monday the same, etc. Therefore, I only learned to cook one thing. Every Saturday they had boiled mutton. I can't remember the pudding. They soon found at this place that I was good at peeling potatoes, I suppose because I was good with my hands. I had never peeled potatoes before. So the young woman put me on to the potatoes for about 40 students. So I hadn't time to learn much else. And then Frank said he didn't like boiled mutton and the caper sauce, which I think is the making of it, he didn't like either.

When it came to ordering meals from Alice, I was not just as bad as mother. At 9 a.m. I would say, "We will have a steak and kidney pudding for lunch today, Alice.""I can't do it," she'd say, "there isn't time." I used to think, "Obstinate old thing."We were both given to frequent prolonged attacks of flu. "Starve a fever," I used to say consolingly and carry her up a cup of bovril, twice a day. When it came to my turn, I would lie in bed and she would get her own back. At 1 o'clock, when I was feeling how I would like something hot and soothing, she would appear in my room with her face of gloom and say, "I don't know what you are going to have for lunch, there isn't anything in the house."

Well, for 15 years we put up with one another and, when she left to go and look after her mother, all my friends said, "What will you do without Alice?" and I wondered myself. Whatever would I do? I didn't wonder for long. At once I got a first class cook – very, very nice to look at and entirely trustworthy and competent. She stayed several years until she married - and as I looked back I thought what a fool I had been to endure the gloomy sulks of Alice, never never again would I be so foolish – and I wasn't. But I must never forget her love for my children. She adored my little girl *(Mollie)* and would greet her with shouts of joy, hugging her. So very different from the quiet gentle girl who was their nanny – Alice's uproarious welcome could be heard all down the road when they came in from their walk.

Pregnancy and childbirth, 1910-1911

The book a woman sent me was by Chevasse. *('Advice to a wife on the management of her own health and on the treatment of some of the complaints incidental to pregnancy, labor, and suckling', by Pye Henry Chavasse, went into 16 editions, published in Philadelphia 1879.)* I have not got it, as F. burnt it. I wished he had burnt it before I read it. It didn't mince matters: "The gentle reader will now suffer unimagined agonies", and so on and so forth. I was paralysed with fear, as I read. I couldn't possibly go through that. I simply couldn't. Not only was there the agony but there was the obvious danger. I had heard of people dying when having babies, but that was only unhealthy sickly people, I thought. Now I realised that every potential mother faced death. Frank did his best and said quite truly that that book was out of date, and completely old-fashioned. He also said that nowadays the use of anaesthetics saved the woman having any pain, and I swallowed this also, only thankful to be convinced. I still feel a loathing for that woman in the old waterproof, though she is dead and I never saw her again.

One thing I got into my head was that I must take exercise. I was so

Phyllis in the sitting room at 75 Flask Walk

accustomed to being out and playing games that I decided to walk over the Heath every day. I went to another station, so as to give me a long walk. I walked every morning with Frank across the Heath, dropped him at the station and then walked home slowly. It was during these slow sauntering walks home that I realised the depravity of the solitary men who haunt such places. As soon as I was off the main path, I would be confronted by a man exposing himself behind a tree. This may be considered an exaggeration but it is not. I had an idea that if I walked incessantly I might be able to evade the terrible fate outlined by Chevasse *(sic)*. So I walked a great deal and, in consequence, produced appalling varicose veins. I asked our doctor to look at them and he told me to wear bandages. He did not examine me at all and asked no questions, and appeared to be just as embarrassed as I was over the fact that I was going to have a baby.

The months dragged on slowly. It was a hot summer. Our house looked due south. It had no back room, so sometimes the heat was unbearable. Oh for a shady quiet garden to sit in. I became tortured with internal irritation. I had reached a preposterous size. Never could I have believed that the human form could have become distorted. But I didn't mind anything until this irritation came along and that got me down. The doctor said there was no cure for it. The only thing he would suggest was to get a sponge of cold water and hold it against my skin. The irritation stopped but I felt unwell and uncomfortable and I couldn't sleep any more.

He *(the doctor)* then went away for his holidays. He would be back in plenty of time, he told me. The baby was due towards the end of June. Every afternoon I walked round to my mother's house to have tea. We were slowly advancing through May, when Alice went to bed with her usual flu. I had engaged a country girl to come and live in, but she was to come after the baby was born. Getting instructions from Alice, who slept at the top of the house, I cooked a joint in the basement. That would keep us going. But Alice persisted in being ill and was still in bed. I suppose I cooked something else. In those days we were accustomed to porridge and fried eggs for breakfast and two full blown meals, that is two or three course meals, twice a day with a good cakey tea in the afternoon. Perhaps the daily girl did the breakfast, while Alice was ill. That was on a Sunday. I walked round on Monday and again on Tuesday afternoon to have tea with my mother, as usual, till the baby came. The heat increased and I toiled about on the Heath, all the time thinking that that was my only way of escaping the agonies described in the book. My mother had told my sister-in-law *(Enid Floud, who was a midwife, trained at Queen Charlotte's Maternity Hospital in Hammersmith)* to let her have a list of things required for the confinement. She did not want me to know anything about the matter beforehand.

[Years later, when she knew that Frank and Phyllis were bound for India, Enid, by then an elderly spinster *(63)*, said that years ago she had missed the opportunity of going to India. She was suddenly invited by two friends of her parents to go out to India with them for about six months. Enid had never been abroad. She had trained at Queen Charlotte's, but otherwise she had seen little of the world, brought up in a country rectory and educated by a series of governesses who had never been educated themselves. When this invitation came, Enid suddenly saw the heavens opened, but, at the same moment a cloud appeared, as she remembered that she was booked for a case 6 months hence. She was very conscientious. She put it to her parents, saying what a pity it was she couldn't go. "Yes", they agreed "what a pity". How she had hoped that they would say, "What nonsense, my dear, of course you must go. You can quite easily get a friend of yours to take on that case."But they didn't and she hadn't the guts to say it herself. She didn't marry and, all her life, she carried about this grudge because she had missed her great opportunity. India in those days was the marriage market for the English young ladies, who did not manage to get a husband here. In India they were known as the fishing fleet.]

One night late in May (the baby was due the third week in June), I could stand the irritation no more. I got out of bed, turned on a cold bath and sat in it. Every afternoon I walked round to my mother's house to have tea. I did not rest nearly enough, but I felt it was not the right method, so I drove myself on and on. I used to go by unfrequented roads and one afternoon, it was late in May, as I walked along, I was suddenly seized with a racking pain. I leant against a wall till the pain had subsided. Then

Enid Ethel Floud

I crawled along to my mother. She said she didn't think I could manage that walk again but I said, "Oh, yes, I should do it every day until the baby comes".

I had one night been driven demented by a headache, beyond words it was, and in desperation I took ten aspirins. I woke up hours later lying across the bed, where I had fallen. I had gone to the spare room so as not to disturb Frank. At breakfast next morning, I felt unwell and unable to eat, so Frank said he would walk down and fetch my mother on his way to the office. He disappeared. I felt very alone. At last my mother arrived. She was flurried. She asked what I felt like and I said "As though my monthly was on". I never felt that", said my mother, "What's it like?" She said she thought she had better get the doctor. My own doctor was away, she must get his partner. I said I didn't want his partner, who was a young man whom I played tennis with. I wouldn't have him. But, as my inside was producing distinct pains, I gave in. We had had the telephone installed. Mother tried to get the doctor but he was out on his rounds, and so was every other doctor she tried. Then she got in a panic. She said, "If only I knew where there was a midwife". "I don't want to have a midwife, I must have a doctor". "A midwife would do just as well", said my mother. "No", I said, "It must be a doctor, I intend to have chloroform".

"You wouldn't have that", said my mother, deeply shocked. "I certainly would", I said, and we started worrying as to what to do, and then we decided to ring up Frank at his office. Mother didn't want to. She said husbands were best out of the way, but I insisted. Suddenly there was a ring at the door and the doctor (not my own) walked in. He had come to see Alice, and so all was well. By this time I thought the baby was going to arrive at any minute, so did mother. So I was deeply disappointed when the doctor said it would be a long time yet, but it was on its way. Frank got hold of my sister-in-law *(Enid) a*nd she arrived at about midday. Our double bed was then taken down and a single iron bedstead put in its place. Afterwards it had to be repaired. I had pressed against the bars at the end of it so much that they were all bow-shaped. My pillowcase was in ribbons as I gnawed it, trying to stifle my groans. "Don't let Frank hear you", was mother's refrain.

The summer had been hot but this day was the hottest of all and by the afternoon a fierce and terrific thunderstorm was raging. Some people were struck by lightning. A chimney pot went hurtling down near to our house. One doctor came in and out. He was pouring with perspiration as we were too, but I was also shivering with cold. Opening my eyes, I saw mother on her knees, clutching the doctor's legs. "For heaven's sake, give her something", she begged. "I can't yet, Mrs. Ford. I can't do it yet." And on and on went the struggle. My mother stayed beside me all the time. I don't think she ate anything. "How did you bear this, mother, six times?" I groaned. "I never had anything like this ever", said my mother.

Sometime getting on for mid-night, I was given some chloroform and blessedly went off. When I came to, the nurse said, "There's your little baby girl in that chair". An armchair was near the bed and, as I turned my head, I saw, propped up on a cushion, a baby. It had a very crooked face and I stopped looking, as I was again seized by a pain. Oh, this is too much, I thought. "It's only the after-birth now," said the doctor, "nothing at all really". All very well for him, I thought. Is this never going to end? Oh! the pain again. "I can't stand any more", I protested groaning. "You haven't got any more to stand", said the doctor, getting irritated. We were all tired out. Another groan, an acute one from me. "I don't know what's the matter with her", said the doctor to the nurse, not intending me to hear. "I think I'd better give her another whiff of chloroform and see...." Oh, blessed word, another whiff and I went off again – not for long apparently. I heard a shout, "It's a boy". This was too much really. Was everyone going mad? I must speak to them severely. Enunciating like a drunken man, I protested very slowly, "First you say it is a girl, then you say it is a boy. You are a doctor. Don't you know the difference?"

The astounding answer came with a guffaw, "My dear child, you've had twins". I looked and there was a boy, my son, being washed in a basin. He was sideways to me and there I saw a miniature Frank. Life seemed very good at that moment.

At 5 p.m. I started a haemorrhage and Enid thought I was going. Frank was anxious for the first time, he told me afterwards. The doctor was dragged out of bed and I was sewed. It was not until later in the day they realised our daughter had been born on May 31st and our son on June 1st. They weighed 6 and 5lbs respectively. They were completely separate, with two after-births. They were "two at a birth", not twins. Considering the doctor had used forceps (quite unnecessary, my own doctor said when he came home), and considering the doctor had no idea that there was more than one baby, it was, I suppose,

Nanny with the twins, Peter and Mollie

the greatest luck that the two babies were not damaged during birth. The girl's face was crooked but that righted itself very shortly.

There is one thing that still makes me rage. I had enough milk for an army – my nightgown and bedclothes were saturated; but the doctor, the young man, said I must not nurse two, with the result that I nearly lost them both, and Frank and I nearly died too from anxiety and exhaustion. The ignorance of doctors and nurses – and their prejudices. I argued with the nurse, Enid. She was very cut and dried, as most nurses are. She had bought two glass cups to fit on my breast to save my bedclothes. "Why not save it and put in a bottle?" I said. "It would not be hygienic", was all she could say. And so it came about that the babies were starved, literally. First one then the other declined to digest any food we gave them, except from me. My milk was all they wanted and it suited them. I nursed them, first one and then the other, then as the one off me was losing weight, I did them alternate feeds. It really was a nightmare – our terrible anxiety and sleepless nights, the babies crying incessantly and my own doctor, the fool, saying that if they cried they must be being overfed. "Cut their food down." After the nurse left, I coped alone. But by this time the milk had adjusted itself and I fed them both. At least they were not sick after me. When they were 3 months and we were all worn out, I got a nanny - a sweet girl, younger than I, whom we loved and who stayed with us 8 years. But that age is so important to their health and to their teeth and eyesight. At the age of one year they were bonny babies.

1914-1918

During the first war mother had a paying guest or two. Many other people were doing it. It didn't reduce one's status very much. People were too busy to talk about such paltry things. So mother took in a very elderly pair. He a retired parson. They were very quiet, gentle frail people. During the war, people who "took the trouble to look for good got it". That is, they got more than the ones who didn't bother. To mother and, as I think, to many lazy housekeepers and many bad restaurants and hotels, the war was a glorious excuse for meagre and deadly food.

One Monday the cold joint disappeared (probably the cat). Mother always had a theory that animals didn't need feeding, they picked up their food. On this occasion the cat did pick up its food. There was a great search for the cold meat and it was found at the end of the garden, the cat having had some pickings off it before the hue and cry began. Mother brushed the meat and put it on the table and no one was the wiser. But the little old pair evidently didn't like Mother's housekeeping, and they gently suggested to her that they did not get enough to eat. "One must keep up one's strength", said the old gentleman. "Why?" asked mother, and he couldn't think of an answer. Mother resented them, just as I think one almost always would. To have strangers occupying one's house is a hard thing to bear for both sides. And in war time it meant real difficulty in providing food. She repeated this conversation to me and commented, "Why should people like that want to keep up their strength? They are no use to anybody – they aren't helping to win the war". That was all that mattered. Mother would have liked to liquidate them if the word had been invented, which it hadn't.

What happened after Hampstead?

Phyllis and Frank left Hampstead in 1913 to live in Epsom, Surrey, at 16 Alexander Road. In 1929 they moved to a bigger house in the same road with a large garden and tennis court. Frank's career went well. He had entered the Board of Agriculture at a junior level in 1894 and, while working there, qualified as a barrister of Lincoln's Inn. He served in a variety of posts before being appointed, in 1920, the Permanent Secretary of the Ministry of Agriculture and Fisheries. In 1921 he received his first knighthood. He was Chairman of the Board of Customs and Excise from 1927 to 1930 and then Permanent Secretary of the Ministry of Labour (1930-34) during the very difficult period following the financial crisis, when unemployment and other benefits were cut by the National Government. Phyllis enjoyed becoming 'Lady Floud' and insisted on her title. She spent her time playing tennis, and took up golf and bridge but her great pleasure was drawing and painting. She attended the Slade School and became a good amateur artist, drawing and painting portraits and landscapes.

In Epsom in 1915 their third child, Bernard, was born, to join the twins, Mollie and Peter. The boys were sent away to school at Greshams in Norfolk, the choice of liberal parents. They both met Benjamin Britten there and played a great deal of music. Both then entered Wadham College, Oxford where Peter read Greats and Bernard History. Peter Castle Floud became Head of the Circulation department at the Victoria & Albert Museum and an expert on William Morris. His wife, Jean Floud, a sociologist, became a Fellow of Nuffield College, Oxford and then Principal of Newnham College, Cambridge. Bernard Francis Castle Floud was a civil servant, a farmer and a television executive, and then became Labour MP for Acton (1964-67). Mollie was an excellent amateur pianist and piano teacher. She married Peter du Sautoy, who became Chairman of Faber & Faber.

In 1934 Sir Francis and Phyllis left for Ottawa, where Frank became British High Commisioner to Canada until 1938, acquiring his second knighthood, a KCMG. Phyllis did not like Canadian society and was delighted when, in 1938, Sir Francis was asked to be Chairman of the Bengal Land Revenue Commission – and she got to India at last. They stayed there till 1940, when the Commission's report on land tenure was complete and Frank was knighted for the third time, as KCSI. On their return, they retired to Ickford in Oxfordshire, where during WW2 they offered shelter to, at various times, their daughter, daughters-in-law and grandchildren. While Frank chaired the Parish Council, Phyllis painted studies, which are much prized today, of the old cottages in the village. They were responsible for the building of Ickford Village Hall, using Frank's connections and Phyllis' energy and enthusiasm, after Phyllis discovered from her milkman that villagers had been trying to save up for one for years. She painted a huge mural to decorate the Hall, showing the villagers doing the actual construction work. At the end of the 1950s they moved to Brunswick Square, Hove, where Frank died in 1965 and Phyllis returned to her earlier love of swimming. She swam in the sea before breakfast every day of the year. She entertained her grandchildren with lively tales of her life in the chatty style of this memoir. She died in 1976 at the age of 90.

Index

* = illustration

A

Albany Street 45
Alexander family 8
Alice (cook) 167-168,
 170-171, 172-173
Allen-Olney, Rita & Sarah
 67, 69, 70, 71, 92
Alvanley Gardens 134
appendicitis 168-170
art galleries 63, 152-153
Ashbridge House 74
Atwood, Jane ('Trissie')
 & Leslie 43
Axminster (Devon) 14, 21, 54

B

Baker, Chas. & Co. 140*
Baker Street 125
 Station 126, 137, 139
Band of Hope 136-141,
 137*, 139*
Bayford House 75-79, 75*,
 76*, 106
Beauclerk, Penelope 119
Bedford College 125-126
Beecham, Sir Thomas 167
Bell, Alfred 75
Belsize Avenue 34
Belsize Lane 34
Belsize Park 64
Belsize Park Gardens 67
Belsize Square 162
Belsize Terrace 15
Bexhill-on-Sea 101-102
bicycling, see cycling
Bird in Hand, The 94
Bishops Avenue 102
boating 126, 141-142, 141*
Bolton, Mr 111
Bowyer, Harriet G 49
Brittany 143-144
Brown, Ada Haydon (née
 Ford) 16, 17, 18, 20
Brown, Florence Ada 18
Brown, Rev. John 16, 16*
Buckeridge, Charles 75
Buckmaster, Stanley Owen
 127-128, 128*
Burlison, John 75
Burnett, Betty 129-131
buses, see omnibuses
Bush, Kate 65
Butler family 17-19

C

cabs 33, 88-89, 94
Cadogan Square (No.23)
 14, 22, 22*, 54-55
Camden Town 74, 94, 147
Campbell, Jock 116
Canada 81, 82, 83, 177
carriages 54-55, 132-133
Caulfield, Philippa (née
 Nevinson) 60, 61
Caulfield, Sydney B K 61
Champneys, Basil 100
Charmouth (Dorset) 54
children's parties 64, 85
Christ Church
 (Albany Street) 45
 (Hampstead) 82, 107
Christian, Ewan 105
Church Lads' Brigade
 85, 112-114, 112*
Church Row 80
churchgoing 98,
 104-109, 161-162
clothes 12, 31, 57-59, 64,
 66, 73, 131, 132, 140
Coburn, Miss 88
College Terrace 15
Congregationalists 105,
 156, 158
Couton, Mrs 78
Cross, Arthur George 44
Crossfield Road 66-67
Crystal Palace 139*
Cumberland Lawn
 Tennis Club 134-35
cycling 61, 69, 102, 111,
 117, 118, 118*, 143

D

Dalton family
 Sir Cornelius N 33
 Catherine E A ('Hetty') 33,
  34, 69, 81, 102, 127, 128,
  128*, 137, 138, 153-154
 Lady Margaret 33, 47
 Mary E N ('Ellie') 44
dances; dancing 99, 100,
 110, 148-155, 156
Dean, Ivy 114
Dearmer, Rev. Percy 109
Dix, Nelly 140
Dolling, Caledon 144
Downshire Hill 24, 34, 157
Downside Crescent 60
Drill Hall 110, 151
du Sautoy, Peter 177

E

East Heath Road 34, 64
Edis, Robert 48
education
 (boys') 34-35, 45
 (girls') 29, 34-35, 64-65,
  66-71, 73-79, 125-126, 128
Egerton Gardens 54
Eisdell, Hubert 81-84, 83*
Eldon Court: site 25
Eldon Road (now Grove):
 (No.2) 24-28, 25*, 29,
  143; garden 42, 43
 furnishings 48, 109
 (No.3) 105; (No.4) 59
Ellis, Harold 157
Epsom 41, 148, 177
Eskhaven 34
Eton Avenue 61, 135
Evans, Agnes 25
Express Dairy 126

F

Farnell family 73-74
 Ellen & Ida 73-79
 Harriette & Rosalind 79
fathers 103-104; see
 also Ford, Everard Allen
Field, Miss 81
Finchley Road 127, 158
Fitzjohn's Avenue 24, 65,
 106, 107, 124, 140
Flask Walk 94, 166; (No.75)
 166, 167*, 172, 172*
Fleet Road 88
FLOUD FAMILY
 Bernard Francis Castle 177
 Enid Ethel 173, 173*, 174,
  175, 176
 Francis Lewis Castle (Frank)
  35, 38, 39, 40, 41, 165*,
  166, 168, 169, 170, 173,
  174, 175, 177
 Jean 117, 134, 177
 Mollie 51, 83, 171,
  175*, 177
 Peter Castle 122,
  151-152, 175*, 177
 Phyllis Allen, see Ford,
  Phyllis Allen
 Rev. Harold Arthur 35,
  107, 108*
 Rev. Henry Castle 35
Foley Avenue 157
food, see meals
FORD FAMILY
 house, see Eldon Road
  (No.2)
 home life 46, 47-48, 52;
  meals 46, 50-52, 106,
  107, 114
 baths 27; cat 43
 servants 15, 26, 36,
  49-50, 65, 89, 123
 finances 21, 52
 (see also holidays; religion)
 Ada Haydon 16, 17, 18, 20

Aubrey Hammick 20, 36,
    36*, 47*, 49, 73, 86-87,
    89, 101, 106, 115, 116,
    118, 121, 160
Bernard St Vincent 32-33,
    32*, 34, 38-42, 45, 47*,
    107, 120, 121, 151, 164
Everard Allen ('Father') 24,
    14*, 15, 15*, 21, 22, 23,
    24, 25, 26, 29, 30, 32, 34,
    46, 47, 48, 49, 51, 52, 53,
    53*, 87, 88, 90, 91, 92,
    101, 101*, 106, 107, 111,
    112-114, 112*, 113*, 117,
    120, 121, 136, 139, 141,
    142, 143, 161, 162, 166
Geoffrey Noel 34-35, 34*,
    47*, 62, 73, 89, 91, 102,
    166
Joseph 15; Katya 166
(Mary) Marjory 13, 29-31,
    29*, 47*, 67, 69, 111,
    111*, 143, 152, 154,
    165, 166
Rachel ('Mother') 8, 12, 13,
    14*, 19, 21, 22, 23, 24, 30,
    31, 46, 47, 48, 49, 50, 51,
    53, 56, 58, 62, 63, 69, 75,
    78, 85, 87, 88, 89, 90, 91,
    92, 99, 100, 101, 102, 103,
    107, 110, 113*, 114, 121,
    122, 123, 125, 131, 133,
    136, 141, 142, 144, 146,
    147, 152, 153, 159, 160,
    161, 162, 166, 167, 173,
    176
Stephen Everard 23, 31-32,
    31*, 36-38, 47*, 54, 66,
    119-123, 119*, 127
FORD, PHYLLIS ALLEN 35*,
    47*, 62*, 165*, 172*
  habits 44-45, 46-47
  clothes 57-59, 64, 66,
    73, 132, 133
  health 31, 65-66, 81,
    85, 132-133, 146-148,
    156, 168-170
  schools 64-65, 66-71,
    73-79; college 125-126
  holidays, see holidays
  socialising 95-100, 100,
    102, 110-111, 130-131,
    140-141, 154-158
  music, see piano; singing
  art 20, 68-69, 135-136
  sport, see hockey; tennis;
  marriage 164-165, 165*;
  pregnancy & childbirth
    171-176
  married life 173, 177
Frognal Lane 100

G
Gainsborough Gardens 134
Garnett family 156-158
  Hilda 78, 157, 163
  Rebecca 157, 158
  Dr William 157, 158
Gayton Road 89
George, The 88*, 89, 147
Gertler, Mark 60, 124
Gorkhover, Katerina 166
Gray, Miss 132, 133
Great Central Hotel 148,
    149*, 154
Griffith, Gladys 39, 140
Grout, Rose 65
Guildford 98-99
Guildhall (City) 85, 86, 113
Guy Fawkes Day 72, 85-87

H
Hall Oak 100
Hall, The (School) 66-71, 68*
HAMMICK FAMILY 8-14,
    10*, 13*
  Constance 143
  Dorothea Constance 144
  Rev. Ernest Austen 95, 95*
  Frances Grace, see
    Spottiswoode
  Georgina Mary 118
  Henry Alexander 144
  Jane Alexandra 118
  John Eustace 11
  Mary Alexander 8, 10*,
    12, 13, 52, 143, 144
  Mary Caroline 9. 12
  Sir Murray 20, 144
  Rachel, see Ford, Rachel
  Robert Frederick 155
  Sir St Vincent Alexander
    11, 119
  Sir St Vincent Love 8, 9,
    10*, 14
  Stephen 20
  Sir Stephen Love 14
  William Maxwell 118, 119
Hampstead
  Cemetery 16
  Conservatoire 61, 117, 135
  General Hospital 170
  Heath 85, 168
  High Street 67, 94, 95, 169
  Junction Railway 60, 87
  Scientific Society 78
  Square 107
  Town Hall 152, 156
  Tunnel 87
Haverstock Hill 89, 94, 147
Hawkey, Misses 163, 164
Heath Drive 128
Heath Rise 34
Heathfield 64

Hempstead (Norfolk) 91-92
Henley 99-100
Herries, Rev. Robert S 57
Hibbert family 95-97, 98,
    99, 101, 109, 110, 124,
    129, 133, 134, 148, 149
  Alice Holden 95, 131, 142
  Georgina 95, 148
  Mabel 167
  Marjorie 97, 98
Hicks, Keith 103
Highcroft 95
Highgate Cemetery 79
Highgate School 82
hockey 98, 148, 154
Holborn Baths 113-114
holidays 87-93, 101-102,
    143-146
Holly Bush Vale 110
Holly Mount 44
Hopkins, Minnie 65
Horton, Rev. R F 105, 107
Hove (Sussex) 79, 177
Hubbard, Mina Benson 157
Hunwick, Mrs 73

I J
Ickford (Oxon.) 61, 177
Jay, Violet 88
John Barnes 158
John Street, see Keats Grove
Johnston family 152

K
Keats Grove 60, 68
Keynes, John Maynard 18
Knight, Ambrose 98

L
Layton, Marion 70
Leicester Galleries 63
Leigh, Miss 126
Lisson Grove 136-141, 138*
Longman family 155-156
Ludgershall (Wilts.) 92
Lyndhurst Gardens 72, 95, 129
Lyndhurst Road 50, 66, 105,
    106; Congregational Church
    105, 105*, 158
Lyndhurst Terrace,
    see Windsor Terrace

M
McMillan, Misses 128
Marble Arch 126, 133
Marelli, Miss 155
marriage, thoughts
    on 158-160
Martineau family 104-105
Masterman, Mrs 141
Matheson, Mr 111
Matthew, Frances 68

Maude, Cyril 169
May, Edna 120, 120*, 134
May family 131, 133, 148;
　Charlotte 131, 132, 134;
　Fred 134, 164;
　Lottie 158;
　Mary Eleanor ('Nelly')
　　131-132, 133, 156, 157;
　Peter Wilson 131, 132
meals 20, 33, 115,
　130-131, 170-171
Michelbouch, Hélène 78
Milford, Sir Humphrey 119
Millar/Miller, Jean E 79
Milton Abbot (Devon)
　8, 9*, 10*, 11, 13, 24
Moorgate, Amy 114-116,
　117, 144
Morris, William 48
motoring 100
Munro, Edie 123
music, see piano; singing

N
nannies 49-50, 148, 175*
Nevinson family
　Christopher (C R W) 60,
　　60*, 63, 124
　Elizabeth ('Lizzie') 59, 62
　Henry Woodd 59, 61
　Margaret Wynne 43*, 59,
　　61-62, 62*
　Mary 59, 62
　Philippa 60, 61
New End 166
Newland-Smith, Rev. N
　72, 108
Niven, [William E G?] 161-162
North London line 60, 87

O
Old Conduit House 75, 75*
Olney, see Allen-Olney
omnibuses 56, 94-95, 95*
Onslow Gardens 54
Oswald House 75, 75*

P Q
Patriotic League 116
Pearce family 99-100
Philharmonic Choir 166-167
piano 16, 17, 20-21, 48, 136
Pollock, [Ella Violet?] 64-65
Pond Street 165
Pooley, Mrs 107
Priestley, J B 134
Prince Arthur Road 129
Queen's Hall 82, 167

R
railways 87, 89-90
reading 11, 53, 135

Redington Road 157
regattas 99-100, 145
Regent's Park 126
religion 17, 46, 48, 98,
　104-109, 115, 163-164
Rhodesia 121-123
Roppey family 37
Rosemount 166, 167*,
　172, 172*
Rosslyn Hill 95*, 105, 106
Rudall Crescent 79

S
Sailors' Orphan Girls School
　& Home 65, 123-124, 124*
St John-at-Hampstead 44
St Margaret's (house) 131
St Mary's, Primrose Hill 72,
　107, 108-109, 108*
St Peter's Church 162
St Stephen's Church 105,
　105*, 113
St Stephen's Hall 165
Salisbury
　(Rhodesia) 121-123
　(Wiltshire) 74, 118-119
Salvation Army 89
Sandy Ring 85
Savernake Road 60
Savoy Turkish Baths 147
Scarr Cottage 60
Scotland 111
servants 13, 15, 36, 49-50,
　55, 65, 89, 96, 123, 129;
　(see also Alice; nannies)
sex 103, 146
sexual harassment 71-72, 127
Sharp, Cecil 135
Shepherd's Path 76, 76*,
　79, 81, 106, 110
Shepherd's Walk 106
Shere (Surrey) 119
Silver, Ida Marion 79
singing 14, 17, 18*, 97,
　166-167
Slade School of Art 60,
　124, 177
social class 53-56 & passim
South Hampstead High
　School 60, 67
Spaniards Road 58, 82, 102
Spencer, Stanley 60, 124
SPOTTISWOODE FAMILY 119
　Adrian George 43, 56
　Frances Grace 11, 12, 14, 21,
　　22, 23, 24, 53-57 passim,
　　55*, 58
　George Andrew 14,
　　53-56 passim, 57, 59
　John 56
　Mabel ('Teeny') 56-57,
　　59, 86, 87

　Margaret Eleanor ('May') 56
　Theodora 55, 56, 166
Spring Path 106
Stuart, Miss 136, 137
suffrage 30, 59-60, 157
Sundays 17, 72, 98,
　104-110, 162
swimming 90, 113, 177
Swiss Cottage 24
　Station 127, 127*

T
Tate Gallery 152-153
Tatham, Florence 50
Tatham, Kathleen 66
Taylor, Mrs 67
tennis 33, 97, 115, 124,
　133-135, 144-145, 144*
Teulon, Samuel 105
Thornly, Dorothy 93
Threave House School 128
Thurlow Road 65, 74, 105
Torquay 117, 119, 143,
　144-145, 166
Townsend, Barbara S
　& Gertrude E C 118-119
Townsend, Gladys 80-81, 82,
　84-85, 96, 97, 98
Turkish baths 147

U
Unitarians 100, 104-105, 111
University College 124
Upper Park Road 16, 20

V
Val André (Brittany) 143-144
Vale of Health 24
Valol, Miss 156

W
Wabe, The 157
Wales, train to 89-90
Ward & Downey 54
Watson, Maud 169
weddings 24, 44, 57, 59
West Hampstead 86,
　87, 120, 134
West Heath Road 131
Wharncliffe Rooms
　148-149, 154
Whitestone Pond 102
Wicks, Miss 67, 69, 70, 71
Willett, William 28, 72, 96
Willow Road 34, 157
Windsor (now Lyndhurst)
　Terrace 74, 75, 76*, 106
Woodd family 64, 85
Woodlands 64
Wooldridge, Miss 126
Woolwich 153
World War One 59, 60,
　158, 159, 163, 175